THE CHRONICLES OF
FRED SMITH'S
FEDEX
PLANTATION

A LEGACY OF RACISM
FRAUD   DRUGS   THEFTS

A true and very revealing story detailing the history, philosophy and inner workings of the Fedex corporation and it's founder and CEO Fred Smith

GARY RULLO

PREFACE

If you are reading this book I may already be dead. I didn't die from natural causes, and not from a heart attack. I didn't have a <u>real accident</u> and I didn't commit suicide. I died at the hands of someone sent to kill me by Fred Smith.

The founder and CEO of Fedex.

In March of 2002 Fred Smith sent someone to my home in Delaware to kill me. And he nearly succeeded. My wife came home and found me semi-conscious and covered in blood on our bed which was also covered with my blood. I had lost a lot. I had an open wound to the back of my head and had been unconscious for hours. She quickly called an ambulance which rushed me to the hospital emergency room and they saved me. The wound was on top of my head near the back and to the right side. My wife was told by the doctors who treated me that most people with a head injury as serious as mine ...die.

Fred Smith wanted me Dead... He had to silence me.

One of the surgeons who treated me in the emergency room in the hospital and examined me a month later had seen many head trauma's and he was "absolutely certain" that someone had struck me on the head from behind. And that because the injury was on the back of my head and slightly to the right, he felt pretty sure the attacker was right handed and struck me while standing behind me. He had volunteered this information to me without my asking him about the injury. He was clearly concerned about my safety and my life. I believe he was also worried that the man or men who had tried to kill me...would come back to finish the job. I have already been "Left For Dead" once.

Will I survive if there is a next time?

The question is, will Fred Smith again send someone to kill me?

I'm sure many people will question why a man of such wealth and success would attempt to kill a common working family man like me. Who was I? Just a little nobody.

To be perfectly honest I had never really thought he would either. But if you read this book completely, you will know exactly why and how it happened and you will have no doubt that he did.

I had been warned by a number of people that he would. Including two Federal agents in two different Federal Law Enforcement Agencies.

Both the FBI and The AFOSI agents were very much concerned that Fred Smith would send someone to "Murder Me" ... and I was to be VERY CAREFUL. They both...said he was a "Dangerous man"

What did they know about him that they couldn't tell me?

I had gone to the Air Force Office of Special Investigations (AFOSI) Agents with evidence that proved a "Conspiracy to Commit Criminal Felony Fraud" against the military, the U.S. government, the CIA and other government branches by Fedex CEO Fred Smith and fellow criminals within Fedex management.

I had worked undercover and helped AFOSI coordinate nationwide investigations that proved this fraud without question with solid indisputable facts. AFOSI forwarded the investigation to Federal Prosecutors (DCIS) in Washington who wanted him prosecuted to the full extent of the law for "Felony Fraud" against the U.S. military and government.

I had put Fedex on ABC's 20-20 with thirty million viewers and in newspapers all across America. Exposed some of his criminal acts and the illegal drugs within Fedex.

I stopped Fred Smith from stealing more than a billion dollars from our military and government while he was betraying our soldiers. This stopped Fred Smith and Fedex from stealing $50,000,000 (that's fifty million dollars) a year from the U.S. government for absolutely NOTHING. And who knows how many million dollars a year from the private sector by using the same Fraudulent Non- existent (never existed) Scam.

On the internet I exposed to the world Fred Smith and his "Fedex Plantation" corporation of Racism and Discrimination programs against Blacks which cost Fedex more than one hundred million dollars in numerous lawsuits.

After that, Fred Smith had his lawyers send me a letter threatening me for the second time, because I had continued to expose the crimes by him and his Corrupt and Racist Fedex Corporation. I knew what I was saying was true and needed to be told and that I had the documentation and tapes to prove in court what I was saying. And I didn't back down.

The TRUTH needed to be told. Or the crimes would continue. I'm sure those things gave rise of anger and thoughts of vengeance by Fred Smith.

But it wasn't until I began to expose his "Illegal Drug Smuggling Operation" ... that he realized he would have to silence me forever. This was a secret that few knew about and none would openly talk about.

I had opened "Pandora's Box."

I had exposed what government investigators and others within Fedex's own management had told me about Smith's drug smuggling. The false picture of a successful smart corporate entrepreneur that people were talking about and had written stories about would fade. Fred Smith would be known as " a Racist, a Criminal and a Drug Smuggler'

He and his Fedex company have spent millions of dollars buying favors from senators and congressmen maybe even presidents for years. Newspapers and magazines wrote glorious stories about his success and the business world speaks so highly of him. And every year Fedex spends millions of dollars on false advertising and telling lies about how great and smart he is and how great Fedex is.

And the REAL TRUTH IS ....Fred Smith is nothing more than a common criminal.

He's a white man born of wealth in the south.

A Racist who grew up on a cotton SLAVE plantation who wants to control Blacks even today. He has killed at least one innocent Black man and left him to die in the streets like an animal. He may have actually killed the man in anger which would make it Murder.

I too, was almost one of his victims. Who knows how many more there are?

The Fedex corporation is the most Racist White Supremist company in America in the last seventy-five years and maybe more.

I will show you the proof.

That Fred Smith was indicted for forging another man's signature while trying to steal his own sisters money.

The TRUTH was coming.

And Fred Smith was not going to allow that to happen.

His threats didn't work, I didn't scare.

So he sent someone to kill me.

When some men are faced with Adversity they turn away and run from it.

When real men are faced with Adversity they look it in the eye.

Before you begin reading this book please realize that I am not a professional writer and have few literary skills. With just one year of college I am honestly poorly equipped to write such a story as the one contained within. Yet, the story inside this book is such a powerful and important one that I am hoping it will make up for my shortcomings as a writer. More importantly, this is a story that needs to be told if only to get the TRUTH out.

I am certain that after this book is out, more books like this one about Fred Smith and his corrupt Fedex Plantation will follow. And even more of truth will continue to be revealed.

There are many wrong and illegal acts committed everyday in the world. Many of these wrong, immoral and illegal acts are committed right here in America. As you read this book you will see and learn that I have stopped at least a few of them. The wrong and illegal acts told of in this book were committed by a very powerful, corrupt and evil man and his even more powerful, corrupt and evil Fedex corporation.

The "beginning of this book" is a little amateurish and awkward because there is so much information and groundwork that I feel needs to be put forth even before beginning the story.

Read through my amateurish beginning and get on to a very revealing story that few would ever imagine.

Judge the book by the story inside …Not by my literary skills.

When I first began writing this book and was talking about it and the DEA picture of Fred Smith's Fedex cargo plane smuggling illegal drugs online … Fred Smith had his lawyers send me a very threatening letter.

When I didn't back down from what I was saying online and was talking about exposing his "Drug Smuggling" in a book … "not surprisingly" I was contacted several times by people who would talk up the contents of the book and wanted to "help me" co-write it and get it published. They would try to get me to send them the manuscript so they could go over it and offer suggestions.

I would explain to them that if they were serious we would have to meet with 'my Lawyer" so we could get a legal contract signed and also to make sure they were not connected to Fred Smith or Fedex in any way.

And they would "always" disappear."

It happened at least twice and maybe three times. Between four to ten months before I was nearly murdered at my home in March of 2002.

Needless to say being nearly murdered did put off the book for awhile, and almost stopped completely the writing and publishing of this book. If you've never been close to death from an attempt on your life while laying unconscious for hours and slowly bleeding out…it would be hard for you to understand.

Had my wife not came home and found me when she did and called an ambulance… I would have died.

Recently I have been talking up my book on "twitter" and it seems that out of nowhere…my computer has been hacked. Yeah. And oddly, I've began to get a few "blocked out" phone calls where no one on the other end answers or speaks but just holds the line open. Just EXACT-LY … like in the months before I was nearly murdered in 2002. Yeah… I'm serious.

So this time I've sent out letters to the FBI and the AFOSI … before they come again. On the following page is the letter to the FBI… NOT KIDDING.

June 11, 2012
Attn: FBI Special Agent George C Venizalas
      600 Arch Street,   8th Floor
      Philadelphia, PA   19106

Dear Sir,

My Name is Gary Rullo Sr. and I live in Middletown, DE. I am writing this letter to you because I have serious concerns for the safety of my life and also for my family.

I am a former Government/Federal witness against Fred Smith and The Fedex Corporation. Years ago as a Fedex courier I was trained to and ordered by Fedex management to "commit Fraud against the U.S. military and a number of other government branches. If not stopped this fraud would have exceeded more than a Billion Dollars and endangered the lives of thousands of military personnel and civilians.

I instead contacted The Air Force Office Of Special Investigations located within the Dover Air Force Base. They asked me to work undercover with them in nationwide investigations which proved 100% Fraud by Fred Smith and his Fedex corporation.

After the newspaper and ABC's 20-20 exposure … this Fraud was stopped.

Shortly after the ABC 20-20 show I was contacted by the Wilmington Delaware FBI Branch by FBI Special Agent Atkins who informed me that Fedex Thieves had stolen a $100,000 Gold shipment from Goldman Sachs that was shipped thru the Bank Of Delaware.

He explained that Fedex management would NOT cooperate and could I help him with the stolen Gold shipment. …which I did as best I could.

During this meeting Agent Atkins also told me that Fedex CEO Fred Smith was a "Drug Smuggler" and the FBI considered him a "Dangerous Man." He said that Fred Smith may very well send someone to harm me…"Murder Me". For exposing his crimes and costing him so much money. He warned me to be VERY CAREFUL.

It was very obvious at the time that he was concerned for my life. And it was almost the very same words that "AFOSI" agents had used to also warn me that Fred Smith was Smuggling Illegal Drugs and a Dangerous man who might cause me harm aka…"Have me Murdered.' They too were VERY concerned for My Life.

In March of 2002 my wife came home and found me covered in blood semi- conscious and nearly dead from a blow to the rear of my head. She called an ambulance which rushed me to the hospital where they saved my life. I had been "Left For Dead." The attack came after a few months of daily midday anonymous/ blocked out phone calls. When only I was home alone in the winter months. The person on the other end NEVER answered but just held the line open to hear me speak. And the day I was nearly murdered the calls STOPPED COMPLETELY. The attack came about noon, the same time as the phone calls.

I have written a book about my experiences at Fedex. (Agent Atkins is in it)

It is a important story that I feel needs to be told.

My concern as my book nears publication …is that I believe my computer has been "Hacked" and I have begun to get a few "anonymous/ blocked un-answered phone calls".

I realize the FBI has a full plate with all the terrorist issues and other serious crimes. What I ask of you… if I should suddenly die within the next year or so…"I did NOT have an accident, I did NOT commit suicide and I did NOT die of Natural Causes.

PLEASE Look into my Death.

Sincerely,

Gary Rullo Sr.

Note: When Fred Smith originally created Fedex he had named it Federal Express. After I exposed some (certainly not all) of his and Federal Express's Criminal Acts, Racism and Discrimination to the world on national television and in the media he changed the company's name to "Fedex." He hoped that the new name of "Fedex" would fool people and make them forget about his and Fedex's thefts of many millions of dollars from American civilians, business's, our military, the CIA and other government branches.

The millions of dollars worth of illegal drugs that are knowingly and intentionally (they know) picked up and delivered by Fedex couriers there daily. The thefts of these illegal drugs and many other valuables including Gold, Diamonds, Furs, Cash and so many other valuables.

And of how Fred Smith and Fedex management betrayed and compromised the safety of our soldiers, our government and even the lives of elementary school children and the American people for GREED.

Changing one's "shameful name" is a common trick used by criminals and prostitutes when they try to hide from their crimes and evil past. They change their names in hopes that no one will notice or remember their past.

Fred Smith's and Fedex's criminal and evil acts revealed in this book were committed while his company used both names.

Throughout this book I will only use the name "Fedex" so as not to create any confusion as to what company I speak of. Because what he and his Federal Express/Fedex Company has done and still continues to do even today... should NEVER be forgotten.

ABOUT THE COVER

The Black man laying in the street…he is a memorial to the Black man Fred Smith killed. Fred Smith struck him with his car and left him to die in the street like a dead rat. When police came to his plantation to question him about the dead Black man Smith lied and said he knew nothing about it. There was extensive damage to Smith's car, blood, a smashed windshield or broken headlights? Certainly to hit someone hard enough to kill them must have made a very loud noise on impact.

And he didn't know? Who's LYING here?

I think the ONLY question is…did Smith kill him on purpose or in anger? Did he intentionally hit him with his big expensive car because he wanted to teach a Black man a lesson? Because he did, the Black man learned the hard way "run away from a rich Racist white man in a fancy car or Die."

It happened in Little Rock Arkansas. That's where the president had to send in the national guard to keep other white racists like Smith and the KKK from killing the poor Black school children … who just wanted an education.

The "Confederate Slave Flag" that's the flag Fred Smith flies so proudly. Just as the KKK and other racists in the south fly it and have it plastered on their pickup trucks. Fred Smith grew up on a southern Slave Plantation. When he went to Yale he took his "beloved Slave Flag" with him where he proudly hung it to profess his love for the Colonial Slave Plantation ways. When whites looked at Black Africans as "less than human" and were to be "controlled by Whites."

Senator John McCain shown taking money from Fred Smith. He's the Ranking member on the Armed Services committee. What is so despicable about McCain? He took money from Fred Smith and his racist Fedex Plantation knowing that Smith and his criminals/traitors within Fedex were guilty of a "Conspiracy to Commit Felony Fraud" against our military and also other branches of our government. He knows they endangered the safety of our soldiers and the American people.

Not only did he take his money, news stories said that McCain had Smith on a "short list" of possible running mates. Imagine having a "Vice President" that committed Felony Fraud against and stole a billion dollars from our government while betraying and knowingly endangering the very soldiers who protect us.

Where would his greed stop? Fred Smith and Fedex would have stolen more than a "billion dollars" from the military and government had I not gone to and worked undercover with Federal investigators to stop them.

John McCain is NOT a hero ..he's a Scumbag Traitor who's also a Racist.

I honestly question how deeply McCain was involved in "stopping criminal prosecution" of Fred Smith and Fedex? Federal prosecutors (DCIS) wanted criminal prosecution of Smith to the Full Extent of the law and the evidence was "Rock Solid". Who stopped it ? Somebody in Washington NOT in the Justice Department. Was John McCain involved the Fraud Scam from the beginning?

He's a Ranking U.S. senator with a LOT of political pull in Washington. He's on the "Armed Services committee."

Did he help Smith and Fedex get the military contracts with the Fraudulent non-existent service against the military?

Somebody helped Smith with military contracts for the Fraud.

AFOSI Agents said Fred Smith "owned" politicians in Washington. McCain is a powerful U.S. senator and the "Ranking Republican Member of the Armed Services Committee" and he's taking large amounts of money from Fred Smith.

Do the pieces fit the ... "Puzzle"?

Blacks in America ....You have a PROBLEM.

Read this and Think.

An even greater concern to "Black Americans"...John McCain is just one of the top echelon of the Republican Party that believe just as Fred Smith believes...that Blacks should be controlled and kept in their place by "Superior Whites."

I've been a registered "Republican" for many years. Not because I believe Blacks should be controlled, or because I think Blacks are "inferior". I'm just a generally conservative thinking guy. I believe you should work for what you get, be responsible and obey the laws. And I know of a lot of people of different races that feel the same way. I like to think and I do believe that is the way with most conservatives and Republicans in the "lower working class" of the Republican party.

But I do not believe that is the way it is at the "Top" of the Republican Party.

John McCain is a "polished" politician. He'll say he didn't know Fred Smith killed an innocent Black man and left him in the street to die like a rat. He'll say he didn't know Fred Smith / Fedex committed felony fraud and stole millions of dollars from and betrayed our soldiers, our government and the American people.

He'll deny knowing Fedex is a Racist company that treats Blacks so bad and discriminates against them. He'll pretend that he doesn't know ... **But he does know, and he agrees with it**.

And he's only a grain of sand on a beach full of Racist Republicans at the "Top Echelon" of the National Republican Party.

He voted against MLK day, then tried again to stop it. But couldn't. And even then it was reported that .... "Republicans" joked about MLK day and called it, "Martin Luther Coon Day". A Racist term for Blacks.

John McCain publicly calls Blacks "Tar Babies." A slur that other "Republicans in the Top Echelon" have used. The truth is that in private conversation with the "Top Echelon" of the Republican Party members he has probably called Blacks "Niggers" and maybe worse many times. And told many "racist jokes" about Black men and their families, even their children. Just as so many other Racist do every day.

But he will NEVER admit to it. At least not publicly.

While Alabama's Republican Sen. Beason just calls America's Blacks "Aborigines". Which I guess means that America's Blacks are NOT civilized. Alabama is KKK country.

These are just a few of the Top Echelon of Republicans that want to "Control Blacks" and keep them in their proper place. Just like "Republican" Fred Smith and his Fedex Plantation.

Sometimes the TRUTH... is just hard to admit.

But probably the best example of how the Republican Party really thinks of Blacks is in an article written in the "Assimilated Press" regarding the KKK. (it's on the internet and you can find it)

In the article dated July 10, 2006 from the location of Pulaski, Tennessee.

*And remember that "Memphis Tennessee" is where Fedex has it's headquarters.

It says KKK Grand Wizard Floyd T Bone Perkins was "Officially Disbanding"   the KKK and they are merging with the Republican Party. Perkins goes on to say that the "Republican Party" has co-opted "all of their ideals" concerning race, immigration and religion.

And that there was no longer any need for the KKK.

He stated that the KKK considers it a measure of their success that the Republicans have picked up their Torch and carried it across the entire country.

He went on to say that the KKK was especially pleased with what the Republican Party did in Florida in the elections of 2000.   And the way they [Republicans] kept the "coloreds" from voting was awe inspiring. And that they [again Republicans] did the same thing in Ohio in 2004.

The article goes on to say that the KKK said, "that they had felt welcomed in the Republican Party for a long time."

Well of course the KKK felt "welcomed" in the Republican party, they just couldn't wear their robes in public Republican Party meetings and they would have to be more careful about whipping, hanging and drowning Black voters as is their tradition.

And right now (2012) both the Republican Party and the KKK need each other to "work together" to get that dammed Black Barrack Obama out of the "White Man's" … White House.

It may sound funny or sad …but it's more true than most realize.

If it weren't so sad it would have been funny to watch Herman Cain earlier this year (2012). The Republican party put Herman Cain out in the public to "pretend' that they would actually let a "Black Man" run for president as a Republican.

It was just a joke that was a "trick"…on the Black voters in America. Just a cheap Republican trick to try to get Black voters away from Obama.   To Fool Blacks into thinking The Republican GOP wasn't a Racist organization.

I'm guessing it started something like this at a Republican think tank meeting, "Hey, I know what...let's let a Black man campaign for president. We'll talk nice about him and say good things about him. We'll make the Black voters think the Republican party will run a Black man for president. And after we get more Blacks thinking of voting Republican ... bad things he's done will "come out in the media" making it impossible for him to continue. And we'll look good to Black voters ... lets do it" And they did.

The Republican Party would NEVER really let a Black man run for president. Yes you will see a few Blacks in the senate and congress. They are the same "token Blacks' that you see in management at Fedex. The Republican Party needs a few "tokens" in these places to make it appear to "Black voters" that they are not a racist organization. Fedex uses the same strategy to play games on it's Black employees too.

It took Colin Powell a long time to realize that. He was smart enough and had much public appeal. To see Obama come out of nowhere in the Democratic party and see them support him must have been disheartening for him.

He realized the Republican Party was for Whites ONLY.

If you look back throughout America's history you will

NEVER see the amount of opposition, resistance and just straight out disrespect that today's Republican's in Washington uses to work against the president Barack Obama. Neither party though opposed in some views, have ever worked so hard to discredit and bring down the other's president.

The Republican party has absolutely no respect whatsoever for Barack Obama... solely because he is BLACK. And they never will. They see his being in the "White House" as a bad picture of possible future Black presidents.

And that scares them.

Everyday in all kinds of media, from bumper stickers, Face Book, twitter, internet, signs...you name it... there are all sorts of "anti-Obama" stuff out there. True, some is from regular individuals that disagree with some of his policies. But just how much is "filtered down" from the Republican party. How much money is "secretly" passed around to fund and promote this "anti-Obama" propaganda? ... A LOT.

No American president has ever had to endure such attacks EVER.

But no American President has ever been Black either.

You won't see a Jew vote for a known "Nazi member" in elections.

You won't see a Black man vote for a known "KKK member" in elections.

Isn't a Black man voting for the "Republican Party" the same thing.

FREDERICK W. SMITH'S FEDEX PLANTATION

A Legacy of Racism, Drugs, Fraud and Thefts

I'm sure many will wonder and ask …was I fired from Fedex?

As you will read later in the book. The answer is <u>NO</u>.

I resigned from Fedex after I finished working undercover with investigators from the <u>Air Force Office of Special Investigations</u> "which is known as AFOSI or OSI" of the Air Force after they completed nationwide investigations of fraud and conspiracy to commit felony fraud against the United States and our military by Fred Smith and his Fedex company. The investigation by OSI agents involved undercover surveillance of classified sensitive military shipments by Fedex all across America and <u>proved</u> a criminal conspiracy by Fred Smith and others in Fedex management to commit fraud against the United States government and the U.S. Military. Fred Smith and Fedex used a fraudulent non-existent CSS service to knowingly and intentionally betray our brave men and women in uniform and jeopardized their safety to fill his greedy pockets. I would have resigned from Fedex sooner but I was asked by OSI agents to stay on and help them until their investigations were completed and forwarded to Washington for criminal prosecution. After OSI finished the investigations I gave Fedex management a formal written two week notice and resigned.

I could no longer tolerate the EXTREME RACISM and DISCRIMINATION against Blacks by a Racist White Fedex management, the CORRUPTION and LIES, and the rampant drug use and thefts of drugs and valuables by both Fedex management and it employees.

Realize this: If while reading this book you begin to think I am being hard on Fred Smith and his corrupt Fedex corporation …every thing I have written is true. I believe that when a man betrays our country and our soldiers like Fred Smith did … he is …LESS THAN DOG DIRT.

And on the same moral level as a PEDOPHILE.

Fred Smith has threatened to put me, my wife and our son out in the streets forever and promised that he would make certain I would never be able to work again ever. He made my wife cry. All because I went to the government about his crimes against our country and our soldiers and I told THE TRUTH.

My wife is a good and caring Christian woman, she loves me, believes in me, and has given me a son. She has done a lot of good things in our church, our schools and in our community.

Let's just say this …I NEVER FORGET and though I am a very faithful Christian… unlike GOD…I DON'T ALWAYS FORGIVE. DON'T BETRAY OUR SOLDIERS OR OUR COUNTRY … AND <u>DON'T EVER HURT MY WIFE OR MAKE HER CRY.</u>

Smith made these threats through his corporate lawyers. And they made these threats to me because they are lowlife bastards. Fred Smith never was man enough to make those threats face to face to any man, because he is a coward. He's like that rich little sissy boy who hides behind his mothers skirt and pays others to do his dirty work.

As you read this book you will see the REAL Fred Smith and how he thinks and believes, how he shaped his Fedex corporation in his image. He spends tens of millions of dollars annually on flashy advertisements, and hires public relations people to not only lie about the quality of their services, but more importantly to hide the many evils and crimes both he and his Fedex plantation corporation have already committed and still commit daily. To me the name Fred Smith belongs on the same pages as Bernie Madoff and Adolph Hitler to name just two monsters that share the same morals and disrespect for human life as he does. You will also read in this book how Fedex management hates Jews and that Fedex management actually bragged that Fedex would ship Jews and their children to the gas chambers.

So yes, I tell the hard truth and what I think about Fred Smith and his racist corrupt Fedex company.

INTRODUCTION

I signed on with the best of intentions as I am sure it was with many. I had been told by Fedex management that Fred Smith was a good man and that Fedex was a good place to work.   Inside this book you will read a lot about racism and discrimination against Blacks, who are often called Niggers by white Fedex management. Enough to turn a good man or woman's stomach. The sad part is that it's all true, and yet it isn't even one thousandth's of the amount of real racism and discrimination that goes on within the FedEx / Plantation corporation everyday.

It may very well be that the Fedex Plantation Corporation is the most racist and discriminatory company in America since the 1940's and maybe even further back than that. Fred Smith's dream was to use Blacks at Fedex as a lower paid,   lower skilled work force because he believes they are of a "lesser human race". Not one bit different than the Nazi's who believed Jews too ... were of a "lesser race."

As for creating the Fedex corporation, which used to be called Federal Express Fred had his racist daddy's money. A lot of people could be successful if they had as much money as Fred had to start their company with.

And the real truth is IT WAS FORMER <u>UPS MANAGEMENT AND OTHERS</u> THAT CAME IN AND SHOWED THE SPOILED LITTLE RICH BRAT HOW TO MAKE THE COMPANY WORK. It was real former UPS management and many others with real knowledge and experience that made Fedex work.

After Fedex was up and running Fred fired most if not all of them as soon as he didn't need them anymore. That way he could lie and claim all the credit.

Or was he involved in some illegal crimes and afraid they might find out ?

Or maybe they told him they wanted no part of his criminal activities ?

While it would be expected that in any company or work place there would be some degree of lying, drug abuse and even thefts ... never in my life would I expect to see the amount of Racism and Discrimination,

Drug Abuse and Thefts, and Corruption that I found so common within Fedex ...not only with their rank and file employees and couriers, but especially within Fedex management.

Fred Smith and his Fedex corporation is being exposed and American's everywhere are seeing the truth slowly coming out, especially the minorities.

Even Fedexs' high paid public relations people can't stop the truth. It took years for the truth to come out about Hitler's extermination of the Jews. And Bernie Madoff just like Fred Smith also told thousands of lies, gave money to and bought politicians like prostitutes, and he stole millions of dollars from so many for a long time before he was caught. Another company ...Enron also used the same tricks.

Now the truth is coming out about Fred Smith's Racist and Corrupt Fedex corporation too.

THE TRUTH IS COMING

Documented Facts about Fred Smith

Fred Smith and other criminals within Fedex and even one or more members of the military were involved in a "Conspiracy to Commit Criminal Felony Fraud" against our military and other government branches. They were in the middle of this fraudulent conspiracy to steal more than a billion dollars from the military and other government agencies when they were stopped.

It's called…R.I.C.O.

In some countries Fred Smith and his gang of criminals in Fedex management would be shot by a firing squad or hung by the neck until dead for their crimes. Because they are not only criminals at Fedex, they are traitors against America and our brave soldiers and should not even be allowed to live in this country.

Fred Smith and Fedex has given Washington politicians millions of dollars so he is free. And we know Politicians are like Prostitutes that are bought to turn "favors"

Read how I found and was sending out "official DEA pictures" directly from the governments' (Drug Enforcement Agency Official) DEA WEBSITE of Fred Smith's Fedex planes flying illegal drugs into America from Mexico and maybe South America. The DEA had even stamped the words "Illegal Drugs" on his plane.

Many of these drugs are sold to and used by children. Imported to your children by Fred Smith.

As a courier I was taught by Fedex management that Fedex / Federal Express was the Number One shipper of Illegal Drugs in America. Fedex management was proud of that fact and bragged about the millions of dollars the Fedex Corporation made from shipping and delivering illegal drugs to drug dealers in America. When I questioned why Fedex allowed this to happen, a member of Fedex management told me, "Fred thinks that most illegal drugs are used by "Niggers", so it's okay" he doesn't care about them. He used the word "Niggers" because it was commonly used by white Fedex management and employees when referring to Blacks.

But Fred's thinking that it's mostly only Blacks that use illegal drugs is wrong. You've heard the saying … "the apple doesn't fall far from the tree".

Fred Smith's younger son Fred Smith Jr. was busted for possession and distribution of "Ecstasy Pills". **A FELONY.** Did he have them delivered to him by a Fedex courier thru Fedex mail?

Were they possibly the same "illegal drugs" that were smuggled into the United States from Mexico by his father Fred Smith Sr.?

Was the use and abuse of illegal drugs the reason why it took Fred Smith Jr. nineteen years to graduate from high school ?

Ecstasy pills are known as the "Date Rape Pill".

An Ecstasy pill is what a no good bastard gives an unsuspecting girl so that he can rape her while she is in a semi conscious trance like state. He secretly slips it into her drink while she is not looking. It renders the victim helpless and with almost no memory of the fact that the bastard raped her without her consent or even of her knowing it. Is young Fred Smith one of those bastards?

Fred's Smiths other Son ...Richard Smith was sentenced to one year in jail when he and a gang attacked an innocent college student while the student was alone and defenseless. He was also much bigger than the victim. Smith said later that without the others helping him he would not have attacked the kid. A typical cowardly Smith. He even needs help to attack kids much smaller than him. Did he learn that from his father?

A woman in Memphis who obviously knows something about Richard Smith quite well reportedly stated that Richard Smith was a "lunatic" and a "maniac."

So I'm sure he'll do just great in Fedex management.

Obviously something's not right with him, because after a formal hearing by his fellow college student peers ... the University of Virginia's student Judiciary Committee (UJC) voted to kick Richard Smith out of the University of Virginia forever. They didn't even want him on campus. Imagine a Judicial Body of "students" kicking another fellow student out of their school forever.

I've never heard of such a thing.

Not only that but nearly a thousand University of Virginia students marched in a demonstration of protest to force Richard Smith out.

You must be an awfully Evil Bastard to draw such hatred from (your own) student body?

Daddy Smith must be so proud of his criminal sons.

They'll fit in well at Fedex. Well at least I hope his sons haven't killed any Blacks **"yet"** and left them dead on the road…like their daddy did. They still have time. Fedex plantation/corporation here they come.

Read how two government investigators from two different federal law enforcement agencies told me that Fred Smith founder and CEO of Fedex was "Smuggling Illegal Drugs" into America. One of the investigators asked my help concerning Fred Smith's drug smuggling operations. How the FBI asked my help with recovering a $100,000 gold shipment and catching the thieves within Fedex who stole it. And you think your Fedex shipment is safe? Yeah Right. If they want your shipment they take it.

What they both said about him and his drug smuggling. Both of them…one an FBI agent and one an AFOSI agent strongly warned me to be careful.

They were concerned for my life.

They said Fred Smith was a "Drug Smuggler" and a "Dangerous Man and he might send someone to murder me."

What else did they know about him that they couldn't tell me?

AFOSI agents said Fred Smith was smuggling illegal drugs into the U.S from Mexico. Smith had access to planes and small air fields in Arkansas. And a whole fleet of Fedex planes just like the one DEA pictured on their website. On that picture of the Fedex Plane the DEA had stamped "Illegal Drugs" on the fuselage.

Another major drug smuggler in Arkansas…Barry Seal was also smuggling Illegal Drugs (marijuana, Cocaine and Quaaludes) into the U.S. from Mexico and South America. Just surprisingly he also had access to planes and small air fields in Arkansas just like Fred Smith. Barry Seal was murdered by Drug Cartel smugglers who he had testified against.

No wonder they were concerned for my life.

Did Barry Seal give testimony against Fred Smith? Was that why he was murdered? Seal and Smith were both in Arkansas and Smuggling Illegal Drugs… did Fred Smith have Barry Seal …"Silenced" too?

Read about how Fred Smith was refusing to allow FBI and Federal agents into his airport loading areas all across America. Was he hiding his "illegal drug" shipments?

You will read how a Fedex Senior Station manager **Stephanie Seberg** in Wilmington Delaware had to be put under bodyguard protection to keep her alive because Fedex Drug Dealers were threatening to MURDER HER.

And Upper Fedex management begged "who" to save Stephanie's Life?

Yeah I tape recorded it… you wouldn't believe it if I didn't.

Is she still Alive?

How drug dealers trust Fedex to safely ship their illegal drugs all across America. NOT UPS, Not DHL, Not USPS …Fedex is the Drug Dealers Shipper.

How anyone can safely ship illegal drugs all across America thru Fedex and for FREE. Taught to me by a FedEx "cargo handler" that was a convicted Federal Drug Felon on "Felony probation/parole?"

Fedex Management brought him in to work as a cargo handler after "his Federal convictions" as a Major Drug Dealer on the east coast.

You'll be surprised what I saw in his car…

Read how … when a Fedex courier did tell management there were illegal drugs in one of his Fedex shipments and that he was going to call the police, he was <u>ordered</u> not to tell police and to just deliver the illegal drug shipment to the drug dealer that was in his own neighborhood where he had children. Fedex was making money on that drug shipment.

They weren't going to lose "revenue" for anything.

The courier instead contacted police who took the drugs and busted the drug dealers. Then Fedex management promptly fired him for not delivering the drugs. He had cost them money. They were concerned that other drug dealers might get afraid and might NOT ship they illegal drugs thru Fedex. Fedex has made many millions on "Illegal Drugs" shipments.

And it's possible … that they were afraid the drug shipment could have been traced back to Fred Smith?

Read how I was told by Fedex management that I was to tell drug dealers that it was okay and safe to ship their illegal drugs thru Fedex…and that their illegal drugs would be safe at Fedex. Also read how Fedex management and couriers many times steal these drugs for themselves for their own use and also for distribution.

7

In this book you will learn that Blacks are thought of as "less than Human and Stupid" by Racist White Fedex management. That Blacks should be thought of as "Pets", you fed them but they were NOT allowed to eat from your table.

That it didn't matter how good a Black employee was or how hard he worked at Fedex, if he was Black ... he NEVER stood a fair chance to advance. Unless he was used as a "Token."

How Black Fedex workers are called Niggers, Monkeys and Baboons etc. by White Fedex management at formal company meetings when there are no Blacks around. And who is going to tell?

Find out about a Fedex management tool (BB&F) used strictly against Blacks to keep them in line and to hold them back from advancement.

Read about Fedex's (NP) equipment. It's "Nigger Proof" engineered just for Blacks because Fred Smith and his White Fedex management believe Blacks are STUPID. and not as intelligent as whites. And the KKK agrees.

And There is so much more in the book

CHAPTER 1

RACISM AND DISCRIMINATION

I am a white man. I am not one of those "ohh I love all black people and think they are all great" kind of guys. I'm just a guy who believes in the old ways of working hard, taking care of his family and being a good and responsible person. If a man or woman has good values, works hard and is responsible it really doesn't matter what color his or her skin is. They will have my respect and I will treat him fairly.

Black soldiers have put their lives on the line to serve and protect this great country we call America for many years. When they come home from their duties of serving our country I believe they should be given all of the same respect and opportunities that any white American receives. Just as equal opportunities to work and be treated fairly in the work place should be the norm for all Americans regardless of color. And not just for the few of a particular ethnic background.

It's been my experience that most companies and people in America feel that way also. In my personal life I've never been around or wanted to be around racist or hate groups or really any radical organizations. I work hard, take care of my family and go to church on Sunday. I have coached summer baseball and football teams and am currently coaching a baseball team at this writing. The wife has been involved in the PTA and other school functions as well as many church functions and I helped when I could. Nothing special about that. Just what I call a regular American guy/family.

I've seen and experienced many interactions between Blacks and Whites and generally both parties worked well together. And many times good friendships came from it. Maybe that's why I was so shocked to see so much racial discrimination and disrespect of blacks by white Fedex management.

I was actually told by white Fedex employees living in the south, but could not confirm, that there are in fact a number of Fedex management and employee's that still belong to the KKK. That they do display that "confederate flag" that symbolizes slavery, in their yards and on their pickup trucks. They said that upper Fedex management is aware of this fact and they are okay with it.

I guess the question I would like to have <u>truthfully answered</u> is ..."how many in Fedex management really do have that white robe and how far up the Fedex corporate ladder do they go?"

<u>We do know that Fred Smith, like the KKK ... loves his "confederate SLAVE flag" that symbolizes SLAVERY and WHITE SUPREMACY OVER BLACKS and displays and defends it proudly</u>.

Just a little more "discretely today".

But we all know that the KKK keep's their membership hidden because they are a "secret organization" that wears hoods over their faces because they have harmed and murdered many Blacks. Many of these Blacks were murdered just because they wanted the right to vote.

I learned first hand early in my employment at Fedex that white management truly believed Blacks were less human than whites. And should be treated as less than human. And that they should be held back and kept at low level jobs and not allowed to be in upper management at Fedex.

That when a Black was allowed into a management position at Fedex it was ONLY so that Fedex could use them as tokens to pretend and lie that they did promote Blacks fairly. <u>Which is a lie</u>.

Sometimes I would hear management talk about good, intelligent and hard working Blacks at Fedex as though they were not even human. Even making nasty racists remarks about their wives and children. I could never be sure if it was already their beliefs before they began working at Fedex or if it was part of the Fedex corporate doctrine. But it was certainly easy to see that it was a belief that they held strongly while in Fedex management.

I came to realize that from talking to quite a number of white Fedex employees and especially white management all across America. Blacks were treated very badly and talked about behind their backs by whites, especially management like I never thought I would see or hear in modern day America.

Sometimes I felt as if I was in the deep south even before the 1950's

Some people will say ... hey, Fedex employs a lot of Blacks. Well so did the white owned slave plantations in the south before the civil war.

Fedex does employ a number of Blacks. But I as a white man who was a "white employee of Fedex" has seen things and heard things in and from numerous Fedex locations that Blacks will never see or hear simply because ..."they are NOT white." So much is spoken against Blacks when they are not present. Then, when they are present the same racists in management will "sometimes" speak nicely to them as though they are their friends.

I can honestly say that in talking to many whites within Fedex management from many parts of the country, I never once knew of one who didn't honestly believe that Blacks were stupid and less than whites.

This next chapter will contain a lot about the racism and discrimination against Blacks and the White Superiority beliefs of Fred Smith and his White Fedex Plantation management.

A lot of people will find some of it hard to believe.

Fred Smith's racists beliefs started many years ago. His father (and maybe even his grandfather) was a racist too. And maybe that is where Fred learned it. His father also known as Frederick Smith owned several business's too. One of them was the "Toddlers House" restaurants. His father actually had a chain of restaurants. That could be a nice story. Except that during the time that his father Frederick Smith Sr. owned the Toddler House restaurants.

Blacks were NOT allowed to eat there.

Fred Smith Sr. had strict and direct orders regarding Blacks.

Fred Smith Sr. said ...

NO NIGGERS ARE ALLOWED in my Toddler Houses.

When Fred Smith's father owned the Toddler House restaurants...if a Black person tried to eat there...they might get shot and killed. They might get beaten and tarred and feathered maybe hung.   If they were lucky they might just get arrested and put in jail. But for certain ..at Frederick Smith Sr.'s Toddler House Restaurants.

NO BLACKS ALLOWED   They might be killed

After Fred Smith's father sold the Toddler House chain to the Dobb's corporation Blacks were finally allowed to eat there. But they knew better than to even try while Smith's father still owned it.

Fred Smith's father was a racists from cradle to grave....I think Fred Smith too. As you read this book you will see exactly why I think...actually know that.

I think to start this chapter off I will begin with an interview I had with a white man who worked for Fedex for sixteen years and was in Fedex management.

For this chapter I will only write about the part of the interview concerning Discrimination and Racism against Blacks by Fedex management.

I had actually intended the interview to be only about illegal drugs within Fedex but the subject of racism came up and the responses to my questions will be a revelation to many but not all. Certainly not to the Black Fedex workers who had these experiences.

In later chapters I will go back to the interview for more documentation concerning drug use and thefts of drugs within Fedex.

This is a very shocking and revealing interview for sure. I had already seen and knew about a lot of racism by Fedex management but there was some information in this interview that was new and shocking even to me.

I did not pay this individual for the interview. As he said...he just wants to get the truth off his chest.

Please understand that I did tape record this interview with his permission and have more than (6) copies of these tapes in different locations (one may be secretly hidden on church grounds) to prove the interview is real. You may also some day hear this actual interview being played on TV or on the radio or other media...maybe...YOUTUBE?

For privacy purposes I will refer to this man as John.

Gary, "John how long have you worked for Fedex"?
John, " sixteen years, I worked as a courier for years then was moved up to management."

Gary , "where did you get your training for management at Fedex"?
John, "Olive Branch, Mississippi."

Gary, "after the training at Olive Branch did you receive any more management training anywhere else?"
John, " some in the King of Prussia District Headquarters in Pennsylvania and often in the station where I was a manager."

Gary, "what were some of the things you were taught by the district director?"

John, " remember, we are always right, never admit wrong. Fire anyone and everyone who causes problems or questions managements decisions. If you can't find a reason to fire someone ...make up a reason and fire them."

Gary, "as a manager who did you report to on a daily basis?"

John, " a senior manager, Mike Mitchell was my senior manager"

Gary, "so Mike Mitchell got his orders from the District Director, who got his orders from the Eastern Region and the Eastern Region got their orders from headquarters in Memphis?"

John, " that's right, not a lot of corporate ladder at Fedex."

Gary, " did your senior station manager ever give you orders concerning the policy on blacks?"

John, " yes, that I was not to hire them. Fedex didn't want a lot of black couriers."

Gary, "so Mike Mitchell, the senior station manager told you straight out that you were not to hire blacks?"

John, " yes, well he called them Niggers. Mike said I was not to hire any Niggers unless instructed by him.

Otherwise I was to tell them we weren't hiring."

Gary, "did he tell you those instructions were from district headquarters?"

John, " he left me with no doubt they were. He certainly implied they were and NO station manager would adopt a policy like that on his own. Orders and policy are sent down from company headquarters. No manager makes decisions on his own, the decisions are made at the top and passed down. Of course some policies are not written on paper so there is no paper trail."

Gary, " were you shocked or surprised at this policy against blacks?"

John, " yes I was real surprised, and I didn't like it but I was younger and I had just made manager and I had a home and a family to provide for. I didn't like it but I was afraid of losing my job so I kept my mouth shut. Also, I had worked at Fedex for a long time and I was used to seeing blacks getting screwed and discriminated against and held back and so forth. What I think really surprised me was that it was company policy ...and yet it did seem as though it always was that way."

Gary, "did he say anything else about blacks?"
John, " well, one of the things was they wanted to avoid was having too many Blacks in management and absolutely none in our station. That they had to have a few as tokens but only as few as necessary."

Gary, "how did Fedex manage to keep blacks out of management?"
John, " easy, give them lower scores on their evaluations, usually on paperwork but it could be anything. You would overlook clerical errors on a white couriers paperwork, and embellish the same clerical errors and other minor things on a black couriers paperwork. Mark them down for things like having their shirt tails out, having a truck door open ...numerous ways of doing it."

Gary, "you mean management intentionally gave blacks lower grades compared to whites?"
John, "I only know what I was told. That it was company policy."

Gary, " do you think you were the only Fedex manager told to do that John?"
John, "no I don't, I'm sure I wasn't. And I know over the years at Fedex I've both seen and heard of many better performing black couriers getting lower performance evaluations than their white counterparts who weren't nearly as good. Even I was promoted ahead of better performing blacks. My paperwork was very sloppy and I did a lot of things wrong that would have kept a black out of management. Yet I was white and they needed a manager so I was promoted ahead of more deserving and better black couriers."

Gary, "when your station manager told you not to hire blacks, did he warn you not to tell anyone about it?"

John, "it was an unwritten rule, we weren't even to tell our wives. It was understood. Just like you NEVER said you liked Jews. Certain things at Fedex just weren't acceptable."

Gary, "wait a minute John, did you mean that saying you liked Jews or had Jewish friends wasn't acceptable at Fedex?"

John, " that's exactly what I'm saying Gary, you worked there, did you ever see a Jew working there? <u>No</u>. Management at Fedex hated Jews and if you said you liked them or said something good about them ...well it just might result in your removal from management at Fedex. They can't always control what the couriers think, but if you're in management and you let management know that you are pro Jewish ... well chances are you'll go out the door before you go up the ladder at Fedex.

You'll find very few Jews working there that's for sure"

<u>Note</u>: I remember a member of Fedex management saying to me when I was employed there that Fedex would ship Jews and their families, even their children to the gas chamber if they could get away with it and make a profit doing it. He wasn't just stressing Fedex's commitment to be profitable. He was also expressing Fred Smith's and Fedex management's dislike, even hatred and disrespect, for the Jewish people in general. I guess exactly like the KKK's hatred of Jews.

He seemed very proud that Fedex would do something like that. Here was Fedex management boasting "We'd ship Jews overnight to the gas chamber". I realize now, that statement was generated out of beliefs within Fedex management in Memphis. What a sick bunch of bastards. I had heard Fedex management say bad things about Jews several times while working there but I had thought it was just them as individuals and not a company policy. Apparently I was wrong.

And I remember thinking at the time ... thank God ... Fred Smith and Fedex wasn't around to help Hitler transport the Jewish people to the Gas chambers. Because I'm sure they would have if they had been there. Hitler and the Nazi party might have been their biggest customer. Fred Smith and his Fedex corporation would gain enormous wealth while boasting and bragging about shipping Jews to the gas chamber to be murdered.

Then again, Fred Smith was raised in Little Rock, Arkansas. A KKK capital, and everybody knows the KKK hates Jews and Blacks alike.

Back to the interview.

Gary, "did you ever question the policy against hiring blacks, did you ever talk to your district director about it?"

John, "well actually I did yes, we were breaking from a meeting in King of Prussia, Pennsylvania. I asked him why Fedex didn't hire more blacks into management or as workers. He said that blacks just don't fit Fedex's mode. That Fedex is a 'young white progressive company' and that blacks just don't fit the mode ... that they would slow down the company's progress."

Gary, "did he say anything else about blacks?"

John, "other things too, but what I mostly remember is his warning me about not telling anyone. He warned me that if I ever told anyone about it that Fedex would come after me, that I would be fired and I would never work for anyone ever again. And that Fedex lawyers would come after me and ruin my reputation. It really scared me to be honest."

*__Note__: When Fred Smith found out I had gone to the government and the newspapers about their fraud against the government and our soldiers, their lawyers threatened to put my family out in the streets forever. They said, tell Gary Rullo to keep his mouth shut about the fraud or we'll put him, his wife and his kids out in the street forever and he'll never ever be able work again. Fortunately the Philadelphia Inquirer did their own investigation of Fedex's fraud. They told me not to worry because Fedex was guilty of fraud and they [Fedex] would have to go thru them before they got to me. They were doing the story. Still I did wonder if they meant "physically" not able to work again?

Back to interview...

Gary, "in regard to black employees at Fedex or even black applicants ... did your station manager Mike Mitchell ever ask you while you were a manager ..."if a black person smelled or stunk?"

John, "yeah he would always ask ... "does that nigger smell or does that nigger speak Caucasian" and he never asked that about white applicants. It was as though all whites smelled fine and all blacks stunk."

Gary, "was it common for you to hear white Fedex management refer to blacks as Niggers?"

John, "yes , all the time as a courier and even more as a manager. When there was a management meeting in which there was no blacks present it almost seemed like it was more of a Klan meeting than a company meeting. It seemed that management was more concerned with putting down blacks than anything else. It seemed they all tried to out do each other with stories about this or that "stupid Nigger". Or how they screwed this or that Nigger. Or how there was getting to be too many Niggers at Fedex etc. It was pretty disgusting to be honest. And when they went out to lunch there seemed to be a contest to see who could use the "Nigger" word the most. It was like old time southern pictures when blacks were talked about and thought of ... as less than human."

Gary, "what other names did you hear management use to describe blacks at Fedex?"

John, "just about all of them, Jungle Bunny, Porch Monkey, Baboon, Apes, Spear Chucker, you name it they used it and often. Just never to a black's face.

Gary, "in your sixteen years at Fedex as a courier or as a manager did you ever hear of anyone being reprimanded for using racial slurs against blacks?"

John, "no, in fact I know of a black guy, a friend of mine by the name of Kevin Brownley who got a letter of reprimand because he said something back to a white woman at the Philadelphia airport ramp. The woman was white and she called him a "Lazy Nigger" and when he said something back to her because she called him a nigger he got a letter for it. She never got any reprimand even though there was proof that she called him a Nigger. Management did nothing to her."

*Note: I also worked at the Philadelphia airport ramp. I can't begin to count the number of times I heard good hard working blacks called nigger, monkey and other insulting names. The blacks were intimidated by whites and white management there. They were taught early on in Fedex employment, that they were less than the whites there and to keep their mouths shut or they wouldn't have a job. Even though they worked as hard or harder than their white co-workers. Many of them had families to support so they put up with it to keep their jobs.

Back To the Interview
Gary, "is there a lot of 'NP' equipment at Fedex?"
John, "I was told there was 'NP' equipment at Fedex.
An engineer at Fedex told me there was 'NP' equipment at Fedex yes. He said that "'NP' stood for "Nigger Proof" meaning that if a black person could use 'NP' equipment, anyone could. Only he didn't use the word 'black'. We had been talking about the tracker/scanners couriers use and he informed me that they were engineered to be 'NP' ... "Nigger Proof". Otherwise (the engineer said) "we'd have to fire all the Niggers at Fedex."

Gary, "was that a common way of thinking by white management at Fedex?"
John, "well in my sixteen years at Fedex as a courier and in management ...it was the ONLY way of thinking about blacks by Fedex management. I was even told that by others in Fedex management."

Gary, "a few years ago I was having a conversation with a white man who was a member of Fedex management in New Jersey. In the course of the conversation he made the statement ... 'BBF the Niggers'. John, what does 'BBF' stand for?"
John, " it was explained to me that 'BB&F' had a double meaning and was to be used by white Fedex management against black employees. It stood for 'Basketball, Boxing and Football'. And it also stood for 'Bullshit the Blacks and Fuck'em'.

Gary, " could you explain to me how it worked?"
John, "Fedex management believed that if a white manager talked to blacks about one of those sports they would win their hearts and minds. That blacks were easily won over and fooled if you spoke sports to them. And they would cause less problems."

Gary, "when you say ... less problems, what do you mean."

John, "less complaints, less GFT's, less lawsuits if they got fired etc. <u>Get the blacks to think the white managers were their friends and they wouldn't cause problems.</u>"

Gary, "did management use this '**BB&F**' tool on whites too?"
John, "no, not really, it was intended to use on blacks."

Gary, "as a courier or as a member of Fedex management have you actually seen a black person held back or not given a job just because that person was black?"
John, "yes Gary, lots of times. Numerous times I've seen blacks come into the station and ask if there was any positions open or was Fedex hiring. And they were told Fedex wasn't hiring or that the positions had been filled. When in fact there were openings but they were only hiring 'whites'. It happened ALL the time.
I'm sure it STILL DOES TODAY."

Gary, "what about management positions, have you actually seen blacks passed over or held back strictly because that person was Black?"
John, "yes, Blacks were passed over for promotions many times just because they were Black. Charles Dorsey is Black and several times he was passed over just because he was Black. He was passed over for a sales position and a manager's position. And he would have been perfect for those positions. He was smart, clean looking, he was tall with a loud clear voice ... in short he was a sharp clean looking Black man who spoke well and clearly. a Good family man too. But he was 'Black' and to management he was just another 'Nigger' who didn't fit Fedex's mode.
It was a shame because Charles was a class guy.
Gary, "I remember when I worked the ILG station in Delaware and they needed a manager on the evening shift. At the time I thought maybe Charles would be offered the job. But what management did was, they brought in a white guy from Philadelphia who had never been in the station before. Did he have much experience?'
John, "very little if any at all. They had to teach him everything and he had to learn nearly everything. Charles already knew everything and he had years of experience and was very good at it. But he was Black and he never had a chance at the job.

Gary, "if Charles had been white would he have been considered for the position?"

John, "he would have had the position he was perfect for the position ... education, knowledge, experience, excellent skills and he was clean cut. He had it ALL ...except he was "Black". They wouldn't even consider him."

Gary, "can you give me another example?"

John, "Sure. There was a Black cargo handler. He had college was also clean and very well spoken. He was working full time as a sales representative for the McCormick seasoning company and doing very well. But at the time they [Fedex] would only hire him on to handle freight part time at night. He was a hard worker. He worked for McCormick in the daytime in sales, and at Fedex he was only a cargo handler part time at night.

A sales position came open in the station and I know he asked management about it but they wouldn't even consider it. Mike, the senior station manager, said, "no way, I don't care if he is in sales, there will be no Niggers in management here."

"He was Black and never stood a chance." Fedex brought in a white guy that didn't even work for the company. Just to make sure a Black stayed at cargo handler. Mike said that company policy didn't want many Blacks in management and he especially didn't want any "Nigger" in management in his station.

Gary, "So Mike would actually say to you that he didn't wouldn't allow Blacks in management at his station"?

John, " yes he did, he actually said a number of times that he didn't [want any dammed Nigger's in his station] that he didn't want to have to deal with them or be around them. This is a common thought with white Fedex management even today. It's just a little more sophisticated today.

I believe there's a group of Black Fedex workers in Memphis that have a discrimination lawsuit against Fedex."

Gary, "what is the lawsuit about"?

John, " it's mostly by Black cargo handlers in Memphis. It seems that Fedex keeps so many of the Blacks in the lowest paying positions and keeps them doing the hardest dirtiest work there. It's more like [slave labor] ... very hard work and very low pay. And they're mostly supervised by whites. No different than the plantation days I guess. I'm surprised that Fred Smith doesn't offer the Black workers beds in the [slave quarters] on his plantation.

Gary, "you know ...basically it seems that Fedex management is telling the Blacks that 'you are too stupid to manage yourself.' That you need to have SUPERIOR WHITE people over you to tell you what to do and how".

John, "not basically, that exactly what they are telling them. Fedex is saying that BLACKS ARE STUPID and WHITES ARE MUCH SMARTER.

A white work force which comprises approximately ten percent of the cargo handlers in Memphis is smarter than the other ninety percent of the work force [Blacks] simply because they are white."

Gary, "if a white manager did an unfair or biased evaluation on a Black employee, wasn't that manager afraid that the Black employee would file a discrimination suit against the company"?

John, " Well that's where the **BB& F management tool**' came into play. Management knew that Blacks were loyal and believed that they could easily be fooled. So if a white manager talked [Basketball Boxing, or Football] to a Black employee and the Black believed the manager was his friend...that manager felt he could get away with giving lower evaluations to Blacks. Although sometimes I think the Blacks knew the white manager didn't like them and they were just afraid of losing their jobs.

Fact is ... the Blacks had to be better, do better and not make mistakes. Many times I made mistakes that a Black worker would have been fired for ...and yet, because I was white nothing happened to me. I've seen it happen a lot that a Black would get fired for doing the exact same thing that a white courier was getting away with and management knew it."

Gary, "didn't it make Blacks feel inferior when they repeatedly saw their "white co-workers" get better grades and promotions? They were doing their best and yet it seems they always came up as being not as good as the whites."

John, "yeah, I guess it did but that wasn't the intention. It was just Fedex's way to keep Blacks out of management. And it made it easier to fire them of course. But also, I think it was just thought of as a way to keep them [Blacks] in line. In the colonial days they used a whip to keep Blacks in line ... at Fedex they used a "Pen" like a Whip." It was a way to keep Blacks in line. Letters in your file, every little thing that might be used to keep them out of management or to fire them.
The "Pen" was used as the modern day Whip".

Gary, "Funny you brought that up ...doesn't Fred Smith the founder and CEO of Fedex live on a southern plantation that has SLAVE QUARTERS on it"?
John, "yeah I read that and others have told me that too"

Gary, " But doesn't Fedex have a Black man as the top personnel guy? Wouldn't he look after the welfare of his fellow Blacks? Make sure they are treated fairly?"
John, "I have no idea what he's up to. But I do know that within the company many times he's referred to as [Fred's House Nigger] and he was there so that Fedex wouldn't have to fear the Blacks because they had one in a key position in personnel. Believe me , he's no Jesse Jackson. I honestly don't believe he cares one bit about the Blacks . He's right there in Memphis and that's where the discrimination lawsuit is. So what's he doing to help his fellow Blacks?"

Gary, "So what you're saying is that he was just a Black man bought off by a rich white man?"
John, "That's exactly what I'm saying, he was bought off. They're paying him good money."

Gary, " John, as a former member of Fedex management and having worked there for sixteen years, what do you think Fedex will do after they find out about this interview?"
John, "I guess like they'll do about everyone else who tells the truth on them. First thing they'll say is that I'm a disgruntled former employee, as some others will think too.

Then they'll try to sue me and you. The threats will come as you have already found out. Maybe they'll bring out a few loyal company Blacks and parade them around so they can say what a great company Fedex is. How they helped so many Blacks.

Fedex does have a very powerful public relations firm. In years past a lot of people believed them. But today more and more people and employees are beginning to see the truth.

And the TRUTH is …Fedex treats Blacks terribly … about what you would expect from a white southern plantation owner. For so many years Black workers at Fedex have poured their hearts and souls into Fedex …and WHITE Fedex management has always screwed them. Called them names, told jokes about them behind their backs, and not only about them but also their wives and children . They even make fun of Blacks in management, all Blacks, but even more so if they were dark Black …the darker a Black was the 'less human" he was. White management actually thought of and treated Blacks as "less then human".

"God it was despicable … it made me sick to my stomach. I only wish I had had more courage to speak up before.

So let Fedex bitch, let them sue me. I've told the truth. Hopefully I will be able to go to my grave with one less burden on my soul. One less feeling of guilt."

Gary, "John, did you ever realize that many of the same Blacks that were discriminated against and screwed by white Fedex management … that were denied jobs because they were Black, were called Niggers and worse, were made fun of and thought of as less than human …were the same Blacks that went to war for America?. That some were wounded … perhaps crippled, that they put their lives on the line while serving our country. Only to come back and be discriminated against and treated as "less than human" by RACIST WHITE FEDEX management?"

John, " yes I realize it …and it's not right."

Gary, "John, as a former member of Fedex management what would you say to a Black employee of Fedex if a white manager came up to him and started talking about "Basketball, Boxing or Football?"

John, "I would tell that Black Fedex employee …not to trust that white manager. Because chances are that manager is just trying to **B**ullshit the **B**lack so he can **F**uck him. I would bet the white manager is BB& F'ing the Black worker. I would tell him, just remember …they are NEVER your FRIEND and NEVER TRUST them."

I have seen and heard a lot of the hatred against Blacks by white workers and management at Fedex. Both while I was employed there and even after I left Fedex and had opportunity to speak one on one with a number of white Fedex employees both regular hourly workers and also members of Fedex management from various parts of the country.

In the beginning I guess I was a little shocked to see so many in management of a national corporation not only outwardly stating their dislike for Blacks. But also actively preaching it and also committing so many acts of discrimination against them. While I'm sure it might still be a common belief in some southern states where many still believe the south should have won the civil war and that slavery was and is a good thing … this is America.

Slavery was rightfully abolished after the Union did win the civil war.

<u>And Frederick W. Smith…Founder and CEO of the FEDEX Plantation needs to learn this.</u>

But I am certain he never will. If pressed to give an official statement about racism and discrimination either by himself or the Fedex corporation as a whole. He and his publicists will spend millions of dollars saying how much they love Blacks, respect Blacks and treat Blacks equally. And try to hide the evidence that proves otherwise. Then they will try to crucify anyone who dares speak the truth about their racial hatred or how badly they treat Black employees there.

Fred Smith might even try to murder a man at his home … if that man speaks the truth about him

But will Frederick W. Smith openly brag about taking his "**beloved confederate flag**" to college with him and how he proudly displayed it on his dormitory wall to express his desire to continue slavery even on his own cotton plantation   How he expressed strongly his belief that the south should be allowed to own "Nigger Slaves" to do the hard and dirty work on their plantations.

Now that he is CEO of a major corporation will he brag about how he believes they should be whipped and beaten when they speak up for their rights? How Blacks should be kept in their place?

Will he try to hide his "beloved confederate flag" and what it stands for? Does he also have that white KKK robe that goes with it?

Hitler and his Nazi's had their NAZI swastika flag that symbolized their hatred for Jews and their belief in Aryan superiority. The KKK and Fred Smith have a Confederate Flag that symbolizes the enslavement of Blacks and white superiority. And he will run Fedex that way until he dies. My guess is his sons will follow his lead and continue to run Fedex in the same racist manner. That is if they can stay out of jail long enough to run Fedex. Fred just does it a little more discretely today. Just as a Nazi will always hate Jews and want them exterminated. So will Fred Smith always believe in white racial superiority over Blacks and continue to fly his confederate SLAVE FLAG and wish for a return to slavery for Blacks. Or at least the "control over Blacks" by whites.

Will we ever know just how many times he stated in private conversations with other white racists in Fedex management in Memphis and other places "Boy wouldn't it be great if we still had NIGGER SLAVES to do our hard and dirty work here at Fedex?" Wouldn't it be great if our Black workers at the Hub in Memphis were all just slaves and we only had to feed and clothe them? After all Blacks don't really deserve real healthcare and retirement benefits or even proper wages."

"Just to do what the "white people tell you to do."

Do I personally believe Fred Smith said that … I honestly have no doubt that Fred Smith not only said that many times, I'm sure he thought that a thousand times more. As I suspect many other whites in Fedex management did too from conversations I have had with them.. And probably a lot more worse things than that about Blacks. If there is anything worse.

One thing life and history teaches us is that a man's deepest beliefs never change. Not even in a thousand years. Does anyone really believe that if Adolph Hitler was still alive today …he would say, " hey I was wrong about the Jews, they're good people and should be treated fairly. I Adolph Hitler personally like and respect Jews"?

<u>NO</u>. he would never think or say that.

On January 31, 1975 Fred Smith hit and killed a innocent Black man in broad daylight and drove off to let him die in the street. He knew he hit him and killed him…Did he do it intentionally ?

He was a rich white southern man who killed a poor Black man in Little Rock, Arkansas in broad daylight. Where most whites in Little Rock just called them "NIGGERS" anyway. When he was later caught and questioned by police he stated that he wasn't aware he had hit a man.

I wonder if he was he smiling when he said that? In his eyes and mind he was telling the truth, he had only killed a "NIGGER" not a real man so he could just keep driving away leaving the man to die in the street like he had just killed an animal. White men in Little Rock didn't have to stop and call police when they killed Blacks. Fred Smith proved that.

Now there might be some naive people out there who might think … maybe Fred Smith didn't know he had hit a man. Well I've seen accident scenes and the damage done to a car when it hit a man both close up personally and also in pictures in the newspapers and on TV, when you hit someone with a car hard enough to kill them it makes a lot of noise and leaves a lot of damage to the vehicle.

Who are we kidding here? <u>Fred Smith didn't stop because it was a Black man he hit</u>.

Does anyone really believe that this wealthy, super smart (according to his well paid publicists) , well educated business man not realize he had hit someone? Did he not realize his car had sustained extensive damage from impact like maybe a broken front windshield, maybe no more headlights, all the damaged metal sheathing (fender or hood) did he not hear the noise of the Black man's body hitting his car as he broke many bones in the man's body? Maybe heard him screaming in pain? Did he not see the body flying thru the air like a basketball?

Who the hell are we kidding …a rich racist white man killed a "poor black man."

And it was okay…He was a rich "white man" in Little Rock, Arkansas.

The KKK has killed more Blacks than that and got away with it. No Big Deal !!! The KKK was very active in Little Rock. Maybe Fred Smith even "hi five'd" some of them in celebration. Maybe he drove home and immediately kissed and saluted his "beloved confederate slavery flag" or maybe even a secret hidden KKK robe? But he certainly had no shame or remorse for what he did NONE.

But what we do know is that he didn't call an ambulance or the police did he? He didn't stop to see if he could help the man. He just left him laying in the street to suffer and die in broad daylight.

How could racism, racial hatred and discrimination be so prevalent in a nationwide corporation with tens of thousands of employees?

Answer : Let Fred Smith be the "Founder and CEO".

So I looked deeper and what I found was extreme racial prejudice handed down from generations. Fred Smith's family had owned plantations where slavery had been the norm and Blacks were thought of and treated like animals. That's why he took his "beloved confederate flag" which is the south's symbol of white supremacy over, and slavery of Blacks to college.

Just as the Nazi's flew their flag because they believed in Aryan supremacy and extinction of all Jews.

Fred Smith's creation of the Fedex corporation with it's constant preaching and practice of disrespect and discrimination against Blacks by it's white racist management is no accident. Rather it is done with planned dictated intent, and is the legacy of Fred Smith and racist white management within the Fedex corporation.

Ask yourself would Adolph Hitler change his beliefs that Jews should no longer be murdered and put in gas chambers until the complete extinction of their race? NO.

Would the Grand Master of the KKK ever tell his followers that Blacks were equal to whites and just as good. That he realizes the KKK was wrong and should respect Blacks and treat them fairly and not harm or kill them anymore? NO.

Would Frederick W. Smith who lives on a southern slave plantation and still believing in and flying his "beloved confederate flag", who killed at least one innocent Black man and left him to die in the street like an animal. He is the founder and CEO of the Fedex Plantation that treats Blacks as "less than human." Where Blacks are kept in their place like modern day slaves …will he ever change his beliefs of White Supremacy over Blacks … NO. White control over Blacks…It's in his blood and in his heart.

And it will stay there until his death.

Thank God America does have a system of courts and investigative agencies in place to stop the organized conspiracy of racial discrimination and hatred by companies trying to enslave certain ethnic groups in America.

Below is just a <u>tiny look</u> at the company wide discrimination and racism by Fred Smith's "Fedex Plantation Corporation". These examples are like a single grain of sand on a beach.

Racial discrimination by the Fedex plantation is most times hidden and covered up by layers of loyal racists in Fedex's management and legal teams. They make sure Fred Smith's desire of controlling and holding Blacks down as far as possible are not only fulfilled but also protected. I would guess that it's hard for many whites that never worked there to believe the extent of racism and discrimination that goes on within Fedex every day or even that it really is "corporate policy" and that it is directed and ordered by Fred Smith.

Following are some, probably less than one ten thousandths of the discrimination complaints by Black employees against Fedex. These are just a very few that were made" through their attorney's, the EEOC and the courts against the Fedex Plantation.

Many times Fedex settles out of court privately because Fred Smith doesn't want records or evidence of his and Fedex's racism and discrimination on court records and exposed to the media's eyes.

Just as the tobacco companies didn't want records of testimony and evidence that tobacco caused cancer. So they threw up every injunction and hid and destroyed every piece of evidence they could … to stop all testimony and evidence against them.

It took many years and many lawsuits to finally get the truth out that they always knew about tobacco causing cancer and were lying about it. So too it is with Fred Smith and his Racist Fedex Plantation Corporation.

Today as always Fedex lawyers throw up every injunction they can to stop the truth and Fred Smith hides and destroys every piece of evidence he can. So no one will know the corporate wide racism and discrimination they commit every day against Blacks especially, but also to other minorities.

He did the exact same thing with documents and evidence when ordered by courts and military investigators and prosecutors to present "all documents and paperwork" concerning CSS shipments of sensitive military equipment by Fedex. He knew as did his fellow criminals at Fedex that they were guilty of not only conspiracy to commit fraud, but also were actually caught in the act of committing fraud against the military.

And if all the documents and evidence were found he and they would spend many years in a federal prison.

His corporate lawyers kept him out of federal prison but that is where he belongs.

Here are just a few <u>FACTS on Fedex Discrimination.</u>   If the truth were known there would be a million.

In May of 2006 government agents of Equal Employment Opportunity Commission (EEOC) did an investigation of the Fedex corporation of company wide discrimination against Blacks all across America. The regional government attorney for the EEOC had to file for a federal subpoena against Fedex to get evidence that Fred Smith and his Fedex Plantation were hiding and refused to turnover because they didn't want the government to find official company programs of racism.

<u>Chester Bailey the district director for the EEOC involved with investigating Fedex publicly stated that, "No employer has the right to systematically deny promotional opportunities to "entire demographic groups."</u> Blacks being treated as "less than human."

Think about what this man is saying. He did the investigation of Fedex's Racism and Discrimination against it's Black workers. He found that Fred Smith had put in a program of "systematic Racism and Discrimination" against Blacks. That is a vital part of Fred Smith's "corporate Doctrine. "Keep Blacks in their place," Keep them at the bottom of the work force just EXACTLY like the Slave owners did to their slaves. It wasn't a few Fedex locations in a few states… it was "corporate wide."

Fred Smith was intentionally keeping thousands of Black workers under "white control." Because he believes that Blacks are "less than human" and that they are "mentally inferior" to whites, that there should ALWAYS be a white man OVER Blacks to tell them what to do.

Just how many confederate flags are hanging in how many homes of White Fedex management?

On August 11, 1997 seven present and former employees of Fedex filed a " racial discrimination lawsuit" against Fedex. In the lawsuit they claimed that Fedex had a disproportionate number of Black employees and far too few Blacks in management. They stated that Fedex corporation discriminates against Blacks by denying them promotions and paying them less. The lawsuit stated that current and former employees were systematically kept out of Fedex management by white Fedex management. They said that Fedex management used "underline discipline and terminations" to retaliate against Blacks who "ask to be treated equally to whites."

"Fedex uses the Pen Like the Whip"

THIS IS FACT:… if you are a Black employee at Fedex and you file a "discrimination complaint" because Fedex management discriminated against you …Fred Smith will do everything he can to have you terminated.

So basically what Fedex is saying to it's Black employees is…if we do let you work here be prepared to be treated like a "SLAVE" with no rights … or we'll fire your Black Ass.

Sounds like the old BB& F program doesn't always work quite as well as Fred Smith wanted.

Still the KKK would be proud of Fedex for trying.

In March of 2005 in St' Louis, Missouri the EEOC had to step in and force Fedex to pay $ 500,000 to twenty (20) Black employees of Fedex Freight East for racial discrimination. It stated that Fedex had denied promotions and assignments based on their race.

That's "Fred Smith's Fedex Plantation" at it's best.

In February of 2002 Myron Lowery who lives in Memphis where Fedex headquarters is located filed a racial discrimination lawsuit against Fedex. Thompson who is Black and a **Fedex employee stated that he was denied promotions within Fedex simply because he was "a Black man."**

Well no wonder he was held back at Fedex Plantation. After all he was a Black man.

Lowery was also a Memphis city councilman and even with his political position and connections he was still thought of as "less than equal" by Fedex management.

There's a lot of confederate flags in Memphis and Tennessee. Fred Smith has at least one and the KKK has many. There's also a lot of white KKK robes there too.

Does Fred have one of them also? He has the flag, why not the robe?

February 2008 …Fedex loses another discrimination suit in New York. It was for $4.5 million dollars

Most people would think that Fred Smith would stop his "Racism and Discrimination" at his Fedex Plantation. But he won't. What he will do is try to "polish his act" to better hide it. So he can keep it going strong.

Then...

On November 09, 2009 The U.S. Supreme court in New York denied Fedex corporation's challenge (<u>injunction</u>) that would have stopped the EEOC from investigating racist discrimination by the Fedex corporation management. So when Fedex or Fred Smith says they are an equal opportunity employer and would welcome an investigation of their company for discrimination against Blacks and other Minorities, ask them why they filed an injunction against the EEOC to stop their investigation of Fedex.

Remember this when you read or here a Fedex spokesperson, even Fred Smith, say, "we are fully cooperating with authorities."

If they did ...they'd ALL be in jail.

Just one more time that Fred Smith and his racist Fedex corporation was trying to <u>hide</u> their racist practices and policies against Blacks.

How much evidence do you think they <u>destroyed</u>?

I bet he wishes he could have just bought his Blacks at the local "Slave Auctions" like in the good old southern slavery days in Arkansas and Tennessee and other states. Just like they were "bought" to work on the slave plantation he grew up on.

He'll never learn...The south lost the war ...and slaves are a thing of the past.

In Houston Texas a jury awarded a Black man $2.9 million dollars, finding that <u>Fedex management retaliated against him after he filed charges of racial discrimination against them.</u>

Around 2002 Mr. Price filed a complaint against Fedex stating that they held him back from promotions simply because he was Black.

White Fedex management then began retaliating against him because he had the character to speak up and state the truth. After Price filed a complaint about the racist discrimination by white Fedex management, they came after him.

He was wrongly written up and reprimanded. **"the Pen is used like a modern day Whip"** for the Black guy. And then they fired him.

I guess they were going to teach "the Nigger" to keep his mouth shut about the racist practices of discrimination within Fedex corp.

Fortunately for Mr. Price this was not 1800 ...or Fred may have had him tied to a post and whipped. Today Fred could only punish him with a "pen" and fire him. Still, he wanted to punish the black man for standing up for his rights.

Did Fred want Mr. Price to say, "<u>Yes Master</u>, whatever you say or want I'll do?" It doesn't work that way anymore. Mr. Price was a better man than that.

Price's attorney Mr. Harris stated that, "Obviously the jury felt very strongly that Fedex needs to learn a lesson and that they have to pay a substantial amount of money to get their attention."

The truth is ...You can NEVER take racism and prejudice out of someone when it is ingrained so deeply as it is in Smith. Just as you can never make a Nazi like or respect a Jew.

Fred Smith still tries to keep his racist "Fedex Plantation" going.

Not only does Fedex management discriminate against Blacks and other minorities within Fedex, They also retaliate against whites in management and force them out, if they find that they are not racists and will not follow Fedex's programs of discrimination. A white man in Fedex management learned that the hard way.

In the case below it sounds like KKK lesson number "101" for the dumb white guy.

*As in this case of a Mr. Ted Maines, a White Man, who had been with Fedex since the eighties and was considered a valued employee of more than (20) years until Fedex upper management found out that he was NOT a racist and would NOT discriminate against Blacks or other minorities. Mr. Maines rose to the position of Senior Manager of Customer Account Services in Florida. He had worked hard thru his many years at Fedex and had gained the reputation as a smart man that had done many great things at Fedex and was a loyal and dependable employee.

* <u>**Until he got stupid and tried to treat a Black man equally and fairly.**</u> What the Hell was he thinking?

Things began to unravel for Mr. Maines when he tried to promote two very deserving employees of Fedex. The problem was ...they were both minorities. One of the employees was a Black man and one was

Hispanic. They had also worked for Fedex many years and also had a history of great work and dependability within Fedex.

Mr. Maines put these two men [a Black and a Hispanic] in for promotions for openings within the company because they had the right experience and deserved it. Fedex's White Vice President flat out refused to promote them and instead put a newly hired "White person" in the position instead. The White was not even qualified and had NO experience" at all.

Mr. Maines, who is white, wrote a letter and complained to Fedex's legal department that the Black and Hispanic men were being discriminated against.

I do wonder, he worked there for twenty years. He must have known better. Blacks were promoted primarily for "quotas and appearances." Fedex must have already met their Black persons "quota for appearances" for the year. No more Blacks allowed, no matter how good or how deserving they were.

That job was only going to ... ahem a "superior white person" with no experience, no qualifications and no knowledge of the job. But they were ...White. For Ted Maines it was a...

Bad move sticking up for Blacks and minorities.

In retaliation to Mr. Maines for trying to do what was right and fair to a well qualified and deserving "Black and a Hispanic man," upper White Fedex management gave him a choice of accepting a demotion of five pay grade levels and to report to "his new subordinate" ... or be issued a strongly worded warning letter and face "immediate termination" for any subsequent mistake.

Which I believe Fedex management would create as soon as Mr. Maines signed the letter.

It would be (I believe Fedex management planned) a chance to get rid of the "Nigger Lover."

Mr. Maines refused to accept either option so Fedex management issued a disciplinary warning letter to him anyway containing a threat of termination.

And also a verbal admonishment stating that the "White vice president of Fedex" wanted him to know that the very next mistake he made... such as "trying to promote a Black man or going against Fedex's corporate wide policy of Racial Discrimination against Blacks and minorities, would be his very last one as a Fedex employee."

Thereafter Mr. Maines was subjected to intense scrutiny, including electronic monitoring. He believes that his phones were monitored and much more. His every move at Fedex was closely watched until he could take it no more. And he was forced to resign from a company he had given his all to ... for twenty one years.

All because he as a "white man" in Fedex management tried to promote a well qualified and deserving Black and a Hispanic.

Welcome to Fred Smiths' "Fedex world or racial discrimination"

When I read about this, "a white man trying to treat a Black man fairly and as an equal, and how he was singled out and was ran out of Fedex" ... I thought back to how my then Senior station manager Mike Mitchell grilled me about my views of equality for Blacks within Fedex. And how he told me straight up that Fedex management didn't want Blacks in management...well he called them "Niggers." But I did get the point. Fred Smith think Blacks are not mentally our equal... that Blacks are inferior to whites.

Are there any Blacks that want to work at Fred Smiths Plantation ?

In December of 2004 a Federal Jury ordered Fedex to pay Mr. Maines $ 1.57 million dollars.

So what, Fedex let everyone in management throughout the company know ...you don't promote Blacks unless told to. Keep them in their place.

The lesson that was taught to other whites in Fedex Management cost Fedex 1.57 million. But Fred Smith thought the "Lesson" outweighed the cost.

DO NOT treat Blacks as equals... End of Lesson.

In San Francisco around 2006 Fedex was ordered to pay millions of dollars for racial harassment against a Hispanic worker and also again when a white Fedex supervisor forced himself on a Black woman and conditioned her pay check upon her seeing him after work. Does that sound like "Colonial era Cotton Plantation slave treatment or what?"

They were Black and Hispanic and easy prey for White Fedex management who doesn't see Blacks and other minorities as equals or even as "real humans."

Instead of talking **B.B. & F.** ...He was trying to force **F. U. C. K. Me.** from what he believed was an "inferior Black woman". Just like it

34

was done on the "southern slave plantations" like the one Fred Smith grew up on.

Weren't the Black women there to serve their "White Fedex Plantation Masters?

In September 2007 Fedex agreed to pay **$55 million** dollars in an "out of court settlement" of a racial discrimination lawsuit. They didn't want to go to court where so much of their dirty racist laundry would be put on court records forever and also exposed to the public. They must have REALLY Been GUILTY on That one!!! **Ahh...Fred Smith's Fedex Plantation pays a BIG one.**

But even that amount of money won't change the racist attitudes of white Fedex management.

The sad truth is, no matter how much money the Fedex corporation has to pay in legal fees, fines, judgments or punitive costs they will NEVER change their ways. Just like the KKK ... Fred Smith and his Fedex Plantation will ALWAYS be a racist organization.

Fred Smith will carry his "beloved confederate SLAVE flag to his grave. It stands for Slavery and White Superiority and Dominance over Blacks. Maybe he keeps it in hopes that Slavery will return. Just as the last living Nazi's keep their flags in hopes the Third Reich will rise again someday and they can start killing the Jews again.

"Cradle to Grave" racists never change.

A Good Story of Unity

Fred Smith and his Fedex Plantation even continues his racism and discrimination against Blacks outside of America.

In a small country called Antigua three Black workers who worked for Fedex had each taken a day of sick leave. The written company policy was that each worker was allowed two days sick pay each year. All three workers had taken only one day each. But Fedex management refused to pay them for the sick day even though they were supposed to get it and had been guaranteed it in writing.

Well surprise to Mr. Fred Smith and his Fedex Plantation. The rest of the "Black workers" at Fedex there went on strike in support of their co-workers. Evidently they don't like RACISM and DISCRIMINATION down there.

Soon other workers not associated with Fedex, but who also work the docks in Antigua joined in solidarity against what Fedex was doing and refused to handle Fedex shipments coming and going to and from Antigua. They even had the Fedex trucks and equipment moved off the port's properties.

Evidently the Blacks in Antigua didn't know that Fred Smith was their all powerful White Master and they were only his lowly Black servants and that they were to do just as they were ordered.

So Smith shut down the entire Fedex Antigua division that had been in operation for twelve years to teach them a lesson.

All this because Fedex tried to cheat three 'Black Men' out of their earned and guaranteed sick pay. Hard to believe isn't it?

Fortunately Antigua has a good and honest Labor Commissioner. Because Fred Smith was forced to pay those "ahem...Black workers" over a half million dollars.

Just because Fedex refused to treat three Black workers like they were real "human beings".

I mean, my God ...what did they want ... to be treated "white men?" Not at Fedex.

I talked to a Black cargo handler that worked at Fedex's Memphis Hub. He said he had been there a couple years. He told me how the white supervisors down there would run all over the Blacks. Said they would holler at them, call them racists names and make them work twice as fast and much harder then whites down there. When I asked him if they [Blacks] ever filed a GFT complaint against the supervisors, he said a few did and they never won but were terminated soon after their complaints were filed. He said the supervisors would just walk up to a Black who was working and doing nothing wrong at all ... and just come out and say, "I'm writing you up for this or that", and just laugh at them and walk away. And then they had letters in their files so if they did complain about being discriminated against, Fedex management would pull out their files and threaten to terminate them on the spot if they pursued the complaint. He told me that a lot of the Black workers at the Hub just kept their mouths shut, did their jobs and tried to not be noticed.

Damm ... sounds just like how a colonial era slave would behave to me.

Evidently at least there…Fred Smith's program of using the "Pen like the Whip" works.

Another Black male working at the Hub told me that he had been working one shift and going to college on his time off. When his supervisors found out he was going to college in the hope of getting a promotion within Fedex they switched his hours in mid term for no reason at all. When he tried to get them to let him keep working the same shift at least until that semester was over they laughed at him and said he already knew how to do what he was doing and didn't need college for that. And that job he was now doing was as high as he was going at Fedex.

And he had to drop out of college losing the credits and also his tuition money.

I remember when I was just starting at Fedex and my trainer was still with me. We were driving in Wilmington, Delaware doing pickups. And we were passing a few Blacks. "Look at those stupid Niggers," he said. He said we [Fedex] had to let them know that the Federal on the side of our truck didn't mean we were delivering money to them. The federal government gives money to Niggers not Fedex he said.

And he started laughing. He went on a rant about how Niggers will always be Niggers "forever" and they'll never change. That they were stupid and lacked the intelligence and ability to be responsible. That Black women should be put on birth control when they hit twelve etc. Said some really nasty things about Black children …and on and on. And I'm thinking…I just started here, don't say anything that might cost me my job…just keep quiet and don't say anything. I needed my job and besides, no matter what I said he wasn't going to change his racist beliefs. So I just kept quiet and concentrated on learning my job.

As one of my earlier duties at Fedex after doing pickups on the evening shift I drove the shuttle truck loaded with our daily pickups from our station in Wilmington, Delaware to the Philadelphia airport ramp. There I unloaded it and helped the ramp crews and other truck drivers coming in get the freight ready to load onto the airplane to fly back to Memphis that night. It was somewhat of a hustle bustle atmosphere as all the shuttles from the local stations were bringing in their freight for the nightly flight out to Memphis.

There was a mixture of about 95% white with a few Blacks driving the shuttles from their stations. While I was working to help get the freight I would often see the guys and a few women there exchanging drugs. I wasn't always sure whether it was coke or amphetamines, crack or maybe even heroin but the airport ramp was certainly it's own hub for drugs that's for sure. Just about every drug out in the street found it's way into the stations and the ramps. The drivers would bring it in from their own stations and either buy sell or trade it with the other drivers coming into the ramp or the ramp crews.

They knew that Fedex would not allow the FBI, DEA or other law enforcement into their airport ramps and that they were safe to deal and use drugs freely there. It seemed common and normal to see them selling drugs or slipping off to the bathrooms or some room and doing drugs. And coming back a few minutes later and loading the planes.

It was at the Philadelphia airport ramp that I learned a trick that Fedex couriers, managers, and other Fedex employees used if they wanted to buy quantities of coke etc. Fedex has a jump seat policy where a Fedex employee gets to ride free on the planes. So they can make drug connections and fly to Memphis then Florida and back to Memphis and fly to their home airport with their kilos of drugs. Basically a round trip by Fedex cargo planes to bring home their drugs. It was Completely and Totally ...SAFE.

And Fedex management didn't care.

Fedex once did a station wide drug test in Atlanta and lost nearly the whole station. A member of Fedex management told me that Fred Smith didn't care if there were druggies doing drugs on the job...just load the planes.

After a short time you get to know the drivers and how they work. Some just kind of lay back and try not to do too much and let the others do the work and some just bust their butts the whole time they're at the ramp. It seemed that the few Blacks coming into the ramp (I never saw any Blacks that were part of the regular airport ramp crew) always worked hard. It never really stood out to me until I saw a white crew team leader holler at a Black driver there one night. We were loading large containers that were going into the plane. We were pulling freight off the conveyor belt and loading it into the cans. Robert was working next to me. He had a little more experience at it than me and he was a little faster picking up which packages went into which cans. Still everything was moving along in a normal pace and nothing was behind.

The supervisor was walking down along side the belt and chatting until he got to Robert. He stood there glaring at him and I knew Robert was feeling it, still he just continued working and I guess he knew better than to open his mouth. After a moment the supervisor told him to work faster. Robert said something to the effect that he was way ahead of the belt and working as fast as anyone there. It was obvious that he was harassing Robert and for no reason.

I said something like "hey man we're doing fine, nobody is backed up and we can only pull freight as fast as it gets here". He looked at me like he was going to ream my ass and hesitated, than he turned back to Robert and told him that he didn't want his "lazy Black ass" getting lazy here at the ramp. Either work faster or don't come back. Then he walked away.

After he left I asked Robert what that was all about. I thought maybe Robert had done something wrong previously and the supervisor was just riding him for that. Robert told me that it was nothing. They always ride the "brothers" like that. When I told him that he should file a grievance about it. He replied that he would lose his job if he did. He told me that he had a wife and a kid and house payments and he couldn't afford to lose his job. Besides he said, it's not that bad ....he said it was like that at his station too so he was used to it. Robert was a good family man, smart and a hard worker.

He didn't deserve that kind of treatment.

After that I realized that when two or three Blacks at the ramp would be working near each other and the supervisor would walk by they would always shut up totally and just work quietly until that supervisor or other white team leaders left. Since there were no Blacks allowed in management there it must have been very intimidating.

There are literally thousands of complaints by Blacks of discrimination and harassment by racist white Fedex management. Unfortunately Fedex management creates a way to terminate the unsuspecting Black employee who does attempt to seek justice and fairness in his or her work place. Then "mysteriously," after the Black worker is fired the complaints of racial harassment and discrimination, both written or verbal, disappears forever leaving no "paper trail" of their crimes.

And no complaints of racial discrimination or harassment.

Remember back in the "interview with John, when he said he was trained" that if an employee causes a problem…"create a reason to fire that employee."

I guarantee you that if "every Black worker" who was ever fired from Fedex was interviewed or investigated it would be found that at least (85%) or more of their terminations came soon after they made a complaint written or verbal about being held back from a promotion or was treated unfairly because they were Black.

I saw this happen in the Wilmington, Delaware station when Mike Mitchell said, "if that Nigger doesn't quit asking about that dammed sales job I'm gonna fire him and he can take his Black ASS and his complaints someplace else." And he meant it. He would never let a Black person in any level of management at Fedex. Mike hated Blacks. But to be totally honest…so did many other whites in management. It was their "Badge"

Fred Smith and his Fedex corporation will deny this and put out all kinds of well orchestrated slick propaganda saying it is not true. And how Fedex is fair to their Black workers and treats them well. And promotes them fairly.

Let them tell that to the thousands of Black workers they fired after those Black workers filed a complaint of harassment or discrimination against his or her "white supervisor."

Let Fedex give the names and addresses of "every Black worker" that was ever fired by Fedex management to say…EEOC or the NAACP and let them interview that "fired Black worker" and watch what happens.

But you know Fedex won't do that. Fedex lawyers file an injunction against the EEOC every time the EEOC tries to get any kind of information. They don't want anybody, the government, private attorney's, judges, media or anybody else to know about their crimes and their RACISM.

Fred Smith and his corrupt and Racist Fedex has hired some of the highest paid lawyers in the country to make sure they keep their crimes secret.

Take the case of Mr. Smith a Black employee at Fedex. He had been employed with Fedex since 1998 at the Santa Clara station in California. He had been a loyal Fedex employee for ten years and he wanted to move up to management. He had repeatedly put in for classes and programs that would qualify him for a position in management. His senior manager did everything he could to make sure Mr. Smith was NEVER going to make it to management.

Mr. Smith had repeatedly seen less qualified whites with less seniority than him move up ahead of him. Finally they did give him a class and he not only met the requirements, he exceeded them in passing the class and actually did better than most of his white peers who did move up into management positions.

But management would NOT give him any more classes that would have proven even more that he was more than qualified for promotions than whites who scored less and had been promoted.

Finally his "white manager" just came out and told him straight up, that he would NEVER be allowed in Fedex management.

After all... this Mr. Smith was Black ..."get back to the cotton fields BOY."

Fedex management realized it was time to put Mr. Smith in his proper place for even thinking he deserved a place within FedEx's "white management". So his white manager gave him an unfair "written warning" for a very minor offense. An offense so minor that it was common practice for nearly everyone in the station to do it. An offense so minor that his station manager and the other white managers at the station saw his fellow "white co-workers" do all the time, and nothing was ever said to them or done about it. The operative word here is "white co-workers" of which Mr. Smith was not.

Fedex headquarters only advanced Blacks to meet minimum quotas (to get government contracts). So the white manager was only following corporate practice, policies and procedures put into place and passed down from Fedex headquarters in Memphis. He would have to put the Black Mr. Smith in his place and make him keep his mouth shut about moving up into Fedex management.

Knowing full well that the warning letter he gave Mr. Smith was unfair ... so what?

Or as I've heard a number of times from white Fedex management, "who the hell does that Nigger think he is? I'll fix his Black Ass."

In June of 2002 Mr. Smith filed a GFT (Guaranteed Fair Treatment) complaint with Fedex management and also a complaint with the EEOC and the Department of Fair Employment.

<u>In July of 2002</u>   (as soon as they found out) Fedex terminated Mr. Smith. They used the exact same excuse to fire him that they had previously used to harass him before.

It was the same offense...not a new one.

His manager had already wrongly wrote him up because he was seeking a well deserved promotion he was well qualified for.   To keep his mouth shut.

After he filed the complaints... Fedex "fired" him for the very same minor offense he had already been wrongly written up for.   WTF ?

He had filed a complaint of racial discrimination against Fedex management... so they got rid of him.

Then they wouldn't even let him attend his own GFT appeal against the termination and discrimination.

How can you possibly argue your GFT appeal if you're not there? It's like being tried for a crime and not being allowed in the court room to defend yourself.

I guess he is Lucky they didn't tie him to a tree and whip him for wanting to be treated like a human being.

Another case...A Rachel Hutchins (a Black Woman) working for Fedex in Bakersfield, California.   She had originally been hired on as part time and was expecting to be moved up to full time employment at Fedex as she had seen many of her less senior "white co-workers" do. Even though they were less experienced and less qualified than her. It was always the whites that moved up to full time positions and got promotions to CSA. She had filed for a position of CSA (Customer Service Agent) numerous times but was ALWAYS passed over for less qualified and less senior "whites."

A CSA position came open and management needed help to fill the position quickly. So management put her in that position ...but only as "temporary status."

She performed her duties very well and every bit as well as other "whites" in the same position who were permanent /full time.

She did this job very well for nearly a year,   then management hired and brought up and promoted whites ahead of her. In the very same position she had been doing very well already. And they moved her back down to part time "cargo handler" the bottom rung at Fedex.

A position similar to that of slaves picking cotton on the cotton plantations like Fred Smith grew up on. She had worked hard for years there, had proven she could do a very good job as a CSA ....but...she was BLACK.

She never stood a chance.

Later on when a yet another CSA position became available within the station... Fedex management gave the position to a "another white" who not only had less seniority than Mrs. Hutchins, <u>but one that Mrs. Hutchins had to train.</u>

If they use you as a trainer ...you must be very good.

Even worse, Fedex was only paying Mrs. Hutchins at the lowly "cargo handlers" rate of pay while she was doing the CSA job daily for nearly a year.

I guess they figured they were only going to pay this BLACK woman the lowest pay no matter what job she did or how well she did it.

If that's not slave plantation mentality ...

I just honestly think that is so sick. It is racism and discrimination at it's worse. How does anyone with even the slightest sense of decency think Mrs. Rachel Hutchins was feeling every day? Here is this Black woman working so hard every day, trying to do her best, and trying to better herself and in all honesty was probably doing far more and a far better job than most of her co-workers ... and to be treated like that.

Like she wasn't even a human being.

Finally when Mrs. Hutchins couldn't take it any more she filed a complaint of Racial Discrimination with the EEOC against Fedex on <u>May 27, 2003.</u>

And as per Fred Smith's Fedex Plantation's practice ... <u>they fired her on January 20, 2004</u>

It must have taken months for the complaint to get back to Fedex headquarters?

Retaliation against an employee for filing a complaint with the EEOC is against the law. Fred Smith trained and ordered his white Fedex management to treat Blacks like this. They are his RACIST WHITE SUPREMIST PROGRAMS that he designed so that he could run Fedex like a Cotton Slave Plantation

He doesn't get it.... These are not the times of his racist father. All of the Fedex lawyers together can't keep Blacks out of promotions and well earned and deserved management positions.

Not Today, Not Anymore.

I thought as I wrote this section about this poor woman and how his RACIST Assholes in management treated her....it's just not right.

I honestly pray to GOD….That he punishes them for this.

This is just…Fred Smith's way of "hiding the evidence." Get rid of those dammed Blacks / Niggers that complain. Make this whining and complaining about us treating them bad disappear.

Thank God he can't tie them to a tree and whip them because I honestly believe he would.

The saddest part of all of this, is that what happened to Mrs. Hutchins and Mr. Smith, happens everyday at Fedex.

And most times Fedex gets away with it.

Rachel Hutchins complaint was part of a $53,500,000 dollar settlement Fedex made with roughly twenty thousand Black and minority workers. Fedex management had kept them at the bottom of their ground crew work force. And would not let them rise above it. To Fred Smith and his Racist Fedex management Blacks and Hispanic minorities were no better than "Cotton Plantation Slaves."

They were to do the hard dirty work, do as they were told and keep their mouths shut about it. They were to be kept at the bottom of Fedex's pay scale except as "tokens."

I've heard white Fedex management say many times they're just …"Niggers, Monkeys, Apes, Baboons, Spear Chucker's" etc.

They'll talk "publicly" about how good they treat all of their Black workers….then they HIDE and or destroy all of the evidence that will prove otherwise. They have their high powered lawyers file court injunctions and every kind of legal motion possible to suppress evidence that they know will prove a pattern and history of systemized company wide programs of discrimination against Blacks.

Because they know that if Fedex was investigated thoroughly enough, it would be found that there are programs in place even today that were instigated and designed to hold back and hold down hard working and well deserving Blacks and other minorities.

It is after all …Fred Smith's "Fedex Plantation."

And this doesn't even begin to take into account all of the thousands of Blacks that either try to apply for a job at Fedex and were told "there are no jobs openings" when there were in fact job openings but only for "white people'. Or that Black man or Black woman who does get to fill out an application only to have it thrown in the trash can and the job given to a white person.

Later on in the book you will read that I contacted ABC's 20-20 about Fred Smith's Fraud against our military and government and told them how Fedex was endangering not only America's security but also our soldiers lives. Even that Fedex management had me "unknowingly" taking large quantities of military explosives into an elementary school, shopping centers and neighborhoods. And they did a feature story on Fedex.

Tom Jerrold did the story that told about Fedex's Fraud and Illegal Drugs. Of course Fred Smith and his Fedex team of liars tried to say they did nothing wrong and that I was just a disgruntled worker that was making it all up. If you can believe the Philadelphia Inquirer and ABC's 20-20 would just take my word for it without investigating the facts on their own.

I didn't like that Fred Smith and Fedex betrayed our soldiers and our country and I started putting some stuff out online about it. Information that was 100% true and that I could substantiate. Fred Smith didn't like it but he knew It was all true. That I had and still do have multiple copies of documentation to prove it. I told about the racism and discrimination and I also put out other information. Some of it involved an official DEA picture of one of Fred Smith's Fedex planes flying illegal drugs from Mexico to the northeast U.S.A. The Plane and picture was on DEA's official website. They still have it.

In the picture was a Fedex plane flying from Mexico to Boston. On the planes fuselage DEA officials had stamped the words "Illegal Drugs." Yeah I got the original... just waiting to see if Fred tries to sue me.

The DEA has it too... send for it.

I've got a LOT MORE documents...not in this book

While I was online on AOL one evening a man came on and started talking to me. His profile showed and he said he worked in Fedex management in Memphis. He said that he was in middle level management and maybe passed Fred Smith or saw Fred Smith about a dozen times a year but had very limited conversation with him. And yes, people within Fedex did fear him. But that he also personally had great respect for him and what he had accomplished.

Then he asked me if I was "white" to which I replied that I was ... why?

He went on to say that I had put out a lot of information about the Blacks being mistreated at Fedex. And was I, "a liberal goody two shoes white guy" that was always sticking up for Blacks and saying how they were mistreated?

He said that he did see the story about Fedex's CSS service on 20-20. He didn't come out and say it was fraud. But he did say that Fred Smith did make a big mistake with it. And he understood that I would be mad at Fedex for what they said about me.

And I thought …what a politician. Don't say he committed a crime and betrayed our soldiers…just say that he made a mistake.

Then he asked me if I had any Blacks in my family. And I replied that I did not, at least not that I knew of.

Then he asked me "then why" was I trying to make Fedex look bad in their dealings with Blacks. That they treated Blacks pretty well considering.

And I asked him point blank….considering what?

Then he said, "can we talk as white man to white man?"

I said, "sure."

He said, that I should try to consider that Fred Smith grew up in the south. And that down here we look at Blacks a lot different than they do up north. He went on to say that whites in the south understood Blacks better that their northern brothers.

And I'm thinking….well this could be interesting.

So I asked what he meant by, "understanding Blacks better?"

He went on to explain to me that back in Colonial times farmers that controlled large farms were considered "Plantation owners" but that the normal labor costs to manage those huge plantations would have been cost prohibitive. And that Africans were brought into this country …only as a means of cheap labor. That they were never intended to be equal or have rights like the whites that settled this country.

And he asked me if I understood that?

I replied that I did already know and understood that.

You've got to understand also that Blacks are not as developed mentally as whites are…he continued.

We, down here in the south understand that.

Too many times the northerners don't quite grasp that fact, he continued.

So I asked him …so when do you thinks that Blacks will be as smart as whites?

And he replied…it's not just that they're not as smart, it's that they're not as civilized…not disciplined …and don't take their responsibilities seriously…like most Whites do.   Some races just never fully develop mentally relative to their white European counterparts he explained.

Then he went on to explain that …the Fedex corporation was founded by a very smart and rich white man who is from the south, who was raised in the south with southern ways and beliefs. Though there is some degree of management from all over the United States the main thrust and crucial areas of Fedex is run by whites mostly from the south that understand that point very well, he stated.

He said that what I was putting online made Fedex management seem like they hated Blacks …and it's not like that.

Then why have I heard all of the nasty remarks about Blacks and why does the word "Nigger" always come out of management's mouths so much I asked. And what about the way Blacks are treated by white Fedex management?

Not too many whites in management within the company actually "hate Blacks" he said.   Yeah, you might hear the 'N' word a lot,   but it may be that some of the lower level managers misunderstood what was being said to them during training sessions or meetings and took it wrongly back out in the field.   It's just that we in management know how to manage our Black employees better than a lot of other compa-nies. Especially the northern based companies where Blacks are more easily accepted.

Fred knows that if you keep a Black Man in "his proper place" he will most times perform better. But that if you give him too much lee-way he can and usually does…go out of control.   Generally speaking Blacks don't have that 'control or discipline' required of management over their actions like say … a white person would.

Do you understand that, he asked.

I replied that yes I do understand Fred's thinking on that.   I just don't agree with it.

Then he went on to put it another way. Look he said, you probably have a pet dog or cat or some other kind of pet.   You love it, you care for it, and you feed it and give it shelter. Maybe it can perform a certain function like guarding your home, or do neat tricks. but you don't al-low it to eat at your dinner table and you don't allow it to sleep in your bed with you at night.

In a way…Blacks are not all that different.

Then he went on … We at Fedex don't hate Blacks at all. We just know and understand their limits.

"You have to understand", he said, "Fedex is a very fast paced technological and complex company, many times quick decisions have to be made that can make us or cost us millions of dollars." Fred will never let a Black man be in the position to actually make that call.

Fedex is his baby. It's too important to him.

So then I asked him "when" or how long will it be before Blacks catch up mentally with Whites.

He explained to me that …you have to understand, just as Blacks develop mentally …so do whites. And that he wasn't sure that Blacks would or could ever actually advance far enough to be on equal footing mentally or intellectually with whites.

I asked him if that was Fred Smith's philosophy and or beliefs on all Blacks… and was that his justification for treating blacks like he does?

He stated …It's not only Fred's beliefs, it's everybody here in Fedex management on down too, or you're not with the company. He said that I had never been in management at a higher level and so couldn't appreciate the difficulties of running a top corporation and keeping it at the top and competitive.

Trust me, we "know how to handle our Blacks."

We talked a little more but I wasn't going to concede to his beliefs or Fred's that Blacks were as a whole inferior mentally. He could see he was not gaining any ground.

Then he hit me with a stumper.

"Look," he said, "suppose someone in your family had a very serious illness, maybe a brain tumor that was very difficult to operate on. If there were nine white surgeons and one Black surgeons…which would you choose to do the operation?

I had to think….it did make me think. I think in all honesty I might have chosen one of the white surgeons. Maybe because I am white and would have felt more comfortable as I would feel that I could get a better read of the white doctor.

Think I thought….wait a minute…

"Well," I replied, " if it were a really serious operation to someone close to me, I would check very closely the qualifications, experience and histories of each doctor. And make my choice from there. If I felt the Black doctor was the best qualified…I would choose him because I would only want the best doctor operating on someone close to me."

He told me I was "copping out." That if it were a serious operation to someone close to me…there was no way I would choose a Black doctor over a white one to do the operation. Come on, be honest he said, it's just you and me…two white guys talking. There's no Blacks here to impress.

By this time I had a few minutes to think. Maybe it was a flash back to a philosophy class I had taken at college. I'm not sure. But I knew the right answer.

I said to him, "two thoughts on that … one, what if there were nine Black surgeons and only one white surgeon?

And two … here's what I honestly think about your question. If someone close to me had to have a very serious operation, I would only have the very best surgeon that I could afford regardless of race or anything else. Otherwise, if the surgery went bad for any reason and I had NOT chosen the BEST surgeon … I would hate myself forever.

Where the hell are you going to find nine qualified Black surgeons… he asked.

And he added an … LOL "Laughing Out Loud"

Obviously not at Fedex I replied.

We chatted a little more. He did try again to convince me that Fred Smith and Fedex had good reasons behind the policies they had in place concerning Black workers. Try not to forget that you are a "white man." And don't be too hard on another white man who is trying to uphold the good ways that were in place down here way before you and I were born.

I thought about what he said, "the good ways before I was born" and realized that he was talking about Slavery.

Then he ended with … about that DEA stuff with the Fedex plane Remember, Fred Smith is a "vengeful man" be careful.

And I thought

Welcome to the world of Fred Smith.

CHAPTER 2

MY FIRST DAY OF WORK AT FEDEX

It was my first day at Fedex and I was looking forward to starting with a big new company. I had been told that it was a good place to work and the pay and benefits were okay. My wife had just given birth to our son and we looked forward to the security a big company would provide.

I had met my new supervisor and he seemed nice enough. It was early afternoon and he had asked me to wait outside in the freight area while he was taking care of something. So I wandered around in the building where they parked the trucks and handled all of the incoming and out going freight.

There was a courier there and he was doing something with the freight in his van. Usually the day drivers went out in the mornings doing deliveries and spent their afternoons picking up freight to be shipped out that night. And the evening drivers were usually newer part timers that mostly did pickups only. Like most others I would start out evenings doing pickups and work my way into a full daytime position as they came available.

I walked over to the driver / courier and introduced myself. "Hi, my name is Gary," I said.

"Hi, my name is Tony," he said, "how are you doing?"

"Good," I replied, "how is it here?"

"Not bad, well at times it's not bad, but sometimes you have to be careful. There's a lot of funny shit that goes on here," Tony said.

I asked him what he meant by that.

Tony looked around and then he said that lot of guys will steal your shit and you have to be careful. That there was a lot of funny stuff that goes on there.

I asked him what he meant by that.

And he looked around the station as if to see if anyone was watching or who might be close by.

Then he says, " well lots of guys here will steal your shit and you have to be careful. They'll go right into your truck and take it if it's something they want, or they'll take it off the belt before it gets to you. You just have to be careful always" he said.

"What do you mean, steal what," I asked, not sure what he was talking about.

"You know, your packages, jewelry, money, drugs …anything they want," he said as he looked around the building. "Man you have to watch your stuff all the time, these guys will steal anything not nailed down."

"But I don't do drugs," I stated, not really sure if this was a trick test or some kind of setup the company used to check their new employees before they sent them out on the road.

Tony replied, " I mean the drugs in your shipments, there's always a lot of drugs in the shipments and these guys take them or part of them and deliver the rest. That way the shipments keep on coming in. You'll learn once you're here for awhile … Fedex ships a lot of illegal drugs, an awful lot."

"Wow I never thought of that," I said, "don't they call the cops?"

"Not very often, most times the guys just take them for themselves," he said. He went on to show and explain how the couriers take the drugs and valuables for themselves.

Then he said, "want me to teach you how to feel packages?"

"What do you mean, " I asked. I had just completed two weeks of courier school training and no one had ever mentioned "feeling packages."

"You know, feel a package to see what's inside," Tony said.

Then he continued, "once you get good at it you can almost always tell what's inside. You know like if it's an overnight letter or Courier Pak envelope you just feel it and see if it's money or jewelry or if it feels like drugs. Lots of times you can just open up the package and take it. Lots of people do it, you can get some great stuff that way."

"You mean that you can tell what a package has in it just by feeling it?" I asked. Not quite sure what to make of this conversation.

"Oh yeah, look," he said as he took out his wallet and put it in a courier pak envelope and sealed it. "Now feel this envelope, you know what a wallet feels like …could this be a wallet?" he asked.

"Well yes," I said, "it does feel like a wallet now that you think about it, but what if it's not?"

"No problem, you just put it in another courier pak and send it on it's way. Nobody knows and nobody cares," he replied. "Look man, everybody does it, a lot of the guys do and some of the girls here too. And you can tell if it's money or drugs too, it's pretty easy after awhile. I've seen some real nice jewelry come out of the freight."

I looked at him and realized that he was probably telling the truth. I also felt that he might be one of the guys stealing from the shipments too. He certainly had a lot of knowledge about it.

Just then my manager came out of the office and called me over to him.

He said ...lets go check out a van and go on a safety training ride so you can start your new adventure at Fedex.

"Great" I said, anxious to get started and yet at the same time I had a little uneasy feeling. The first impression at the real job wasn't what I had expected.

After a while the feeling passed as I tried to prepare myself mentally for the job.

It's funny though, as I look back, even on my first day I somehow sensed that Fedex was not really the company they painted it as being.

I guess partly because of the fact that on my first day of work, I learned that Fedex Couriers and managers steal a lot of drugs and valuables from Fedex shipments.

The next day I reported for the evening shift. I was going to be training with the courier whose route I was taking over. He had done his time on the evening shift and proven his abilities and now he was getting a newly opened position on day work.

His job right now was to get me ready to take over his route.

His name was Tom Anglin and he was a straight kind of guy. He was serious about his job and he did it well. His route covered an area in the south and northeast section of Wilmington, Delaware. And also slightly above Wilmington and to the east out to the Delaware river. The route consisted of private residences, businesses, and even a factory or two.

During the evening we were given a pickup to do in the lower part of Wilmington. As we pulled up to the address there was some Blacks standing on the corner and they glanced over at the van. Tom told me to just stay with the van as he went to do the pickup. While I was sitting there one of the Black guys looked at the van and then at me and nodded to me. It was just a nod as if to say hi.

I felt comfortable because I had worked in Wilmington several times when I was younger.

Soon Tom came back to the van and put the shipment inside without incident. As we drove away Tom glanced at the people on the street. Not only the guys on the corner but also the families and children outside their homes. Then he began a tirade about how stupid Nigger's were. And how when they saw our vans they thought that we were delivering "welfare checks" to them, and he began laughing.

"Nigger's are stupid and always will be, that's why they'll never get anywhere" he stated as if he were stating a known scientific fact.

Then he went on about how Niggers were lazy and always stealing and how you always had to watch your truck when they are around.

I asked him if that was why they sent the "two of us" to do this pickup tonight, and he laughed.

"No." he replied, "they wouldn't pay two couriers to do a single pickup no matter how many Niggers were around.

I said something like "maybe if they had jobs, they wouldn't be hanging on the corners, and that I had worked with Blacks before and thought they were good workers."

Tom replied that our company isn't going to hire Niggers. They don't like them and only hire one or two to keep the government quiet.

After returning to the station that evening I helped the others get the freight ready for the Philadelphia airport. Where it would be loaded onto the airplanes and flown to Memphis for sorting. Then it would be flown back out to delivery locations across America.

When we were finished and I had punched out I walked out to my van that was parked in a fenced in parking lot. I started it and pulled out into the highway to go home. There was wind coming in thru the passengers side. Funny, I didn't remember having the window open when I arrived. No, I couldn't have left it open. I remembered that I had even locked the doors. Then as I looked over to see if the window was down, I realized that someone had broken my window. I checked under my seat for my radar detector and it was gone. How could that be? My van was parked in a fenced in parking lot. There had been no one in the yard but my co workers.

The next day I asked a few guys in the station if they had any ideas of who might have done it. A few guys said it was a bummer and that I had to be careful with my stuff here. One courier just smiled and said, "welcome new guy". I asked him if he honestly thought that it was a courier that broke my window and stole my radar detector.

He replied that yes, it probably was. That it was nothing new and that "lots of stuff was stolen from our parking lot".

Lesson …Never trust a Fedex courier.

It wasn't long before I was running my own route with the other evening couriers. I went in around 3:30 PM and returned to the station around 7:30PM. Then I would help sort the freight with the other drivers and get it ready for the trip to the airport in Philadelphia. They called it the "Philadelphia Ramp."

I had learned a lot in just a few months and felt comfortable on my route and I was often asked to help other couriers that were backed up and couldn't make all of their own stops. I didn't mind and it helped to make the nights fly by faster.

Still there were many things that I saw in the station and even heard on our radios that made me a little uncomfortable and uneasy. It just wasn't a place where you could let your guard down.

It seems that there was always a lot of talk both in the station and on our truck radios about illegal drugs and drug shipments at the station. There was a LOT coming thru the shipments and guys were taking it. Management was involved in it too. Most of the talk was about Pot and Cocaine.

Sometimes I had to wait for the "drug talk and deals" conversations to stop before I could get a pickup address or information on a real shipment for a customer.

The daytime couriers were always talking about what drugs they had found in shipments or were selling from shipments and sometimes just stating how good a particular drug was that they had stolen from a shipment. Initially I wondered what would happen if a manager had walked into our dispatcher's room and heard the conversations.

Before long I found out and realized that the managers were involved too.

Sometimes the conversations and deal making were so long that they cost me time making pickups and or put me behind my schedule. But

I knew better then to complain or it would put my job in jeopardy. It might also result in my personal vehicle being damaged or an attack on me and it would be "me" who was fired.

Probably the most concerns I had was the drugs and drug paraphernalia leftover in my truck from the previous couriers. It was common to find left over joints or empty cocaine or speed baggies where the daytime couriers had gotten high during their daytime deliveries. Maybe even started their day that way. Sometimes the marijuana joints were whole and were just set aside next to a lighter for the next day. Or there would be partial bags of coke or speed left over set in a corner in plain view and could easily be seen if someone came into the van. A few times I even found spoons with residue on them. And yeah I knew what that meant.

My problem was I couldn't throw them away or the couriers whose stuff it was, would be pissed. And I couldn't go to the supervisors about it because they had already said that they got high with the couriers too. I know I had seen them high a few times in the station but didn't know what there were on.

So most times, no actually always, I was left to drive around all night with illegal drugs in my van and I didn't even do drugs. I did decide that if illegal drugs were ever found in my van and I was accused of having them, that I would request a drug test. I wasn't sure if it would work but it was all I had.

Soon I just began putting the pot and other drugs in the box where we kept the labels. Everybody used them daily and I figured that eventually the courier whose drugs they were would fine them when he went to use the labels. I guess it worked but I never really knew for sure. I went into "don't ask, don't talk about it," mode.

Lesson One ...Always check your Fedex van for illegal drugs.

Another thing that bothered me after I had been there for awhile.

Sometimes when I pre-tripped my van before going out to do pickups that night I would find opened and empty overnight letters and two pound Courier Paks. They would usually be in the small trash cans we keep in the truck. I didn't really pay any attention to them when I first began noticing them. Sometimes there would be a half dozen or more envelopes opened. They had the three letter destination code written on the side and it said "ILG" which was a three letter code for our station. That meant that somebody else in the United States had sent these envelopes to our (Wilmington...ILG) station. Sometimes they would have another three letter destination code on them which meant that a courier had picked up the envelope from a customer or a drop box and opened it up and stole from it before he brought it back to the station.

One night as I was doing pickups it finally dawned on me what was happening. The daytime couriers who did deliveries were opening up envelopes and stealing from them. As I thought about what was happening I began to get mad. If management had a complaint from a customer about stolen valuables and found the opened envelopes in a van I had used or was using they would accuse me. And I would lose my job.

Too many of the couriers and management were doing drugs together. They would be protected and I would lose my job. Yeah, some people would say that I should demand a polygraph test if I was ever accused. But it wouldn't work like that. Druggie management would take care of their druggie couriers. I would be accused and fired all in one. So I just decided to check my truck real close before I left the station. If I found any opened packages or envelopes I would throw them out immediately. The illegal drugs and drug paraphernalia I would leave alone but the opened packages I threw out.

I later learned that unlike Fedex UPS has a program in place that severely limits thefts of it's shipments. UPS has a group of people that come into the station and off load the freight from big trucks and then load the delivery trucks. After the trucks are loaded the "loaders" walk out to the parking lot and get into their vehicles. The UPS delivery men don't load their trucks from the conveyor belts so it is hard to steal there.

While at a Fedex station the couriers stand by the conveyor belts when the big freight truck is unloaded and grab whatever freight they want as it passes by and throw it into their truck. If say a TV, electronics device etc. or other package comes down the belt and a courier thinks they might want it, they just grab it and throw it in their truck.

They do this while loading their trucks with the freight that does belong in their trucks and it isn't noticed. Then after they leave the station to do deliveries they open the package or envelope. They can slip what they stole into their vehicle after they get back to the station or they can have someone meet them on their route and take it.

It works well at Fedex.

For instance, suppose I am the third courier from the big truck's rear doors and as the freight comes down the conveyor belt I see a TV or computer coming by. I can just grab it and toss it into my truck and nobody would know. The courier on down the line that was suppose to get and deliver that shipment never even knew that he was supposed to get the "TV or computer" coming down the line. And he doesn't know another courier just stole it. Then the courier who stole the TV continues loading his freight into his truck and then drives away out of the station. He can stash it somewhere or call his wife or friend and give it to them. NO record of the TV or computer etc. …and no record of who stole it,

It sure is fun shopping on the Fedex conveyor belt I've heard them say. It's even more fun doing it at Christmas time. If you want to do it and the right freight comes in, you can do almost all of your Christmas shopping while at work and conveniently from the conveyor belt. Plus the presents are FREE.

Merry Christmas from Fedex's customers.

I remember hearing variations of this line a number of times from Fedex couriers. One night for instance while some of us were talking about how busy we were and how it was hard to do Christmas shopping with all the stores being so crowded. One courier bragged, " hey I do my best shopping right here on the belt …the prices are great (free) and it saves time. Why go anywhere else?"

A lot of couriers were doing it too.

After I was there a short while one of the managers asked me if I would drive the freight up to the ramp at the Philadelphia airport and help load the airplanes. I was still considered part time so the extra hours sounded great and of course I said yes. I enjoyed working at the ramp. There were couriers coming in not only from Philadelphia and Delaware but also from New Jersey and sometimes even Maryland. Loading the planes was a hurried and rushed event but it was okay.

What surprised me most there I think was that you could buy almost anything at the ramp. It had an open market atmosphere where you could buy TV's, computers, jewelry and any drugs you wanted. Right out of Fedex's shipments. Because most of the stuff was stolen from Fedex shipments by the couriers, but some guys were just bringing in drugs to sell from the street too. After I worked there a few weeks the guys were pumping me to see what drugs or valuables I brought to sell or what I might have stolen that day or week. Maybe what good shit (drugs) I had gotten from the shipments lately. There was so much stolen valuables and illegal drug selling and trading going on I usually just replied "not today". Many times pot was offered for free because so much was stolen, but the harder stuff like cocaine etc. was usually only offered for sell or trade for other valuables that were usually stolen too.

At the station most of the daytime couriers didn't come to the ramp so they were taking the stolen stuff home and selling it or keeping it for themselves. But when they did drive to the ramp they were selling wholesale to as many as they could. I can't begin to count the number of times I was offered TV's, computers jewelry, radar detectors and the drugs… anything…any quantity you want it…a courier would supply it. Or you could just walk into the bathroom and they'd share what they were doing.

There was no question that ramp management knew what was going on and I'm sure at least some if not all were involved too. So there was no way I was going to open my mouth about any of it. I just kept quiet and did my job. It was going on long before I got there and it kept on after I left. I wasn't going to change a thing.

There was a mixture of about 95 % whites and the rest pretty much Blacks. But the whites left no doubt in anybody's mind that they ruled. They would force the Blacks to do the harder jobs and talk shit to them while they did them. And they would talk about Blacks being stupid and slow to other whites even while they stood right in front of their Black co-workers. It was very insulting, but it was also intimidating to the Blacks too. It was their way of keeping the blacks in line. A white courier or ramp manager would look a Black worker right in the eyes and say something like, "what's up Buckwheat?" Sometimes something even worse and the Black guy knew that if he said something back he would lose. And the loss might be his job.

I once heard a white supervisor there say to a younger and newer Black courier who had only been to the ramp a few times …" hey bro, I bet your daddy picked cotton faster than that. Now come on bro, you gotta move faster than that if you want to work here, this ain't no cotton field." Then he said something like we load air planes here, you ever been on a plane bro? They go way up in the sky. The black courier just kind of took it and laughed. But I knew he had been crushed inside.

Different place, different circumstances… there would have been a fight. But here at the ramp. He'd just lose his job and he needed his job. Several times I told some of the Black couriers they were good men, worked hard did a great job and would be an asset to any company, "why don't you guys file a grievance or talk to the local NAACP. I explained to them that they didn't have to take that stuff, that it wasn't the 1700's.

I was working on the conveyor belt at the ramp one night just pulling packages off it and throwing them in the cans for loading. A burly supervisor came over and said a few things to me about nothing really.

They he asked me if I had heard that a school bus had ran off the road and into the river. I told him no I hadn't …and asked him if any kids got hurt?

He replied that yes they were and that it was a shame. I agreed with him feeling bad and thinking about the children.

Then he said that it was a school bus that was half full of Blacks kids and all of them died. "It really a shame," he said again. And he sounded sincere.

It was something no one likes to hear, and I thought how bad the parents must be feeling. I told him something like, "I don't know what I would do if something like that happened to my son."

Then he smiled and said, "yeah, you know what the real shame is ? The real shame is that the bus was only half full … of Black kids."

And he started laughing as he walked away to tell his sick joke to the other white couriers working there.

A few days later I heard that same sick joke being told on our 2 way Fedex truck radios at work. A number of couriers were adding they laughter and adding racists comments to it. I think we had two Black couriers out on their routes at the time. They could and probably did hear that joke and there was nothing they could do about it.

I was still considered a new guy and not even full time yet and I wondered how can you could even tell a joke like that in the first place, there isn't anything funny about that. And also, how can you come back to the station and work alongside a co-worker who is Black and know that he probably heard it?

Or maybe even be the white courier that made some racist remark over the radio that only added to the sickness of the joke? Of course it did help to have racist white management in control of the station. So there really wasn't much the Black couriers could do about it.

Some nights after I left the airport ramp and drove back to the station some of the couriers would be hanging out in the station well past the time they had clocked out. There was a ping pong table and I guess it would have been cool if they were just playing ping pong or hanging out. But a lot of the times they weren't playing ping pong they were getting high and making drug deals. And they felt safe doing it while inside the Fedex station. They could lock it up, no police could come in. And they could do and sell all the illegal drugs they wanted and even trade or sell stuff they had stolen that day from shipments. And the truth is that they probably kept a lot of drugs in their trucks anyway.

Often times they would offer me drugs to share or buy right in the station while we were working, sometimes over the radio, but I always said no thanks can't afford them or whatever. I've watched them do pot and coke right in front of me at the station and I just shake my head.

My First Job Evaluation at Fedex

It had been about three months since I hired on as courier and it was time for my job evaluation. At Fedex they call it a "check ride" and it's when a manager rides along with you on your route to see how well you do your job. Then he gives you a rating by using the numbers (1) thru (6) in several different categories.

The manager who hired me was out on disability (so we were told) and I had been assigned a new one. He was a short balding guy with thick glasses and a big smile. His name was Colin Baines and he lived in North Wilmington in Delaware.

Before we left the building he asked me if I had checked the van to make sure I had all of my supplies for my route. I had and told him we were good to go. Then after we left the station the first thing he asked me was if I knew where my first stop was.

To which I replied yes, and proceeded to drive to it. I had worked hard to learn my route and the area in order to be a good courier. Dealing with the customers was easy.

As we rode along the route my manager began to open up about his employment with Fedex and his family. His wife had just given birth to their first child and he was as proud as he could be. And it just so happened that his house was located within my route. Then he said something that just made me shake my head one more time.

Colin looked at me and said, "if we have time tonight we could stop by my house and get high."

I'm thinking...here's my manager who just told me he had a new baby, he has me out for a job evaluation ... and he wants to go "his home" and get STONED.

What's wrong with this picture?

I hesitated, I knew he was serious. Colin wanted to get high. I didn't do drugs and actually drank only a little. It's my job evaluation...what do I say?

Colin looked at me and asked, "you do get high don't you Gary?"

I had known he was a stoner, other couriers had told me that they got high with him and on more than a little pot. Not only out on the route and not only at his house, but a number of times while working at the station.

To me he was just another DRUGGIE.

Still, I took the political way out. I just replied that I never had time on my route, that I was just trying to be a good courier and do a good job.

He wasn't giving up that easy. "Well then we'll see how busy we are tonight, maybe we'll have time to stop by my house for a few minutes," he said.

Colin was bound and determined to get high. He kept offering ways to cut times and even push off a few pickups that I would normally get to other couriers. It wasn't about being more efficient, I was already very efficient in running my route in the shortest times, it was all about cutting corners so that we had enough time to stop at his house. Problem was...I was just as bound and determined NOT to get high.

I don't need that shit to feel good. I had a great wife and family, it really doesn't get any better than that. I don't care what the druggies say. I made sure that we were too busy to go to his house and get stoned. Manager or not, job evaluation or not, I wasn't getting high.

At about the middle of the shift I had a pickup at a private residence. It was an elderly woman and she had a small box about the size of a shoe box. It was about a pound maybe slightly more but certainly less than two pounds. You learn weights pretty good when you handle them everyday. Or put more simply ... it's not hard to guess a pound of lunch meat if you're a butcher. I explained to the woman that I thought it weighed about a pound maybe slightly more but that I had to charge her two pounds. unless she had a scale which she didn't and she seemed okay with my estimate of slightly over one pound. And that I had to charge her for two pounds.

After we left her house and I was putting the shipment in my van I handed it to Colin and asked him what he thought it weighed. He held it for a moment and agreed that it was under two pounds. Then he said, "but you could have told her it was over three pounds and she would have to pay for four."

I said, "But Colin, it wasn't even two pounds,"

"It doesn't matter what it weighs, it's how much you can get. If you told her that it weighed four pounds and she paid for it, that would been more money that Fedex made and the more Fedex makes …the more we get in bonuses."

"Got it, "he asked, "remember REVENUE …bring in all the money you can every time."

"Yeah I got it," I said.

The Lesson Was … If you are a courier for Fedex CHEAT the customer for every penny you can. You may get a bigger bonus.

But I was not going to cheat my customers no matter how much bonus I might get. And I'm certainly not going to cheat some elderly woman. I still to this day can't believe he would do that to her. But he would and probably has hundreds of times.

No wonder Fedex moved him to management. No morals, No integrity, No honesty. It was an old lady

Just Money, Greed and Profit.

It was becoming more apparent everyday. Fedex puts up a good front and then they lie to and cheat their customers and steal every penny they can from them.

I have worked for other companies where I had sometimes disagreed with some of the things they did or maybe even some of their policies. Everybody does. But at least the management in those companies believed they were doing the right things for the right reasons, and they did it with integrity.

But NEVER anything like this. At Fedex they thought everybody was fair game and Fedex was the "Great White Hunter."

Later that night while still being evaluated I got a dispatch to go to a small company called Mercantile Press in Wilmington. It was a printing company. Normally I would do their pickup about once a week. It was a good stop and they were friendly there. They were very particular about their work and they were always on time with their shipments and the paperwork was good.

Being Ordered to Commit FRAUD and .....The Fraudulent CSS SCAM

But tonight they had a CSS package shipment for me to take. I had never done a CSS shipment before and when I was in courier school their instructions about handling one were ambiguous. It seemed at the time that they taught two different ways to handle and do a CSS pickup. There was so much to learn at courier school and little time to learn it and it was kinda just brushed over.

The first time the instructor told us to handle a CSS shipment special and to keep it in your sight always.

The second time we went over the procedure to handle a CSS shipment we were told to just handle it like a regular common freight shipment.

I figured that since these shipments were usually special and important and cost extra to ship there must be some kind of special care they got.

I was soon to learn the truth.

Because tonight I was to learn that you tell the customer that we do give the CSS shipment "special handling.".... But that the second way, was the way it was actually handled. In other words the CSS service NEVER existed, except on paper so Fedex could steal millions from their customers. Fred Smith and his fellow criminals at Fedex were involved in a Conspiracy to Commit Fraud and Steal Millions of Dollars. A Felony

It wasn't sloppy handling, not a misunderstanding, not just one single manager doing something wrong ... it was company wide. It was FELONY FRAUD.

Fred Smith and Fedex management knew exactly what they were doing.

The owner of Mercantile Press came over and greeted both of us. Then he began asking both my manager and I about the handling of a CSS shipment. He asked if every person that has possession of the shipment would be signing for it and would it always be attended to (in sight) and or locked up at all times as the girl on the phone had told him.

I knew what the manual said about the proper handling of a CSS shipment and so I assured him that it would be.

He said that he had been complaining to Fedex about our couriers constantly losing his shipments and they suggested that he use our "CSS" service. Because CSS service would "insure" that his shipment would never get lost or stolen. (it would also get an additional $25.00 for Fedex for handling his package like a common shipment)

Then he asked me to explain exactly how a CSS shipment was handled. I was standing next to my manager and as he was giving me an evaluation on my job performance that night I knew I had to get it exactly right the first time. There was a section in my evaluation that details specifically with product knowledge and I would be scored on it so I had to get it right the first time.

So I started...

"Well Sir, after I fill out the airbill I sign this 'CSS tally record' to show that I do have possession of the shipment and exactly at what time it is. I'm not allowed to let it out of my sight and unsecured so when I leave this stop I have to take this shipment directly back to my station and give it to a "Customer Service Agent" (CSA) at my station.

That person will sign the 'tally sheet' also with the date and time just as I did. And then that person will put the shipment in a locked secure area to maintain it's safety. Then later tonight it will be given to a courier and he too will sign and date the 'tally sheet' and take it to the airport ramp where he will give it to a "CSS specialist" there. That "specialist will also sign and date the 'tally sheet' and place it in a secure area with the other CSS shipments to be flown to Memphis for sorting. The CSS specialist in Memphis will also sign and date the 'tally sheet' to let us know it got to Memphis, and make sure it is forwarded onto the receiving airport.

A CSS courier there will get the package at the airport of the city it is going to and that courier will also sign and date the 'tally sheet' and take it to the destination station that will deliver the shipment.

The station that delivers the shipment will have the courier that finally delivers the shipment sign and date the tally sheet also.

That delivery courier will have the person (the recipient) who finally takes possession of the shipment sign and date the tally sheet for the shipment.

That way every person who had possession of your CSS shipment has to sign a 'tally sheet' to show who had the shipment and when. "It's a great service."

The owner of Mercantile press seemed pleased with my explanation but he also still had concerns about whether or not someone at Fedex might lose or steal his shipment so he added ..."okay, please don't lose this one, it's important," and he turned and walked away.

After we were alone I asked my manager Colin, "well how did I do with my CSS explanation," hoping I had said what I was supposed to and gave a correct answer.

"You did fine," Colin replied, "your answer was perfect."

After I finished filling out the other airbills we went back to my van. I put the packages in the back of my van and began writing on a three letter code for the cities to which they were going.   It's like putting in the Zip Code but instead it's a three letter station I.D. code that tells the sorters in Memphis what station it goes to.

This is how Fred Smith and Fedex STEAL MILLIONS

Colin asked me, " do you know where your next stop is Gary." He was making sure I already knew where my next stop was going to be. He would do that occasionally as we drove along my route.

I replied, "sure I do, I go back to the station to drop off this CSS shipment."

"No, your next stop is up the road to your next customer" Colin said.

I was caught off guard. I thought I was supposed to take it back to the station like I told the customer and the way the manual says.

So I turned to Colin and asked, "what about the CSS shipment?"

"Don't worry about it," he responded, "just handle it like a regular shipment."

"Then what's the difference between a priority one shipment and CSS service shipment." I asked.

Colin replied, "there is NO difference between CSS and priority one shipments Gary." Then he added, "well about (5 - 10) million dollars extra for Fred's Smith's pockets. And when Fred's pockets are full ... what falls out we get in profit sharing."

I didn't take that CSS shipment back to the station like we had told the customer we would. Nor did we ever take a CSS shipment back to the station like Fedex promises their customers they do and charges them dearly for. It wasn't a mistake, it wasn't just Colin and a few others within Fedex. It was a company wide conspiracy to commit Fraud

66

against and steal many millions of dollars from every unsuspecting customer they could scam. All across America.

That day was the first day I came to realize that Fedex was a criminal organization headed by Fred Smith. In time, I have learned, as you too will learn, that Fred Smith is a criminal and he uses the Fedex corporation as a front and a means, to commit even far worse crimes than this.

We finally finished up my route hours later and came back to the station.

What a night, my manager had tried hard all evening to get me to go to his house with him to get high. While I was trying to stay busy on my route so we didn't have time to and …"couldn't". Then he had instructed me to, and basically ordered me to commit an act of fraud, which was a felony. And all this and more … while "He" was giving me a job evaluation.

Well at least I did get a good job evaluation.

By the way, in case you're wondering. Last time I heard… Colin had been Promoted and was working in Liberty District Headquarters.

After I had backed my van up to the conveyor belt and we had gotten out I asked Colin who I would give the CSS shipment to. Who was the CSS person in the station that takes signs for and takes charge of the CSS shipments I asked.

Colin replied, "There is none, just throw it on the belt with the regular freight and go do your paperwork. They're no different than P1 freight…just extra money for us."

So I put it on the belt with all of the other common freight and walked away to do my paper work which was far away, and totally out of sight of my freight. So, not only did I honestly not have a clue of what happened to that valuable shipment… neither would most of the other people who did temporarily (but unknowingly) have possession of it know.

Later that night a courier would take it to the airport ramp along with the other freight and guess what …he wouldn't even know, as he never knew, that he had a CSS shipment thrown in somewhere with this regular freight. He never signed the 'tally sheet' and never even saw it. Didn't even know there was one. At the Philadelphia ramp it would be thrown on the belt with the other common freight. And there someone hopefully would throw it in a can … without ever seeing or signing a 'tally sheet'. I bet I've done that exact thing a hundred times, maybe a thousand times without knowing …while working at the Philadelphia ramp and loading cans for the cargo planes.

Nobody at the ramp even knew about the CSS shipments or what they were …as you will read later on in the book. That's the way it was "really handled" until the CSS shipment was eventually (hopefully) delivered to the intended recipient. Unless someone stole or lost the shipment along the way… it was done this way EVERY TIME. Then someone at Fedex would tell BIG LIES as to why they can't find the shipment.

The truth is….

CSS shipments were not handled any different than a common freight shipment that costs much less.

It was FRAUD. To bring stolen money to Fred Smith's pockets. And it was NEVER intended to Exist.

Here was a nationwide corporation that had somehow gotten many great stories written about it in a lot of magazines and they were for the most part LIES.

The Fedex company was just a corrupt racist organization that was committing crimes all across America.

Shipments were being stolen, Customers Lied to about the weight of their shipments, The Phony Non-Existent CSS service and tens of millions of dollars worth of Illegal Drugs knowingly and intentionally picked up, handled and delivered by Fedex couriers EVERY day.

These couriers and cargo handlers were doing exactly what they were trained and ordered to do by Fedex management.

I guess it just proves that …if you pay enough money to Congressmen, Senators and slick advertisers, public relations people and lawyers …you can get away with just about anything in America.

As one attorney explained quite bluntly to me. Fred Smith and his gang at Fedex are committing crimes that fall under the RICO Act enacted by government lawmakers in Washington to combat organized mobsters. And in fact many times it was those same lawmakers who were involved in or with the R.I.C.O.

For those who don't know what RICO is: **RICO stands for Racketeering Influenced Corrupt Organization**

That would be Fred Smith and his Criminal organization within Fedex.

Think it's not so ? Wait till we get further along in this book and you will learn some things about Fred Smith that he never wants anyone to know about.

Things that I exposed ... that would make Fred Smith try to kill a man in his home.

Fred Smith and other criminal elements within Fedex had come up with this Fraudulent CSS service that was FELONY FRAUD. They were using it to steal from tens of thousands maybe millions of customers all across America, even the United States government, our military, the CIA and many businesses.

It was Fraudulent Scam that even Bernie Madoff would have been envious of.

The phony CSS service NEVER EXISTED and was NEVER intended to.

When a customer sent s regular shipment with Fedex and paid about double maybe more for the CSS service, they got NOTHING extra for it. And Fedex couriers, management, everybody at Fedex all across America was telling the best lies in the world to commit these crimes and steal millions of dollars for "Fred Smith."

They all knew it was fraud and they ALL lied about it.

And Fred Smith and his criminal gang were just raking in the millions.

A good score and comments on my check ride evaluation.

I had gotten a good evaluation on my job performance by my then manager Colin Baines. Evidently he was impressed with my abilities, knowledge of our services and dedication to my job. He had written that I should take on more of a leadership position on my shift. It was the beginning groundwork on the way to a management position at Fedex. Colin had spent time with me and he liked what he saw simple as that. And since Senior Station Manager Mike Mitchell read all evaluations he decided to have a closer look at me after reviewing mine.

Evidently Colin had mentioned to him, while going over my evaluation, that I had a liberal attitude about Blacks. That I might hold beliefs that Blacks were equal to whites and should be thought of and treated fairly. A red flag had gone up about me. The senior station manager was questioning me and trying to determine my beliefs regarding Blacks. I had already known he hated Blacks and somehow I just guessed that he was pumping me for my views about them before ever considering me for a future management position. Fedex wasn't going to knowingly bring in a white manager that they already knew held liberal views regarding Blacks.

When Mike asked me specifically what my views were regarding Blacks I knew right away where he was going.

To be honest I just kind of hedged my beliefs in that area of conversation without giving my real thoughts about the issue. I had a family, I already knew things could go south for me if I proclaimed my beliefs of fairness and equality to Blacks. There was no question I would not get a position in management, and I could live with that, but it was more of a concern for my job.

So I just kind of shifted the conversation to working hard for the company, doing whatever was asked of me, being a loyal employee and stating that all employees at Fedex should have those qualities.

He must have given up on his concerns because he ended the conversation with something like, " Colin says you did good on you're evaluation and he thinks you'd make a good shift leader, keep up the good work and do what you're told to do. Just remember, I just don't want any Nigger lovers here in the station and Memphis (Fedex headquarters) doesn't want any either. Just remember that." He was making his point white man to white man, without putting anything on paper. Just as I'm sure it was done at many other Fedex locations all across America.

I'm sure that many people reading this must wonder is this guy for real or is he just putting out a lot of stuff to make Fedex look bad. I assure you what I have written is true. There was a time when I too wondered if it wasn't just a few racists who were using their positions in management at Fedex to promote their individual prejudice's. But after I had seen and heard it in so many different places and positions within Fedex I realized the evidence was all there. This was hard to believe this is America in the twenty-first century and here is Fedex management operating like it's the 1700's hundreds.

Only Fedex today uses a "Pen" like the modern day "Whip" to keep Blacks in line.

It was okay to do drugs and get high on the job but NOT if you are Black.

Then we got a new courier in the station and he was from Louisiana he said. And he was Black. What a surprise. We didn't have but a couple of Blacks in our station and though it was good to see, I wondered why all of a sudden management hired one. I knew that from the senior manager down Blacks weren't welcome And so one had to wonder why? I was told that he was a "token" and that Fedex was doing a lot of government contracts now and that they would have to hire on a few more Blacks to present a picture of fairness and equality. Just in case the government or somebody else complained about the disproportionately low number of minorities at Fedex.

His name was Ted and he was to be our new courier and also a CTV (Container Truck Vehicle) driver to drive the bulk freight up to the airport at the end of the night. He was a quick learner and he learned his routes and job pretty quickly.

He also got high at work as did most of the couriers and managers there. Sometimes with the other white couriers and I guess that made him fit in better. As it seemed just about everybody was getting high either in the station or out on the routes.

I was a few years older and white and didn't feel the intimidation he did. If he got high with the others it was his link to fitting in with the other white couriers at the station. I'm not saying he didn't do drugs before coming to our station, Because I have no idea either way. I saying that by doing drugs with the guys in the station it helped him to fit in. At least in his mind. There was a commonality in their drug use.

And don't even think about Fedex management pulling a station wide drug test. Fedex did one in one of their stations once and lost (80 - 90%) of the station including management. Upper management at Fedex said they would never again do a station wide drug test. Let them do their drugs ... even on the job, but just get the packages delivered was the way my manager explained it to me.

There was a lot of pressure on him and I know he had to have heard some of the racial remarks about him, maybe even to him by management. He tried hard to fit in and I guess he did get along with some of the white couriers...but very few. A number of times I heard them refer to Ted as "that Nigger from Jersey," and a few times as " the Black motherfuckin Nigger." Once I asked a daytime courier what Ted did or what did he screw up? His reply was that Ted was just another "fuckin Nigger." And he said it just like that. I worked a route next to Ted's and I worked with him at night loading freight. I thought he was okay and I never saw him get ignorant or out of the way with anybody. Some of the couriers that were getting high with him would talk okay to him when they were high, but if they were straight and they saw him in the station they gave him a cold shoulder and talked about him like he was dog crap. There were a LOT of guys and some girls there doing a whole lot more drugs than he was. And a lot of them were also stealing from shipments, so why was he "black balled' ...oh, he was Black.

Once my van was close to Ted's and we were both getting ready to go out on our routes. One of the station managers by the name of Jerry Salomone came by me and walked over to Ted and began talking to him. I don't know what the conversation was all about but I did hear Jerry getting louder and suddenly I heard him say the words ... "you God dammed Niggers" in mid sentence. It was clear that he was lecturing Ted but I wasn't sure what it was about. Just that Ted was taking it all in and not saying much. I had thought that Ted must have done something real bad that Jerry was chewing him out for. I'll never know I guess but I didn't think that Jerry had to call him a Nigger.

There's better ways to get your point across. I never heard any rumors about Ted stealing anything and if it was all about drugs....Jerry was one of the biggest druggies in the station and was stealing from shipments. Even I had seen Jerry high quite a number of times. Actually seen him go outside to his car and get high with other couriers and seen him have white powered drugs in little baggies, of some kind on his desk in the station right out in the open. Other couriers told me how he [Jerry] and other managers had stolen illegal drugs out of shipments many times and either sold them or did them or both.

After I had time to think about it I realized that Ted was in a tough spot. He was from another part of the country and wasn't used to being in the northeast. I doubt that he had any family up here except his wife and it was obvious that he wasn't welcome here in the station. But I think that was a reality to many Blacks at Fedex.

The routes were getting busier in the evenings and I guess in the daytime too. For my part I was glad that we had more stops. We ran a little faster but we also wound up with more hours at the end of the week. I had a family to support so any extra work was good to me.

But some of the other couriers on the evening shift were complaining. To this day I don't understand why, but some of the couriers on my shift thought the routes were getting too busy and they were working too fast. My manager Colin came out one day and asked me if I thought we were working too hard and were the routes getting too hard. I looked at him and smiled. I told him hell no, I'm getting more hours and I'll take all I can get.

Then he asks me, " no problems?"

"No, Not at all," I replied. Having more stops only makes my night go faster. Then he said something like ... "okay great, you're the only one not bitching."

About a week later Mike Mitchell was in the station while I was getting my truck ready to go out. It's smart to get in about (15 -30) minutes early to make sure you're good to go.

Mike came over to my truck and asked me how it was going.

I told him life was good.

And then he asked me how the route was going and I replied that it was getting busier and that was good. And that it got me a few extra hours a week which was real good. Mike said that some of the other couriers were bitching that the routes were getting too busy. And did I feel that way too?

I replied that I was good. And that sometimes Larry the dispatcher would have me help a few other couriers that got backed up and behind on their routes but that I didn't mind. That it was no big deal. It was just work. What we got paid for. I did say that the cargo handler was a little rushed at the end of the night. He was responsible for making sure the freight was loaded properly into the CTV and the shuttle truck and things got a little hectic because the freight was coming back to the station later.

And I guess that set Mike off.

Because ....

There was a sales position open in the station and it was posted in our work area. Evidently the cargo handler had put in for it. He had college and was working full time in the daytime as a sales representative for the McCormick seasoning company.

The problem was... the cargo handler was Black.

Mike went off about how the Blacks want the titles but couldn't do the job. He said something like..."that Nigger will never get above cargo handler in this lifetime. Fucking Niggers, always wanting more and don't want to work for it. They're too stupid and have no discipline.

"I wouldn't have a single Nigger in this station if I didn't have to. But we have to have the fucking "tokens", it's ridiculous."

Then he went on to state..."if that dammed Nigger doesn't quit asking about the 'sales position' and quit his whining I'm gonna fire his Black Ass and he can take his complaints someplace else." And Mike meant it.

The truth is, the cargo handler was actually well qualified for the job.

He had college, was very knowledgeable of our products and was already in sales with another company where he was doing well. And he was a great guy and a good family man. Clean looking and well spoken and made you feel comfortable around him right away. He just wanted to stay with Fedex and make it to full time. He was a hard worker and one of the very few in the station that didn't do drugs at all. He had foolishly thought that if he put in his time and paid his dues that when a promotion to a higher position came available he would get a fair chance at it. It wasn't going to happen. As I think back I wonder just how many times this kind of discrimination went on at Fedex everyday all across America ... by racist white management within Fedex?

Because Mike Mitchell was not alone in those beliefs and in fact it seemed quite common among management at Fedex. One member of Fedex management once explained to me that Fred Smith and Fedex didn't like Blacks being a station manager at all. They believed that if a Black were in the position of station manager ...there would be no one there to keep them in line. He actually stated to me that Fedex upper management told him in a conversations that there should always be a "white man" over the Blacks at Fedex. But that he was not to discuss it with others. He said that Fred Smith believed Blacks lacked the intelligence, discipline, initiative and generally only did what they were told to do and no more. Not one bit more.

Then he hit me with something like ...come on Gary what black business leader do you know that started his own successful business? I knew there are many but didn't have any names to throw at him at the time. Later on I thought of Michael Jordan, Oprah and a few others. But it wouldn't have mattered. He was from the Philadelphia area and he was a station manager. I think he was German.

Was he lying? The question I would ask is ... why would he lie about that?

Well obviously Mike Mitchell bought into that program 100%. But I didn't.

I grew up in a mixed neighborhood. I learned quite young that there are good and bad in all races. I had played with and against Blacks in sports. Had fought with them and against them while growing up. They were people like everybody else and they had their good and bad ways just like everybody else. You can't just say all Blacks are bad people and you can't treat them all badly just because of the color of their skin.

Yet at Fedex it seemed that many times the white couriers always got away with things that the Blacks never could. One peep from a Black courier at Fedex and he was put on the 'short list' automatically. It wasn't "if' he would get fired….it was "when" he would get fired. And everybody knew it because it was common knowledge.

I was now the regular shuttle driver to the Philadelphia airport ramp. It gave me extra hours and more money. So it was good. I drove a IVECO truck to the airport. It was Germen I think. A little awkward to drive but it was okay. It was pretty simple. I would back up my truck to the belt, unload the freight in it and go park it. Then I would help load the cans from the belt and sometimes into the plane. All in a nights work.

I had gotten used to seeing the guys dealing and doing drugs, and the stolen stuff etc. I went in and did my job and came home.

Then one night I saw something that bothered me even after all I had seen there. I had just helped a couple of guys pull a can off a CTV truck from one of the Philadelphia stations. As I glanced back they were looking at something one of them was holding in his hands. They made a comment and then began laughing. Not sure what they were looking at but curious as I enjoy a good joke too. I walked back into the truck and asked what was so funny? What am I missing?

"Show Gary," one of them said, "he'll get a kick out of it."

So the one guy reaches into his pocket and pulled out two Polaroid pictures of a nude girl and held them out for me to see.

"Nice," I said, "one of your girlfriends?"

"Nah, just one of my pickups," he replied, "she sent four of them to her husband, he's in the Marines in California."

Then he continued, "when I went to do the pickup, this real nice looking girl answered the door, she asked me three times if anybody ever opened the 'Overnight Envelopes."

He said that he told her no one ever goes into Fedex's mail. That is why everybody uses us. Because the mail goes thru every time and no one ever messes with it. He even told her that was why the drug dealers use Fedex.

At that they all began laughing. And even I had to chuckle at that.

He said that she then took the Overnight Envelope into another room and put something into it and sealed it before bringing it back to him. Then she asked him again if he was sure no one would open it and he assured her no one would.

After he left her place he pulled over on the side of the road and opened the envelope to see what she sent to her husband. She had sent him four pictures of herself nude. And a letter telling him how much she missed him. And how she was going to make love to him when he came home. He told us that she said it ALL in her letter to him.

He said that after he read the letter he picked out the two best pictures of her and put the other two and the letter into another Overnight Envelope and sent it on to her husband...he said her husband was a lucky bastard.

I looked at him standing there with a big smile on his face and I just couldn't hold back. Here was a soldier's wife sending him something very personal between them. Hell, the marine could be dead tomorrow fighting to save our lives and this clown who probably had never even been in the service was going thru his mail. Mail that the soldiers wife had sent him. She trusted the courier who promised her privacy on a letter to her husband and he betrayed her.

He was a Bastard and a real low life piece of shit.

I said to him, " do you really think that's cool man, to go into her mail? She was sending it to her husband who was a soldier that's protecting your ass."

"All come on man," one of them said, "she'll never know."

"Yeah Gary, it's no big deal, what's it going to hurt," said another.

"It's not the point, stealing shit is one thing but stealing a soldiers pictures of his wife is pretty low. Don't you guys have any friends or relatives in the service," I asked.

None of them said anything more and soon we were all back to work loading freight into cans. But they knew I was pissed. They tried to be friendly with me and act like it was no big deal. But I would never again think of them as just a bunch of guys I worked with. They were low life.

After that I was left out of a lot of conversations. Ones that I'm sure involved drugs or stolen valuables. If they were talking about something they thought I shouldn't hear, they would change the conversation if I was close enough to hear.

If I had gone to management at the ramp and told them that a courier had stolen the pictures they wouldn't have done anything. They would have asked the courier off the record if he did. He would have said no, and the issue would have been dropped. End of inquiry.

And I would be 'black balled' from working at the ramp forever. The word would get out that I squealed on a courier for stealing from a shipment and that would be the end of me being there. There was just too much thefts and drugs going on there. It was the norm ..one of the perks of working at the ramp. You could buy anything there. The customers shipped it and the couriers and management stole it.

That's the real story of "supply and demand. The unsuspecting customer supplied the drugs and or valuables and the couriers stole whatever they had a demand for. It works so well for those at Fedex.

It's as simple as that.

Later on in the book you will read about a "stolen $100,000 gold shipment."

Who said being a Fedex courier didn't have Great Perks?

The wife and I thought it was time to move into a bigger house and though she didn't think we could yet afford one I did.

We spent some time looking and found a new development going up near us with several models that we liked. After some haggling we decided on one that we both liked and put up a down payment and then all we had to do was find a mortgage. It was an exciting time. The current house we were in was new when we bought it but it had already been built when we bought it. This time we would get to see a dirt lot turn into our property and watch the house go up. We could walk thru it as it was being built. It would be fun.

I mentioned to one of my managers that I had to have some financial papers filled out by him and he said that the senior manager Mike Mitchell would do it. That he always did it. I wasn't looking forward to that as Mike was usually in a sourly mood and not a very personal guy. He was also an alcoholic and I was told got high often with his girlfriend at the station who was also a courier. They said she had a "bad reputation" but she was half Mike's age so I guess it worked for him.

It took a few days to catch him in the station but when I finally did. I asked Mike when he had some time would it be possible for him to do a financial statement for a mortgage application for me. I thought he might just say to drop it by his desk and he would fill it out. And hopefully he wouldn't lose it. He asked me if I had it with me and I replied yes and he told me to get it and come into his office. I got the paperwork, but when I went into his office I told him I had to get out to run my route. Mike said to just sit down and we'd get this shit over with.

And he added something about banks being a pain in the ass.

Of course I agreed with him. After all he was doing me the favor. We were going over the pay rates and hours and he knew I was supposed to already be out on my route but he didn't seem to care at all. He had been with Fedex almost since day one when their planes flew nearly empty and they were running on pennies. He knew exactly what was happening on my route better than I did.

We both talked a little light talk and I think it was something he said that made me ask a question I had always wanted to. Usually he was very intimidating but today he was in a good mood, probably better than I'd ever remembered seeing him.

I said, Mike that story we were told in courier school about Fred Smith being completely broke and the company going to fold the next day.... They told us in courier school that he flew to Vegas and won $350,000 - $400,000 that night ... do you really believe that?

Mike looked at me, put down his pen and said, you're the first bastard that ever had the balls to ask me that. He got a whole lot more than that but he didn't win it on a table. He got a hundred times that much.

Then he went on to explain to me that during the prohibition days, the people that made the booze many times couldn't or didn't have the ability to deliver it so they hired people that delivered the booze for them. He said that Fred had the planes and the air strips so he hired out to fly the drugs across the border. He made a deal with "people."

Does he still do it today ... I asked.

Mike finished the last of the paperwork looked up at me and said .... Get the fuck out of here.

In all honesty I never did believe that story that he won all that money in Vegas at the very last minute before Fedex collapsed nah... not that naïve. But I really didn't know how he came up with that much money if he really did. I just figured it was some way he didn't want to or couldn't ... talk about.

At that time I didn't care. I was a happy camper, my mortgage went thru and the family and I were getting a new house. A bigger house with a bigger back yard. And the wife was already telling me that I had to build a deck on back of it. And it wasn't even built yet. Geez.

About a week after Mike had filled out my paperwork in his office I was out by the belt getting my truck ready to go and he walked over to me. He had that serious sourly look on his face that we always saw. He came up close to me looked around and said..."that conversation about Fred ...it never happened. And if I hear a single word about it, you're fired. Got it?" Mike said. He actually seemed edgy about it.

"What conversation, I don't remember any conversation," I replied. I knew what he wanted to hear.

"Hey by the way, I got my mortgage. thanks Mike, thanks a lot" I said.

And Mike walked away. It was obvious he had told me something he wasn't supposed to. Why he would reveal something like that to me I have no idea. We weren't friends, he was my boss and not a friendly boss to anyone...nothing close about us. Maybe it was just something he let slip. Maybe it had been on his mind for a long time and it was finally his chance to say it. Maybe he just had to tell someone and my question gave him a chance to say it. He had been in the company of Fred Smith a number of times in Fedex's early days, and I'm sure he had a some VERY private conversations with him over the years. He had seen a lot of things go on and things happen within the company. For all I know he may have actually seen drug shipments come into air ports or stations, maybe even the Philadelphia airport. Who knows? When you are in on the ground floor of a company's startup you see things that are wrong or illegal and they are "forgotten about" later on. Never to be spoke of. Never to be shared with anyone.

One thing about Mike Mitchell...he was never a man of bullshit. I'm sure he would lie for Fred or Fedex if he had a reason to. And he would have no problem at all doing it...but he was never a man to bullshit. It

just wasn't his style. He told it straight forward and if you didn't like it…
Fuck You.

There was a posting on the bulletin board. It was for a couple of back up CTV (tractor trailer) drivers for when the regular driver was on vacation or out sick. Usually when a new position comes open in the station anyone who is interested checks around to see who is interested in it and what their chances are of getting it. One other courier signed up for it and a few days later after no one else did I put my name in.

I had a good bit of experience driving tractor trailers and still held my CDL license and I knew that the two weeks training would be no problem for me.

The other courier who put in for it was a younger Black guy by the name of Anthony. He was a good kid and was that single good looking ladies man kind of guy.   I think he was hired on just ahead of me and had been a day time courier.

But being younger and Black he also took a lot of flak at the station. When he asked for directions to a business or about a stop on the radio somebody would always make a sarcastic remark to him. Tell him he had to get smarter etc.   Most times they gave him as little help as possible and usually just a rough idea to make him sweat.

It was funny, in his world outside the station he was a young light skinned Black guy who had great looks, a nice car, a good paying job… high prestige. In the station he was just someone who they put down and made smart remarks to and about.   And yeah they sometimes messed with his supplies in his truck. They must have thought it was funny.

Still he endured it.

Anthony and I were told that we were to report to the Philadelphia airport at the ramp to begin CDL training. And there was another courier reporting from another station. It was a woman in her late twenties and she was out to prove that she could drive a tractor trailer. She was actually pretty dammed gutsy and out to prove she could do anything a man could do.

The instructor was an older Italian guy.

He introduced himself and said that he had previously worked for Roadway Trucking which was one of the biggest trucking companies out there. He greeted us all and then introduced himself as Anthony and asked us what our names were.

When the young Black Anthony said what his name was, the instructor stared at him for a second.   It was that "disapproving look" and then he said to him. Well I'm not going to call you Anthony, I will just call you Tony. Then he started talking about the training course we would be taking.

He probably didn't even realize that from then on throughout the course whenever he spoke he only looked the other woman courier and me.   It was pretty apparent that he wasn't happy training a Black guy to drive a tractor trailer, and especially a young Black guy that had an "Italian Catholic" name.

Since Anthony and I had come from the same station we were already friendly and had talked a number of times before. I didn't realize it at the time, but that would benefit Anthony later.

In an effort to not confuse readers with two "Anthony's' I will call the younger Anthony who was in training…"Tony".

He asked me after about three days of training …if I thought Anthony the instructor didn't like him? I tried to give him a political answer and said something like…well, I wouldn't worry about it too much. Then I added that I probably knew more about truck driving than Anthony the instructor did and I would make sure he passed the course.

No matter what. Anthony made it obvious that he had a dislike for the younger Tony and Tony felt it. And it made him nervous.   But I knew I could get Tony thru the course okay because I had trained others to drive a tractor trailer before.

But this time it would be more of a challenge because I had to work around a very racist and bigoted white instructor who was in charge of training and he really wanted to fail the young Tony simply because he was Black..

Occasionally when we took breaks the Italian Anthony and I would be alone. And most times the talk would be him and I talking about previous experiences with truck driving. After about a week of training when Anthony and I were alone one day, he just came right out and asked me, "don't you have any other white guys in your station who want to drive a truck?" It seemed both an attempt at a humorous barb at me and also a complaint because he was having to train a Black guy to drive a tractor trailer.

I replied no, "no others signed up for the position."

Then he went into a tirade about how "Niggers" can't drive as good as whites and how he didn't like training them (he called Tony a 'young buck nigger') and how he didn't like being around them. He said he didn't understand how a Nigger could wind up with a good Catholic Name" and that it bothered him. Then he smiled and said…he didn't even like the smell of Nigger's.

Then he added again, that he really didn't like having to train one and that he was going to make it as difficult on young Tony as possible. And hopefully he could make Anthony quit.

I had my work cut out for me. The instructor was trying to force Tony out of training and he was in charge.

And I was trying to get him thru training.

The training including both text books, videos and actual driving. Since I had been around tractor trailers for many years most of it was old hat. When the older white Anthony made mistakes while training us, I sometimes explained his mistakes to him and we would sometimes openly disagree in the class room. When we went back to the books to check, most times the books showed clearly I was right and a few times it could be taught either way. It was obvious he didn't like it when the books showed that I was right. He just did not have the experience and knowledge he said he did.

The sad part was that young Tony knew the instructor didn't like him and he was too intimidated to ask the instructor to go over specific information again. When I saw that…I would ask the instructor if he would he please go over that part again. Because "I" had missed something. I had more time behind the wheel than the instructor and already knew most of the information but I wanted to make sure young Tony understood. The white girl was totally confident and if she had a question she asked without hesitation. She was not one to sit back.

Out in the field when the instructor explained a certain move or driving procedure that he wanted us to do he looked directly at the woman and me. Almost never making eye contact with the younger Tony. Almost like Tony wasn't even there.

One day we were out in the parking lot where we practiced the different driving maneuvers. The instructor came out and set up cones and told us we were to drive backwards in a snake pattern thru them. Then he told me to get in and show the other two how to do it. I had a lot of experience backing up tractor trailers in far worse situations than this so it wasn't a big deal to me. I got in pulled forward a little to align the trailer before starting and then backed thru the cones. A lot of experienced drivers could have done it. Then he turned to the woman trainee and gave her some directions and helpful hints and told her good luck. She struggled a little but she did get it right.

Then he turned to Tony and said he was next. When the instructor began giving Tony instructions on how to do it I couldn't believe him. He was telling him to do it a different way then he had told the woman. And it wasn't the right way.

When Tony tried to back thru the cones he couldn't do it the way the instructor told him to. Nobody could have. I walked over to the truck and told Tony to just pull forward of the cones and he did. Then I climbed up on the side of the door and told him how to back thru the cones the correct way. He looked at me and said that the instructor had told him to do it a different way. I said, I know, but you can't do it that way. Just try it like I told you to and you can do it. He tried it my way and he made it the first try. He had a great big smile on his face and he was so happy.

Later that day Tony asked me why would the instructor tell him the wrong way to back up thru the cones. I just told him that maybe he wasn't that good.

The fact was…the instructor Anthony had given the woman the right instructions to help her succeed.

But he gave Tony the wrong instructions intentionally hoping he would fail and he did the first time. What I didn't tell Tony was that the whole time he was struggling and trying to back thru the cones and failing when using the directions the instructor gave him, the instructor was laughing at him and calling him a stupid Nigger.

And he laughed as he said, "that Nigger ain't gonna pass this training course."

There were several times that the instructor did that to Tony and every time he would laugh at him and call him a stupid Nigger and make fun of him. And swear that Tony wouldn't pass the training course. But never to Tony's face.

All the while Tony was doing his very best to pass.

Well Tony did pass the CTV tractor trailer training course. And though he never did get the chance to drive a Fedex CTV tractor trailer very much I'm sure he would have made a very good driver.

Ohh … just to let you know. I was trained to drive a tractor trailer by a guy by the name of Willie Burl. He was the truck driving instructor at

ICI Americas and he was very good. He was honestly as good or better then any truck driver I saw at Fedex.

Oh yeah …He was also a Black man. Great trainer to <u>ALL</u> and a great guy.

So training was completed and it was back to work at the station. I would be used as a fill in CTV driver when needed and that was fine with me. I knew that in time I would be a regular CTV driver bringing the freight to the station from the airport in the morning or at night taking freight from the station to the airport for the flight to Memphis headquarters for sorting. I would wait my turn while I drove the smaller shuttle trucks up in the evenings.

<u>Learning just one more way how Fred Smith and Fedex steals million</u>

It was about 7:00 pm and I was nearly finished my route for the evening. The dispatcher Larry said he needed me to help Carol on her route. That she was a little backed up and needed help.

Can you do that for me Gary … Larry asked.

I told him I could and that I had one more stop then I would call him for the address.

Larry told me thanks and something about always being able to count on me.

He was getting the help he needed and he was saying nice things to me. Larry knew all of the routes at our station better than anybody. He also knew how to work the couriers to get the most out of them. He had been in dispatch for awhile and he was very good.

After I finished my last stop I got a Pepsi and called Larry on the radio. He told me the extra stop was at 1210 Market street in Wilmington, and it was on the fifth or sixth floor. He said the stop was for a law firm and added that he appreciated me helping him out.

In about ten minutes I was there and when I found the right floor I realized why the other courier needed help. There was about thirty or forty Courier Pak envelopes on the floor. There was no one in the office area and the envelopes were just laying on the floor. This is a common practice when the stop is a regular one. The customers just leave the Courier Pak Envelopes and Overnight Letters on the floor and the courier does the paper work when he or she gets there and leaves a receipt copy in the door.

All of the shipments were Couriers Pak envelopes that night. The standard cost is $25.00 for each two pound shipment in a Courier Pak. After two pounds you were charged extra.

I grabbed a few and began writing up the forms (air bills) on them. The contents inside which was mostly paperwork weighed about one pound and maybe a few weighing slightly more than a pound. When I had finished about ten of them the regular courier arrived. She gave me a big "hi" and asked if I had been there long.

And I replied …only a couple minutes. Then I asked her if she was always this busy here at this stop.

Sometimes more and sometimes a little less Carol said, adding that it seemed like a lot as a 'last stop'. Then she said that "it's crazy the way they make us run around like this. I don't mind working, but to do this route I have to speed all over town. And one of these nights I'm going to have an accident she said.

I told her that I almost always had to speed to make my route work too.

Then she asked me how the wife and kids were. Carol was always so nice and considerate. I often wondered how she put up with all of the stuff going on with the drugs and stealing at the station. She didn't go to the Philadelphia ramp very often if at all so I doubted that she was aware of what went on there.

She was in her second marriage. This time to an older man who appreciated what a wonderful woman she was. We would often talk about our spouses and children. She had a daughter by her first husband I think. And she was very proud of her. Carol was very determined to do well in her life. She wanted to go daytime where the money was better and also she would be able to spend more time with her daughter at night.

We chatted back and forth as we worked on the envelopes trying to get them done as quickly as possible so we could hurry and get back to the station.

Finally we were done writing up the airbills and I took out a magic marker and started coding up the Courier Pak envelopes for delivery. It's a three letter code a courier puts on a shipment that tells the sorters what city and state the shipment goes to. I had to read the airbills to see where each shipment went to. I noticed that she had written four (4) pounds and five (5) pounds in the spaces where we fill in the weight of the shipment. I said to her, "Carol this Courier Pak is only about a pound and you marked it at (4) pounds and it's definitely less than two pounds.

I had thought that she had made a mistake.

"Oh Gary, you know what they tell you about marking up the packages heavier than they are. Everybody does it, you know that."

Yeah I know, I said. Colin told me to do that too but I don't do it.

I just write in what it correct weighs nothing more, I explained.

But Carol was persistent. "Yeah, but you know what they say ... make all of the money for Fred that you can. And some may come back to you someday", she said.

"Suppose these guys catch you writing up more than the envelopes weigh", I said.

"Oh they won't know, nobody checks the airbills. I've been doing it since I've been doing this pickup and no one's ever said anything about it yet. The managers know it and the courier that trained me taught me to do it, just like all the other couriers do it too" she said.

And she was probably right because she kept lying about the weights and no one ever raised a stink about it. In fact after that night I would occasionally check the packages coming down the conveyor belt at the station and at the airport ramp. And many times I would see the airbills on packages written up at much higher weights than the packages actually weighed. It was easy to do because many times the customer wasn't even there when the courier picked up the package. So the courier was able to lie and put in whatever weight he wanted or what he thought he could get away with. And then, even if the customer did catch it the courier would lie and say ..."oh sorry, I must have made a mistake."

When Carol and I finished with the last pickup we headed back to the station and unloaded the freight onto the belt. Then we would help load the bigger packages into the cans for the tractor trailer ride to the airport ramp. Ted would drive the CTV up and I would take up the bags full of Courier Pak envelopes and Overnight letters.

And the fraud and thefts and the stolen money just kept rolling in. Literally tens of millions of dollars stolen every year by the Fedex and their "loyal thieving employees". I was actually taught to cheat and steal from our customers by my managers and even by our training instructors in "courier school" just as thousands of other couriers all across America have been and continue to be.

But I couldn't do that.

I'm sure it's easy to be a "profitable company" when you have thousands of people all across America stealing money for you from your customers every day and night.

What I find interesting....

Here was Carol, who before and away from Fedex would be a normally honest person with good values and integrity who probably wouldn't cheat a soul. But because of the training and pressure put on her by management and a very good brain washing program ... She had become nothing more than a common "Liar and a Thief" who cheated and stole from people old and young without the slightest degree of guilt.

I guess the only real question to ask would be ..."how far will she or any other Fedex employee sink because of that pressure and brain washing?"

Tonight was Friday night and everyone at the ramp would be partying HARD. It was ... an open market tonight, any drugs you want they had, and if there's anything else you'd like to buy from the shipments just ask. Maybe an eight ball of coke or a hundred count of amphetamines, maybe an ounce or even a kilo of pot if you've got the money. And don't worry, if they don't have it with them on the spot they can make a call and have another courier bring it there in a just few minutes. All guaranteed to be the best on the street. Just speak up and place your order. "Watches, radar detectors maybe a TV or computer. Fedex customers ship it all so the couriers can steal and sell it all....and at a great price."

It was a circus no doubt. A lot of couriers working at the ramp would hold valuables and drugs that they had stolen from shipments during the week until Friday to bring them to the ramp. They knew that on "payday" people had more money and were coming to buy.

To me it was just wrong to steal. But I also would have been concerned about getting fired and having to go home and tell my wife that I had been fired. The reality was that it just wasn't couriers buying stuff stolen from shipments ...it was also management too. So who....was going to turn anybody in for stealing?

All were involved.

I just went in to work, got the extra hours and went home. The manager at the ramp seemed to like me and I did my job. He told me that he liked the way I busted ass and helped get it done to get the planes out on time. So no problems for me at the ramp.

Do your drugs, steal all you want…just leave me out of it.

The benefits of being a "Drug Addict" who shares with management at Fedex

We were at the conveyor belt unloading the evening freight when a Fedex van comes barreling in through the doors. The driver slams on the breaks and slides about five feet and stops about a foot from the belt. His van was pointing towards the belt and not backed up to it like it was supposed to be. It was angled towards the belt and not even straight. Several other couriers who were working near the belt were as startled as I was.

It was another courier by the name of Al Ferrier. He was either drunk or on drugs. We had seen him like that numerous times and we often wondered how he hadn't killed someone while working or even while off duty and in his own vehicle. He usually came to work looking like a skid row drunk. His shirts often had food on them and or was dirty and his pants looked like he's had them on for a month. I honestly don't remember that I ever saw Al in clean clothes and looking cleaned up. And it seemed a lot of guys moved away from him to get away from his body odor. Several of the couriers told me that his paper work was often unreadable. And he would often come into the station at the end of his day and had to borrow money because he had spent customers money when they paid him in cash. He even tried to borrow money from me numerous times. I always said no.

Al was always doing and stealing drugs with the other couriers and managers at the station so they always covered for him. And I sure he shared whatever valuables or drugs he had stolen from Fedex shipments with the managers too.

So management covered for him….he was their drug buddy.

Supposedly he had more accidents than all of the couriers put together in the station. I often saw him doing drugs in the morning before he left the station. Usually with Jerry Salomone but with other managers too. He would be on drugs when he came to work then do more drugs with others in the station or parking lot before he left the station. Sometimes he could hardly walk but the other managers didn't care. After all they were usually high too. Often when Al was too messed up to do his pickups I would hear the dispatcher on the radio begging another courier to do them for him.

It was just one big party at a Fedex station.

After Al had gotten out of his truck he went over to the paper work slots and laid his paper work on the table and walked out to his car and drove away. His freight was still in his van, none of it was coded and we had to go over his airbills to fix them. His paper work that he handed in wasn't finished at all and the manager just said to not worry about it because Al could do it tomorrow.

They were drug buddies…Al would be okay.

Things were moving along at work and my route was getting pretty smooth even if I had to race around like a race car driver. We actually used to refer to race day phrases to describe our nights. But we made it work. When Carol and I finished with the last pickup we headed back to the station and unloaded the freight onto the belt. Then we would help load the bigger packages into the cans for the tractor trailer ride to the airport ramp. Ted would drive the CTV up and I would take up the bags full of Courier Pak envelopes and Overnight letters.

I had settled into the routine and it was just another night at work for me.

Opportunity To do daytime deliveries…

One night about an hour into my shift the dispatcher told me to call my manager Colin Baines when I got a chance. When I called Colin he asked me how it was going. I replied that things were not bad, not bad at all. Then I asked him what he wanted.

Colin asked me if I wanted to come in tomorrow and do deliveries and I said yes. I asked him what area route I would be doing. It was important because you do not want to be running around trying to make all A.M. deliveries by 10:30 am and be in a route area that you did not know well. Colin explained to me that the delivery route I would be doing was mostly in the same area that I did as my pick up route.

We both agreed that since I would be doubling back that I was to just take the freight up to the airport ramp, unload it and come back to the station.

He left me with a reminder…"remember no failures, the regular courier doesn't have failures …got it.

At the time I thought he was just reminding me to work fast and hard to make sure I made every AM delivery on time. Tomorrow I would learn the 10:30AM commitment time was just another lie.

I came into the station a little before seven AM. Then I checked my van to make sure it had gas in it and was loaded with all of the supplies I would need.

Soon the CTV truck came down and we were busy loading freight off the belt.

When the freight was all loaded into my van and I was setting up my route Colin came over to the belt where all of us were. He told us all to come over away from the belt so he could talk to us.

"Look you guys, I got a call yesterday, a woman called here to say that she saw a courier smoking a joint at 10th and King street around 11:00 AM.

And at that everybody started to laugh.

Colin smiled, go ahead and laugh, but you guys know you don't want a urine test and I certainly don't. I have a family. I don't need to have a call come down from district headquarters asking me questions. So I'm telling you now .. It's stupid to light up a joint in midday or any time in the middle of town, certainly not 10th and King street. That's all I'm gonna say. You guys are big boys, act like it. And he turned away and left.

And I'm thinking to myself …are these guys that stupid. Smoking a joint in front of City Hall in the middle of the day. That's exactly where the courts are and where a lot of cops are always coming and going in and out all day long.

I turned to a courier standing next to me and said, "is that crazy or what?"

"Ah, no big deal," was all he said.

And to him I guess it wasn't a big deal or to the other couriers either. They were all joking about it on their radios as soon as they left the station. Illegal drugs were a big part of work for them. They weren't going to stop smoking in town just because a woman called. So what.

I got into my truck and headed out to make my deliveries. No time to think about the dummies smoking pot in front of City Hall. They were smoking it every where else why not there.

I was running my ass off trying to make the 10:30 AM commitment time for the P1 freight. I didn't want to have any failures. A failure is when you don't deliver a P1 shipment by 10:30 AM and I didn't want any. If the other courier was doing it without failures I would too.

When 10:30 AM passed and I still had P1 freight on my truck I was disappointed. I realized that the other courier had been running the delivery route for a long time and it was only my first day doing it, but dammit I was running hard and I was fairly familiar with the area. I should be able to make it happen. And here it was past my time and I still had ten stops to do.

I pulled up to my next stop and ran inside, "sorry I'm late," I said to the receptionist.

"You're not late, the other guy rarely gets here before 11:00," she answered back.

"You mean he's not here before 10:30," I asked dumfounded.

"No, he usually gets here between 11:00 and 11:20 sometimes later, " she said. "so you're doing fine," she said as she signed off on the package.

I still ran back to the truck for the next delivery.

I'm not doing too bad after all I thought to myself. But it was too late to fudge the times on the delivery sheet. I did however mark up the next nine deliveries in about (15) minutes according to my delivery sheet. Of course anybody looking at my times would know that they were fudged and not the correct times.

When Colin looked at my delivery sheet he said something like ... the last nine looked good. He knew I had learned "the lesson". and I did get the point.

No failures no matter how much you have to lie. I got it.

I ran deliveries on that route several times after that And every time I had to put down false times every time I got close to the 10:30AM commitment time. I'm not really into lying, especially something as simple as that. And probably too I was concerned about getting fired for lying on my timesheet. But if that is what they wanted either I lied or I didn't get the day routes.

As Colin said ..."make Fedex look good at any cost."

Taking care of the Senior Station Manager

There were occasional odd jobs to be done around the station and I was pretty handy with tools and management knew I never turned down extra hours. So when I was asked if I wanted to come in the next day to put shelving together of course I said yes.

It was around 9:00am and I had started putting the shelving together when I noticed that there was some packages on the belt. I glanced at them I saw that they had our three letter code (ILG) on them and that they were ours to deliver. But they were mostly P2 freight which meant that those packages didn't have to be delivered till 5:00 PM that day. And there were few P1 shipments among them that had a 10:30 AM commitment.

At about 9:45am another courier walked in thru the bay doors . She put her bag on the belt and said, "hi." Her name was Ailene. I had heard that she had a really bad reputation but I really didn't know her that well. As she began putting the freight in a van I realized that it was her freight and that someone in management had apparently set her up with a "special route" of mostly P2 freight. It was set up that way so that she could come into the station at 9:00 am. It was only supposed to be P2 freight and I may have found out that day why she had such an easy laid back route to deliver.

When she had almost all of the freight in her van Senior Station Manager Mike Mitchell came over by the belt and he seemed mad at her. He asked her why she didn't call dispatch to tell him that she would be late.

She just kind of shrugged at him. Then Mike told her to come into his office when she had finished loading her truck. He looked very pissed and in a bad mood which was common for Mike.

All Ailene said was, "yeah I shoulda called Larry" who was the dispatcher.

She could tell I had seen the whole thing.

Then she shocked me when she said, " it's okay, Mike's EASY. I'll just get him high and give him a blowjob and he'll settle down"

Then she went into Mikes office and closed the door.   When they came out about a half hour later they were both smiling.

So I guess she really was serious.

A REALLY GOOD QUALIFICATION FOR FEDEX CARGO HANDLER ?

Things were always changing at the station. The black cargo handler was gone and had been replaced by a "white guy". Had Mike kept his promise?

He wasn't in our station …did he complain too much?

The new cargo handler was Tom and he was coming in from Philadelphia …they went thirty miles to get a white one that they could train to be a cargo handler. And there were plenty of Black ones only a mile or less away.

Tom did seem to be a nice enough guy. But what did come as a surprise to me was that he was a "Convicted Drug Felon" and that he was still on "probation or parole" I never found out for sure which one. According to Tom, he had served five years in a federal penitentiary for selling cocaine. He said he had been running a big time cocaine operation and had been busted by the feds for selling it by the kilos. There had always been a tremendous amount of illegal drugs coming into and through our station. The thought that some of those in management in our station including Mike Mitchell might have brought him because of his drug connections did occur to me. Several of the other couriers in the station basically said that in conversations. It was the perfect setup. Shipping drugs overnight safely and profitably with Fedex.

People on the inside and people on the outside.

I've had some time to think about it now and I have realized a few things I didn't before … I think back to the day Mike Mitchell told me that Fred Smith was smuggling illegal drugs into the United Stated for the drug dealers …how much did Mike really know, and was it possible that he had somehow been involved in Fred's drug smuggling operation that he spoke of. Was it Mike who had brought in and set up Tom. He was a known and convicted big time drug dealer. Did Mike bring Tom into the cargo handlers position to handle drug deals and shipments? Tom said he had contacts up and down the east coast. Was Mike looking to connect with them also? Why else would Mike Mitchell bring in a convicted drug dealer who was still on probation to work not as a courier, but as a cargo handler where he could have full control of all drug shipments coming into and going out of the station?

It was the perfect setup. Tom had all of the drug contacts. Anyone could fly illegal drugs…even bombs thru Fedex airport ramps with almost complete impunity. And it was common knowledge that Fedex employees would fly to Florida and buy kilos of illegal drugs and fly back home with complete safety and no bag checks of any kinds. Because Fred Smith absolutely forbid the Police, FBI, DEA and other Federal investigators into his facilities.

Tom was an outgoing guy and he would tell you most anything about himself if you worked around him long enough.   I usually saw him when we were handling freight in the evenings while we were getting the freight ready for the run up to the airport, so we did our share of talking. He did lead an interesting if troubled lifestyle and he was never too embarrassed to talk about any of it.   While he was telling me that he was married and had five children … in the same breath he would be trying to sell me a kilo of cocaine and telling me how much money I could make on it. When I would decline his offer he would ask me if I knew anybody that might want some.

Tom often bragged that he could even ship the drugs to a customer for free and completely safe from police through Fedex if they wanted.

That is as long as he got his money first.

I was curious of how he would do it so I asked him.

"Well," he said, "you can drop off the drug shipment into a Fedex drop box. That way no one can catch you shipping it.   Then you mark the airbill to 'bill recipient, or third party', or just use a phony credit card number or check . By the time Fedex sends out the bill the shipment will already be delivered. When you address the shipment for the recipient you just use the address of a neighbors house where no one is home in the daytime.

Mark the airbill to be dropped off by the courier so no one has to sign for it. Then you have the person you're sending the drugs to watch the house for the drop off. And when the courier drives away he just walks over and picks up the drug shipment.

And even if the cops should be following the shipment, the buyer just has to say that he was picking up the package for a neighbor so it wouldn't be stolen. So they get their drugs fast, free and safe."

I asked him if it really worked and had he personally done it that way.

"I've done it and yeah it works," Tom replied.

Well I thought, that was certainly a safe way to deliver illegal drugs all across America and the best part was …it was free.

As I've heard so many times by management, couriers and other workers   at Fedex…"we're the Number 1 shipper of illegal drugs in America."   And another phase they commonly used…"at Fedex was "we deliver more illegal drugs to homes everyday than anybody." At Fedex, management and workers were always so proud as they made that statement.

One thing that Tom said he had done did really make me think if maybe it was a better idea to stay away from him. He told me how he nearly killed a fellow inmate while in prison. He said that the inmate wanted a pack of cigarettes from him. Tom decided to kill the man instead. So he put an iron in his pillow case and when the man wasn't looking he struck him as hard as he could on the head until he fell unconscious. Tom said he thought the man was dead or dying when they took him out in an Ambulance. But that somehow he lived.

You had to believe a lot of what Tom said. He had a wife and five kids, and was driving a Mercedes Benz, had a Rolex watch and always carried a big wad of money. Yet he was only working part time and his rate of pay was about $8.00 an hour.

<u>A funny story (well maybe not so funny).</u>

City Bank (a credit card company) moved into our complex and soon became a customer. Many times their shipments weren't ready to go until later that evening after even the latest pickup times. Because Tom lived in the Philadelphia area and was close to the airport ramp. Tom would often put their Courier pak envelopes into the trunk of his Mercedes and race up to the airport ramp. He used to say and laugh that often times he would be racing up interstate Route 495 on his way to the ramp at 130 MPH with the Courier Pak Envelopes from City Bank and kilos of Cocaine in his trunk at the same time. I used to wonder if he was serious until one night he took me out to the parking lot and showed me two kilos of cocaine in his trunk. He said he had a lot more than that in his trunk lots of times. He had shown other couriers in the station too. I guess he was looking for buyers.

I'm really not sure why, but after Tom had been a cargo handler for some time he decided that he wanted to become a courier. Maybe the heat was on him, I'll never know. For whatever reason Mike Mitchell gave him the okay. So it very well could have been the heat.

I had never thought that Fedex would allow convicted drug felons to be couriers especially while still on probation or parole. I guess I just thought that Fedex would not allow a courier that was a convicted felon and still on probation or parole to go into peoples homes and offices/businesses alone. It just doesn't sound like a good idea. And now

I wonder how many convicted felons Fedex does have as couriers, that have easy access to private homes and businesses?

Then again, Fred Smith has been indicted for forging another man's signature to steal millions of dollars, has killed an innocent Black man, and I have been told he was a "drug smuggler" by the OSI and the FBI and even one of his own managers. So I guess the "drug felons" on probation fit in well. Maybe he has a "soft spot" in his heart for those also involved in some of his illegal activities. For all we know Tom could have been "unknowingly" selling some the very illegal drugs Fred Smith was smuggling into America. Certainly Fred wouldn't want to hurt or hinder those moving his products.

You're ONLY a Lazy Courier if You are Black

We had been loading the freight for the trip to the ramp one night and in our usual hurry when the driver from the Dover, Delaware station came thru the doors. Her name was Helen. She was late and almost didn't make it in time. She said ,"sorry," then started on about a driver being late getting back to the station in Dover. One thing that I noticed about her right away was that she reeked of pot. You could smell it twenty feet away. And she had that... I've been a druggie all of my life look.

I would see Helen often after that night and most times she would either be high from pot or cocaine or speed or whatever pills were available that day. She would offer to sell me and other couriers whatever we wanted... pot , cocaine or speed ..(she called it crank) because she said it cranked her up.

She would say, " I've done every drug on the street baby. What ever you want...I've got it." I never bought anything from her and I think she finally gave up on me. But we did talk often. She talked more I think because she was always high on pot or speed or whatever the drug of the day was...or as Helen called it "drug dejour".

She would tell me who was doing what drugs in the station and one time I asked her how she knew all of that because she was working out of the Dover station which was forty miles away.

"Gary," she said, " didn't I already tell you that I've done drugs with just about every body in the station. Trust me I know exactly what drugs everybody is doing.

"Does everybody in the station do drugs," I asked her one time.

Her reply was that yes, just about everybody. There are so many couriers and managers at Fedex that do drugs that nobody ever turns in illegal drugs when they find them. That's why the drug dealers ship thru Fedex…they know we'll never bust them, we just take our cut.

Then she stated a mantra I had heard many times before at work … "Fedex is the Number One shipper of illegal drugs in America." we NEVER turn in Drugs or call the police…NEVER.

I knew it was true. Some of my customers on my evening shift were shipping drugs but I had gotten used to it. I had mentioned it to several of my managers at work and they only wanted me to bring the shipments to them so that they could steal them. Never call or contact the police. Jerry Salomone told me several times to "bring them to him, so that he could sample the drugs to make sure they were good enough to be shipped through Fedex. After all," he said with a laugh, "they didn't want any cheap drugs to be shipped through Fedex, only the best," he would say with a smile.

Helen wasn't the only courier who drove to the Dover station. Sometimes it was Charles. I believe that he had the route before Helen and that she filled in for him while he was on vacation or needed a break for the Dover run. Whoever had that run would start at Wilmington and take all of the freight to Dover in the morning. Then did a delivery and pickup route before heading back that evening with the new freight which included freight from the other couriers already down there. It was a long day but a good money run.

One evening I was loading the freight on the conveyor belt to go to the ramp and Jerry Salomone came over. He wasn't the normal evening manager but he had been in the station for awhile and he just decided to walk over and chat I guess.

Though I remember that at the time I had thought he may have come into the station to do a Drug deal.

While Jerry was there Charles came rolling in with the freight from the Dover station. He was running a little late because another courier from there had gotten back to the Dover station late. Charles looked tired and I asked him if he had a long day. He shook his head and said how it had been crazy down there today. He helped get the freight onto the belt and then walked away to do his paperwork before going home.

After he had gone into the office and out of ear shot, Jerry said, "that fucking Nigger, if he did ten stops a day he's say he had a hard day.

That's ALL they do is whine and complain.   A hard day's work would kill them."

I didn't know Charles well as I'd only seen him in the station a few times. And I asked Jerry, "is he lazy?"

He replied, "they're all lazy, I've never seen a Nigger that knew how to work hard yet," then he walked away.

I thought about that …there was a white manager who did an awful lot of illegal drugs and who stole drugs, and God only know what else he stole, from Fedex shipments. And he's calling a Black man who worked fifty plus hours a week …"a lazy Nigger."

What's wrong with this picture?

In time I did get to know Charles. I learned that he wasn't lazy at all. In fact I thought that he worked as hard or harder than most other couriers in the station. In time I learned to like and respect him. He was a regular guy who took great care of his family. He was smart and he did a great job. Actually he did more than was ever asked of him and certainly more than he was supposed to.

If it wasn't for that dammed "skin problem" I think he would have made a great manager. You know the "Black skin" problem. I guess it was a problem he couldn't fix.

They had promoted whites ahead of him when the whites were no where near as good or qualified as Charles was. Of the two whites I can think of specifically, one was a drunken drug addict with a horrible driving record and a lot of lost and stolen shipments, and horrible paperwork. Who would wind up missing in the middle of the shift. The other was a white guy with almost no experience and only a very few if any route deliveries.   How could he train a new courier?

Charles was a seasoned and dependable veteran with many years of excellent service and great product knowledge who had gone far above the job requirement many times. Of course we don't know how many times he was cheated on his evaluations by racists white managers. My guess is a LOT.

I guess Charles was destined to be a courier ……. after all he was a 'Black' man.

Fedex Druggie Couriers…Rip Off Mafia Dealer
One day I got a call to do a pick up at Vinnie's Pizza in Claymont. It was a small pizza shop in the Northtown Plaza shopping center. Vinnie

was the owner, he was a smaller Italian guy. And he seemed like a nice enough guy.

Vinnie would ship out an Overnight Letter and most times he wasn't ready when I got there so he would offer me a soda while I waited for him. Sometimes when he wasn't busy we would talk while I waited. The talk was small and usually about family and what I did for fun. In time I began to realize that Vinnie was involved in drugs and was feeling me out. I think he was trying to determine what kind of person I was. I don't know if he was trying to find out if his drugs were safe with me or was he considering offering me some action with his drug business. I can't say either way for sure but he certainly did ask a lot of questions about my personal life and habits.

Vinnie would send the Overnight Letter to Brooklyn, New York and he would staple the entire edge of the Overnight Letter. And I do mean the entire edge about every half inch or so. Several times he asked me if they x-rayed the shipments in Memphis where the sort was. I had heard that question many times before Vinnie. The customer would often imply that they were shipping picture film but you knew why they were asking. They had illegal drugs in their shipments and were afraid the x-ray scan would show it. I always replied that NO there were no x-ray machines in Memphis or anywhere else that I knew of.

Vinnie seemed pleased with my answer and he seemed to relax more. He called for me to do a pickup about once a week and occasionally twice a week. He would usually wait till I got there then he would get the O.L. ready and always stapled it around the edges. He kept a 357 revolver and a shotgun in the back area where he prepared the O.L. One time I was kidding him about the stapling of the O.L. and he picked up the 357 and said, "nobody messes with my stuff."

I got the impression he was trying to tell me something and I did understand.

I did the pickups there for awhile. Then I began noticing several hard core looking type guys there. They were definitely Mafia types. I could have been wrong but I don't think so. They just looked and behaved exactly like we perceive Mafia people would be and act. Maybe the movie people were right after all.

When I went there to do a pickup they would just be sitting or standing around, not working and not eating, just kind of eyeballing the people as they came thru the door. Always the same one or two guys.

One I remember very well was a big Italian guy that always wore a big gold necklace and he looked right out of the Godfather picture. He even made me nervous.

I get a BIG TIME Mafia Experience

But evidently some of my courier buddies in the station had figured out what Vinnie was up to with his drug shipments. One evening when I arrived to do a pickup Vinnie motioned me back to the area where he got them ready. When I got back there Vinnie stuck the 357 in my stomach and said, "Gary you tell you're motherfucking druggie couriers to keep their hands off my shipments. Cause if they don't they're going to end up dead." Vinnie was mad. Evidently someone at Fedex was ripping off his drug shipments. And it certainly wasn't me.

While he held the gun in my stomach I explained to him as calmly as I could. That I NEVER messed with anybody's shipments and that I didn't even do drugs. It was obvious that he was mad and very serious. He had a loaded 357 stuck in my stomach. And the big Mafia guy was up in the front of his store. I could have wound up rolled up in a carpet. Evidently they were stealing large quantities from him. And he had had enough.

I told Vinnie that I would spread the word to leave his shit alone. Or they would get hurt bad. I also told him that I would take special care of his shipments and try to protect them as best as I could. I think he believed me and he did realize that I had nothing to do with any of it. Which I didn't. He was a drug dealer...yes I figured that out. But to my knowledge I never saw any of his drug shipments coming in. I think I was just doing the pickups for the money going to N.Y. The daytime couriers were delivering his drugs to him. They were the ones stealing them.

Before he even took the gun away from my stomach Vinnie said, " okay Gary, you handle that for me. Tell those thieving couriers to keep their fucking hands off my shit and to steal from somebody else. **Or I will kill them.**"

The whole thing had caught me off guard and yes I was somewhat scared, but not nearly as scared as I would have been if I had been involved in stealing his drugs. And I think Vinnie saw that, and maybe he really did already know that. Maybe he was just using me to get the word back to my thieving druggie co-workers in the station.

Still, I thought about it. Wouldn't that just be great. I don't even do drugs, wasn't stealing anything … but especially Vinnie's Drugs… and I could have been the guy getting killed because of them.

What the hell are these guys stupid? The couriers on either end of the pick ups and deliveries had to know this was Mafia Drugs they were stealing …these people will kill you for stealing their stuff. They won't call your boss and tell them to fire you…they'll just kill you.

Was it really worth it.

And to be honest, I didn't say anything to the other couriers at my station. I wasn't sure just who was doing the stealing and it would only bring in more attention to Vinnie's drug shipments. And then they would NEVER get through to him. All the couriers would be looking to steal his drugs

In case you're thinking …"Well I would have called the cops on Vinnie". No you wouldn't have…that would have been flat out stupid. I had a family and this was Mafia.

I look back and laugh about it now but it wasn't really that funny that night. And it was some time later that I even told my wife about it. Only after some time had passed. I was that regular guy who just went to work, I had a family. I really didn't need that shit in my life. Still, I get to say that 'I really had a Mafia guy put a gun to my stomach.' That's serious bragging stuff at my Catholic church's socials.

Vinnie still kept making his regular shipments to Brooklyn. But there was a time when he stopped calling for the evening pickups for awhile. I hadn't really realized it as my route was always busy and getting busier.

Then one night, out of the blue he called and I went back for a pickup. He called me back to the area where he regularly did the Overnight Letters. Vinnie looked like he was or had been very sick, he had lost weight and was pale. I said something like, "what had happened" because I hadn't seen him for awhile? He hesitated for a moment then said that he had been sick. That he had Pneumonia and he certainly did look like it. I asked him if he was going to be all right and he said yes …he would be okay. Slowly the pickups at Vinnie's stopped coming and I didn't even realize it.

It didn't occur to me at the time but his shotgun and pistol were both gone. And previously he had always kept them out in the open where they were easily accessible and could be seen by anyone coming into the back area of his store.

<u>What a Fedex Courier might give a Young Girl working at McDonalds?</u>

Time was passing and I was just settling into being a courier and taking care of my family. My evening route kept getting busier and I figured it wouldn't be that long till I was doing deliveries on day work.

One afternoon my supervisor Colin came out into the freight area and passed out a bunch of trinkets to the couriers going out on the evening shift. I was handed about two dozen small velour pouches with the Fedex name on them. Hand them out to your best customers we were told. They were little (2" X 4") mirrors inside the velour pouches. And they looked like the little cocaine mirrors you see the drug users use when they snort cocaine in their cars. One of the couriers joked that it was Fred's way of saying that it was okay to do cocaine while working. And they all laughed at that.

Some of the couriers said that they were going to keep all of the mirrors as souvenirs for themselves. I thought that I would keep a few and give the rest away to customers. Some of my customers had been there before I got the route…I would give them the mirrors first.

Later that evening I had a very rare few minutes to grab a burger. There was a McDonalds right on my route so I pulled into the drive thru and ordered. When I pulled up to the window to get my order and pay for it the girl working there asked me for a mirror. She was all of sixteen years old and looked younger.

I looked at her and wondered how she knew I had mirrors to give out. I thought …what the hell ..she's just a young school girl why not. I reached into my bag and grabbed a mirror and pouch and handed it to her. Saying …"here you go," or something like that.

She reached into the pouch and pulled out the mirror and looked at me and said, "where's the rest?"

"What," I said, I honestly didn't understand what she meant.

"You know," she said, "the other guy put some coke (cocaine) in with the mirror."

"The other guy put cocaine in the pouch with your mirror," I said in disbelief.

"Yeah," she said, then she said that she had gotten cocaine from the other courier before.

"Well I don't have any and I certainly wouldn't give you any if I did, you can't be much more than sixteen," I said.

"I am sixteen," she said as she handed me my burger and shake. I just shook my head and drove away. I didn't want to know any more. For all I knew he was also having sex with her and I didn't want to know that. For that I would have called the cops. Both were bad... but if he was having sex with her I couldn't deal with that job or not. And if he was drug connected in the station which I'm sure he was, I would be forced out if I ratted him out. And I really didn't want to know which courier it was that would give a sixteen year old girl cocaine. I could guess of which one of three it was...but I didn't want to know.

The Making Of A Fedex Manager ...

As I said earlier Al Ferrier was probably the worse example for a courier that I have ever seen. Many times I wondered how he kept his job. On so many occasions I had heard the dispatch say that he had been out of communication for hours. It would usually happen in the afternoon after he and other couriers would be doing the harder drugs instead of a real lunch. The dispatch would be calling for him on the radio to do a pickup at a customers business or house and Al would not respond. Then the dispatch would start asking his drug buddies where they thought he would be. And none would say. Probably because he was too wasted to drive. Then the dispatch would give the pick up to another courier who wasn't too wasted to do it. They had a regular routine.

And management was doing the drugs right along with him so they took care of him and let everything go and covered for him.

And then the "I can't believe this shit happens."

I was coming in on the evening shift and some of the guys were talking about Al. He was wasted on drugs and had another accident, he'd had so many I couldn't count them all and or I lost count of them all. Normally you were supposed to be gone after three accident's unless you were drug connected to management. I think Al had about twelve, and maybe more, but he was certainly "drug connected' to management.

The other courier's were laughing and one of them said that if Al lost his drivers license's they would probably just make him a manager. And they all busted out laughing at that and I did too. It was the funniest thing I had ever heard. Most times Al couldn't even tie his shoe laces or buckle his belt and they were going to make him a Fedex manager? But I didn't realize the courier was telling the truth.

Well …say hello to Al Ferrier, the new Fedex manager. He had gotten a well earned promotion. He had put in some years and didn't miss that many days a month, was only late once or twice a week, was only missing on the job about once a week. And he usually only stole drugs and valuables from his route…and only occasionally from other couriers shipments. Well… usually only if it was still on the conveyor belt when it came past his truck. But then it was first grab first serve for all of the couriers. "Freebie Time" as they called it. The best part was he would only do drugs a couple times a day on his route. And he did do some pickups and deliveries in between.

Damm he certainly was the stuff Fedex managers were made of… Fred Smith would be proud.

When I told some of the guys at the airport ramp that they were making Al a manager they all laughed too. One of the handlers said he remembered when they found Al passed out in the cargo area of a 727 plane one night. He said that if they hadn't found him amongst the bags of Overnight Letters that were in the tail section and got him out of there he would have died on the flight to Memphis.

Al would be the new Fedex manager at our station.

In the Meantime Jerry Salomone Fires a Black Courier. Jerry just calls them "Niggers"

I was getting my truck ready by the conveyor belt when Jerry Salomone who is normally a daytime manager came over. He had a big shit eating grin on his face. Like something great had just happened for him.

"Hey did you hear," Jerry asked.

I knew what he was talking about, bad news travels fast, but I pretended like I didn't.

"I finally fired that fucking Nigger, it took me awhile but I got him. And in time I'll fire all of them," Jerry said.

"Who do you mean," I asked.

"You know, that fucking Ted Autry," Jerry replied.

Then he went into how he was glad that he fired Ted because he was a Nigger and how he hated Niggers. He always called Blacks (Niggers when they weren't present). He went on to say that he would fire every one of them if he could. That he didn't even like to be around them.

I had known that Jerry hated Blacks from past conversations with him. He stated that he "didn't even want any dammed Niggers in his station." I had heard that from all the White managers there...it wasn't anything new at Fedex. He said they were too STUPID and LAZY to work for Fedex and that most in Fedex management felt that way too. That's why Fedex only hired as few Niggers as they could get away with (his words, not mine). And only hired a Nigger into management if they absolutely had no choice for quotas etc. for government contracts. He had numerous times gone into that "Black Mantra" of ... Niggers are lazy and stupid and they only cause problems etc. that I had heard from far too many whites in Fedex management. I don't know if they attend classes on hating and abusing Blacks or was it on a company memo somewhere that Fedex management gives them to put on their medicine cabinet mirror to look at every morning before going to work.

Sometimes it sounded like a broken record...with almost the same words over and over again.

Maybe it's a KKK verse they had to memorize?

I don't know. But it gets old quickly.

He told me, that he always gave any Black that he did an evaluation on ... as low a score as possible. Fuck'em he said, "If they don't like it go somewhere else."

I'd heard the same stuff at the Philadelphia airport ramp. To my knowledge there were no Blacks working at the ramp. Only the few Blacks that came in as couriers for the night to help load the planes. They said they wanted it whites only.

Management there always referred to the Newark, NJ station as the 'jungle where the monkeys and baboons' worked. It was predominately Black couriers there I think. I've never been there just heard about the Newark station from guys at the ramp. One Christmas a driver came in from the Newark station and told us that a bunch of "Niggers" had been fired for stealing. But that he didn't think any of the whites stealing there were. There were whites stealing all the time at our station and the ramp. Did they just not get caught?

For Instance ...A Courier with a Sharp Nose for Drugs One night while I was working the Philadelphia ramp. I was standing next to the conveyor belt sorting incoming freight to be put it into the big metal cans that would be flown to Memphis for the final sort and then flown back out to the destination stations for delivery.

There was a small Italian girl next to me. When all of a sudden she starts jumping up and down and yelling ..."I smell Pot". " I smell Pot," she yelled again, "I can smell it a mile away." Then she jumped right up on the conveyor belt and started walking around and smelling the freight. One of the supervisors yelled at her to get down because she might fall.

And she yells back at him, "aww come on, you guys got the last ones. Come on let me have this one. I found it first."

And everybody laughed, even me. "Come on, "she begged. And all the time she was sniffing the packages on the belt. She looked like a beagle sniffing the ground for rabbits. It was really quite funny to watch to be honest. Finally the supervisor nodded his head up and down to indicate that it was okay, she could have the Pot this time. But by now she had competition. Other couriers were also sniffing the packages and trying to find the Pot too. It was a general rule at the Philadelphia ramp ... whoever found the drugs first had first dibs on it.

Of course if it were a larger find it was usually split up between those closest to the find. With the exception that management usually got their cut even if they were somewhere else and away from the find. It was just a simple rule that stood in most situations similar to this. Management "always" got their share and it fell under the rule of "Rank has it's privileges" aka ... RHP.

It didn't take her long to find the Pot. In just a few moments she grabbed a box and yelled, "Jackpot." It was a box slightly smaller than a cubic foot. She held it to her nose and took a deep sniff and then yelled, "ALRIGHT." real loud. Then she started tearing the box open. Other couriers ran over to where she was as she started opening the box. They all held their breath while she opened it like it was a Christmas present or something. I was about thirty feet away and was truly amazed by her skills at finding the Pot and the way they all got excited at the drug find. After she opened the box and determined that she did indeed make a great find she climbed off the belt. Then she and some of the other couriers went into the back to split up the Pot.

It had been a good night to be working the ramp. They had gotten quite a bit of Pot and the plane did somehow get off on time. Maybe it was even loaded safely?

I know that some of the Pot was turned into smoke before they left the ramp that night. After all, it did have to be tested to be sure it was a high enough quality to be shipped and delivered by Fedex couriers.

Numerous times at the ramp I have watched both couriers and supervisors grab shipments of drugs off the belt. They would open the boxes and Courier pak envelopes to see what kinds of drugs they had inside. Sometimes they would take all of the drugs and do them right there while working and loading the planes. And if they did load a plane and leave it unbalanced ...ohh well.

* Going back to a part of the interview with John where I questioned him about Illegal Drug shipments, Drug Thefts and Drug Abuse by Fedex couriers and management I will show you...it happens all of the time.

** And remember that I have tape recorded this interview with John's permission ... and I have numerous copies.

Back To The Interview Concerning Illegal Drugs
Gary, "have you seen a lot of drugs shipped thru Fedex?"

John, "yes , quite a lot, at Fedex we bragged about the illegal drugs we shipped ... management, couriers, everybody. **We were the 'Number One shipper of illegal drugs in the whole United States.** Management knew,   it was considered <u>REVENUE</u>. Basically everybody in the company knew, especially management,   because they knew the numbers." (how much revenue Fedex made on illegal drug shipments)

Note: Which means upper management including Fred Smith was counting on the "revenue" from illegal drugs being shipped through Fedex.

John, "I remember this one young fellow who got fired for telling the police there was drugs in a shipment. It was in Arizona and the drugs were being delivered to his neighborhood. He was married and had children living there. He told his manager that a package was a drug shipment. His manager told him not to open it but to just go ahead and deliver it to the drug dealer. Instead he took it to the police, When the police opened the package they found the drugs. His manager fired him because he took the drug shipment to the police rather then deliver it to the drug dealer."

Gary, "sounds like Fedex looked at illegal drug shipments as revenue."

John, "yes it was looked at exactly as revenue. Fedex ships an enormous amount of illegal drugs daily. If the drug shipments were even five percent of Fedex's total revenue and the total revenue was a couple billion dollars ... well five percent of a couple billion dollars is a heck of a lot of money. It's almost like a BIG private account."

Now I ask you to remember back to what Mike Mitchell, a Senior Member of Fedex management in the Wilmington, Delaware station said about Fred Smith flying to Las Vegas and making a deal with people there to "Smuggle their Illegal Drugs" into the U.S. from Mexico for them.

Realize that some of the Illegal Drugs being shipped and delivered daily by Fedex couriers all across America has to be some of the same "illegal drugs" that Fred Smith was smuggling / flying into the U.S. from Mexico? It was common knowledge that Fedex was the number one shipper of illegal drugs in the U.S. And it was forbidden by Fedex management to report the shipments and delivery of illegal drugs to the police. It could cost you your job. Not so at UPS, DHL, USPS or Airborne. Why?

Gary, "earlier you mentioned an incident about illegal drugs at the Philadelphia Airport ramp concerning Fedex employees, could you tell me about that event again?"
John, "yeah, they were loading an airplane and they found some drugs that they thought was cocaine. They decided to get high and also figured that the cocaine would help them load the plane faster. There were three managers and three loaders. But what they thought was cocaine was actually very strong heroin. They nearly died of a heroin overdose."

Gary, "and these people were the ones responsible for loading the airplane? What were their titles? And was anything ever done to them?
John, "they were three managers, a ramp agent and two floaters. And NO, none of them was disciplined for it."
I have personally helped load and secure cargo freight on Fedex planes at that Philadelphia ramp. What most readers probably don't know when they read about these planes being loaded by " out of their minds drugged up management and others" loading these planes is ...

the cans are the size of huge garbage dumpsters and weight thousands of pounds. They are supposed to be individually weighed before they are even taken onto the planes. They are positioned by weight in specific locations and secured so that they cannot shift or roll around in the plane. These are huge jet cargo planes and if they are not properly loaded and make the plane off balance it will crash after take off. If the cans are not locked down a hundred percent they can come loose and shift and cause the plane to crash. And kill many people on the ground in their homes.

And yet, many times they are loaded by Fedex loaders while high and wasted on drugs daily. I have seen it many times.

I worked the Philadelphia ramp for months and every night I worked there I saw Fedex couriers and Fedex ramp management loading these planes while wasted on drugs. It was the norm, not the exception. Sometimes I wondered just "when" not if but "when" would they load a plane so badly and wrong (off balance) that it crashed into a city and killed people.

The sad truth is … just as John stated above Fedex upper management did nothing to the loaders and managers who nearly died from the heroin overdose that they stole from Fedex shipments. These people were taken to the hospital and medical reports were made but Fedex management covered it up and pretended it never happened.

What if…the plane they loaded had crashed and killed people ?

Gary, **"John have you seen a lot of illegal drug shipments at Fedex?"**

John, **"Yes many, all the time as a courier and as a manager. Having worked there for sixteen years I believe Fedex couriers carry millions of dollars of illegal drugs on a daily basis. In fact I know they do."**

Gary, "have you ever seen Fedex employees use illegal drugs on the job or in the station?"

John, "Many times, It's an everyday thing at Fedex. A lot of times couriers or managers would take a portion of the drug shipments so that the drug dealers would continue to make their shipments through Fedex. That way they had a regular supply of whatever drugs were being shipped.

Gary, "without naming names, have you ever seen Fedex management using drugs on the job or in the station?"

John, "yes I have on numerous occasions".

Gary, "have you ever seen couriers or management steal illegal drugs
from shipments?"

John, "yes many times, both couriers and management at Fedex."

Back to story …

"Fedex would ship Jews to the Gas Chamber"…

We had gotten a new manager for the night shift. It was a new guy
named James Herestofa. He was always kind of distant… and projected
that…"I'm better than everyone else attitude. He wasn't someone you could
easily have a conversation with so I usually just stayed away from him. He
did seem to have a serious nose candy (cocaine) problem, but he always put
on a front when I was around. The "I'm the man in charge so I'm smarter
and better then everyone else here. And don't you forget it attitude."

I think he was German but I really have no idea.

I do know, and I will always remember a statement he made one
night that really shocked me. There was something said about a driver
either at UPS or Fedex finding a head in one of their shipments. There
was several of us standing around and commenting on it and how weird
it was. Herestofa just came out and said that Fedex management would
ship Jews to the gas chamber. As long as they could make money doing it. He went on stating something about Fred and upper management hating Jews anyway and they'd have no problem doing it. The
thing was, he didn't say they would ship "anybody"…he specifically said
"Jews." What did he know of Fred Smiths and upper Fedex managements dislike and hatred for Jews that wasn't known to the couriers and
lower employees.

Was there some secret beliefs within Fedex management that espoused a hatred for the Jewish people?

If you look back to the interview with John you will see that deep
within Fedex management there had always been a strong hatred for
Jews.

As John said…"if you were in management and you said you liked
Jews…you would be fired."

You have to wonder if there was a "secret organization" Fred Smith and possibly other members of Fedex upper management belong to? Why would they hate Jews so much that they would deny them employment and even think about shipping them to the Gas Chambers? I certainly never saw a Jew while working there and NEVER ever heard of one working there. Didn't Hitler do enough harm?

Somewhere is there 'that" secret organization ..possibly more horrible than the KKK and worse than the Aryan Nation. Was it one Fred Smith joined while at Yale?

Don't have problems with a Drug Dealing Courier that's connected to Management.
The beginning of the END

I was pulling into our company parking lot in my personal vehicle. I accidentally hit a co-workers car bumper. The hit was a small one and did not even leave a scratch on my vehicle, but his bumper which had been damaged from a previous accident was knocked loose and had to go to the repair shop. Since there was no marks at all on my bumper and no one saw it happen, I could have easily parked in another spot and no one would have known that it was me who hit his car. It would have been so easy to do. But I couldn't do that. I wouldn't want someone to do that to me, and I just couldn't do that to someone else whether I knew them or not.

So I went into the station and told Larry our dispatcher that I had hit one of the guys car. But that I didn't know who's car it was. When I described it he knew immediately who owned the car and he called him to let him know. I waited at the station until he got there so we could exchange insurance papers etc.

I had talked to him previously a few times and even had driven his van on the evening shift when he was done for the day. But I had always tried to use another van than his. The reason was simple, he was selling and doing drugs with the couriers and management at the station. He could do no wrong.

A number of times I found baggies of cocaine in his truck when I took it out. He was using and dealing drugs and if I used his van it meant that I was usually driving around with his drugs in the van I was driving that evening. Not what I needed or wanted. He had tried to sell me cocaine a few times and he knew I didn't do drugs. Yet he still persisted. "I've got the best stuff around and I give a good count…just ask the guys in the station," he would say.

His car would have to go to the shop to be repaired. Should have been simple, my insurance would pay for the repair and the rental of a car similar to his.

Isn't that the way it is supposed to work?

He contacted my insurance company and they told him they would pay for the rental of a car similar to his. But he rented out a much bigger and nicer car for much more money than insurance company rules allowed. Then he got into an argument with them and tried to get my insurance company to pay the extra costs. After they repeatedly refused to pay the additional cost of the more expensive rental car he came after me to pay the extra.

I asked him why he had rented the more expensive car and he wouldn't answer. He had been at fault just a few months earlier when he hit another vehicle while driving. So I asked him if he paid the other driver extra money to rent a more expensive car and he said no. So I then asked him, then why, he would expect me to pay extra. And again he wouldn't answer. He was doing a LOT of illegal drugs and that may have been why he was acting like such an ass, or just maybe he was the bullying type?

I just told him flat out that I had done the right thing when I told him I hit his car and no one had seen me do it. That I could have easily gotten away with not telling him and to appreciate that I was an honest man.

Then he tried to extort the extra money from me while we were at work. I told him that my insurance would have and did pay for a car rental similar to his. And I again asked him why he rented out a much bigger and nicer car than his when he knew they wouldn't pay the extra cost for it?

Finally he began coming up to the conveyor belt when I was alone and say he would hurt me if I didn't pay him the extra money. And that he would have management cause problems for me. At first I thought he must be out of his mind and told him to just get away from me. I knew that he was selling and doing drugs with management and that he was very connected to them thru drugs. And I knew that if we fought at work I would be the one who lost his job

I had hoped he would try to take it outside off company property so it would just be him and me but he never did. I even suggested we settle it off company property, but he would always disappear when it was time to quit. He was physically a lot bigger than me and was probably used to bullying people around. So you would think he would have met me outside work. Still, I never saw him or heard from him when we weren't on company property. I knew he was single and had nothing to lose and I had a family and a new home. But for some reason he only started trouble at the station.

Then one night while I was working up at the airport ramp two couriers got into a fight and both of them lost their jobs. I then realized I had to at least make a formal complaint to my manager at the station in hopes that it [getting fired for fighting] wouldn't happen to me. I was in a difficult situation because my manager and the other managers were also buying and doing, maybe even stealing, drugs with him.

I was in a tough spot.

I explained to my manager at the time Jim Herestofa how it started. I explained that I had done the right thing and now this guy was trying to extort money from me and start trouble at work. And that he had threatened me physically while at work. I said that I was a big boy and could take care of myself, I just didn't want to lose my job when he started a fight with me.

If anything happened off company grounds it was between him and me, but that I didn't want to lose my job because of some druggie idiot starting a fight with me at work.

I could see as I told Herestofa that he couldn't and wouldn't do anything. They were drug buddies. He said that he would talk to him and get back to me.

Yeah Right ...probably while they were snorting down a big white line.

Herestofa never said another word about it. Funny how I knew that was going to be the case. The threats at work continued and I tried to ignore them.

One day when I went into the bathroom to wash my hands after pre-tripping my van. He came in a few seconds later and again demanded money. I explained that I was sorry I had hit his car, but that it had been repaired and fully paid for by my insurance company. That he had no more money coming from me or anywhere else. And that he may as well forget about trying to get money from me because it wasn't going to happen. He turned around and left the bathroom.

I finished drying off my hands and left the bathroom and   as I was walking down the hallway he came around the corner and attacked me without saying a word.   When he had previously threatened me I had kept my guard up, but this time he had waited for me around the corner and when I got to the corner he sucker punched me a few times.

And I was on the ground.   I never saw it coming.

I had to go to the hospital to get checked out. I was told I had a concussion and a badly injured shoulder and I was sent home. My manager Herestofa wasn't in the station at the time, was probably out getting high as usual.   Later that evening he did call me at home and after I told him what happened he said that since it was Friday to just come in Monday and they would take care of it.

WELCOME TO FEDEX'S...

TAKE CARE OF YOUR DRUG BUDDY GAME

When I reported to work Monday a different manager by the name of Al Ferrier handled the assault. (he was also a drug buddy) He told me that the other driver said I must have fallen and that he never saw me.   Then Al Ferrier hands me a letter and tells me that the managers decided to give me a letter for "disruptive behavior".

I asked him, "what is this letter for?"

"Well, the managers all talked it over and decided to give it to you," he said. (while they were Snortin Up) I bet.

"But what did I do to get a letter," I asked.

"Well we just thought that you should have it," he replied again.

"But what did I do ...that I should get a letter for," I asked again.

"What disruptive behavior did I do," I asked again.

"Well I dunno," was all he said.

"Was Mike Mitchell (the senior station manager) in on this decision to give me a letter," I asked.

Al said that yes Mike knew all about it, and that he agreed with the other managers.

I couldn't believe it. The other courier had bragged that he was drug connected with the managers and that they would take care of him.   I had tried so hard to keep everything okay, I didn't want to lose my job because of some stupid drug addict.   I had never backed down from a fight in my life no matter how big or how many they were. And now that I hold back just to keep my job, I get a letter for "disruptive behavior" when everybody knew he attacked me and I never even fought back.

I didn't expect honesty or fairness ...but this was unbelievable.

I went over the chronology of events with Al just to make sure he knew and more importantly, that I knew he knew.

I said to Al, "you mean that after he threatened me right here in the station for months, and after I went to Herestofa about his threats, and Herestofa supposedly talked to him about it, now he jumps me here in the station and I have a concussion and have to go to the hospital ...I'm the one who get a letter for "disruptive behavior"?

"Well, that's what we decided to do," Al answered.

But even the other courier said I didn't do anything wrong I said. How about that?

Al just looked at me.

"Did he get a letter for disruptive behavior too," I asked.

"No" ,he said, "only you."

"So I'm asking you again Al, what did I do to get this letter for disruptive behavior?"

He said, "you can file a GFT "Guaranteed Fair Treatment" grievance if you like." But I can tell you ...it won't change anything ... management at Fedex does what it wants." he continued.

The last line about management should have been an "alarm" to my ears, but I was so mad at the time I wasn't thinking straight.

Well, I'm going to file that GFT grievance I stated and I walked out.

I'm sure readers are thinking this is ONLY a local station problem here and that Upper Management will fix the problem...do the right thing? Think Again.

The next day I handed Al a GFT grievance letter. When an employee files a GFT they are were supposed to get a response to it within five days by written company rules.

A week later when I didn't get any response I asked Al about it.

"Oh that," he said, "I threw that in the trash can."

I said that I would write another one. And I told him that it was supposed to go to District headquarters.

Which he already knew.

"Well, I don't think it's going to go anywhere." he replied.

So I filed another one and got no response from that one either. Then I wrote directly to District headquarters and included the GFT letter and explained that Al Ferrier had thrown away the first two I wrote. I included a complaint about the managers in the station. That they were using drugs and should be given drug tests etc. That the whole station should be given drug tests.

I had talked to a friend who was a veteran at Fedex and he expressed doubts that I would get any justice from upper management. He told me that I could forget a drug test for the station. That once in Atlanta Fedex had so many complaints of stolen shipments that they did do a station wide drug test and lost nearly the whole dammed station. And that Fedex management swore that they would NEVER do that again. Let them do illegal drugs all they want....no station drug tests ever. He had wished me luck but expressed little confidence that management would be fair or do what was right.

Look how they fuck over the Blacks everyday he said...they'll never change.

And he was right ...management at District Headquarter did nothing.

So then I wrote to the Regional Director and got nothing. Then I even wrote to Fedex's Headquarters in Memphis. Nothing.

I could never understand why they would let a few small managers do so much wrong? It was so obvious, even to them throwing away my first GFT's. Why was it so much of a big deal to really investigate what happened in the Wilmington station?

What did Mike Mitchell have over FedEx / Fred Smith in Memphis that they would cover for him in such a small little thing.

THE ANSWER...
Mike Knew That Fred Smith Was Smuggling Illegal Drugs Into The Country. And that made him untouchable. Mike could do whatever he wanted. Simple as that. That's why Mike could always do anything he wanted to. And he never worried about anybody. He knew the secrets.

Meanwhile back at home while all of this was going on I received a letter from "guess who" sent by U.S. Mail. It was a letter with threats of death and newspaper clippings about people that had been crippled and killed. Also there were clippings of people getting fired from their jobs. The letter told me to pay the money or else I would wind up like the people in the clippings. I didn't even tell my wife. I was hoping that someone in management would step up and do the right thing. I guess I really was naive. The letter for disruptive behavior was going to be in my file forever.

The courier actually tried to run over me in Wilmington while I had my three year old son with me. It makes me so mad I can't even talk about it for fear of what I might still do. The police were called and they did an investigation and said they would arrest the courier and that they would prosecute him. That is what the police officers who investigated told me.

Then Fred Smith / Fedex brought in a big money lawyer and a got a judge that looked and acted more like a five dollar street whore. And he got away with it. Smith was a veteran at this. He had already ran over and killed at least one Black man and who knows how many more and he has gotten away with. So something like this was old hat to him. He knew just where to put the money to get the case go his way. The evidence was good and it should have been an easy case to prosecute ... but the money was paid, the police changed their stories. ...No Conviction.

After the trial was over and the courier got away with it. Just like magic a job came open in the Dover station. And guess who it was offered to. I had been branded as a non-druggie and non- thief who wouldn't back down.

They wanted me out of the station. I guess it was better than being fired.

The catch was ...always before, the courier who ran the Dover run started at the Wilmington station that was only ten minutes from my house and ended up there at the end of the day. Because they were afraid of me being in the station I would have to drive the thirty miles to the Dover station in my personal vehicle. And work out of Dover.

It was okay, I could handle it.

CHAPTER 3

FRAUD AGAINST THE MILITARY AND

GOVERNMENT

I WAS TRAINED AND ORDERED TO COMMIT FRAUD AND BETRAY THE MILITARY

Sometimes the Lord does work in Mysterious Ways.

As I said earlier, my manager Colin Baines told me to commit my first act of Criminal Fraud against one of my customers. And as bad as that was, it was only against a "civilian customer."

When actually Colin taught me to commit several different criminal acts against my customers. One was lying about the real weight of a customers shipments. So that Fedex could charge the customers far more than they should honestly pay. That criminal act alone allowed Fred Smith and Fedex to steal hundreds of millions of dollars from their customers every year.

Colin also trained me (ordered me) to treat a CSS shipment just like common freight. And he was fully aware that Fedex was charging the customer extra money for a service that NEVER existed ..except on paper. He actually stood there while I explained the correct way to handle a CSS shipment to a customer and then after we left the customer, he told me to handle the shipment like common freight.

Colin actually ordered me to commit "Fraud"

A Felony!

Fred Smith uses Fedex to Betray America's and Conspire to Steal Billions

In Dover I was going to find out that Fred Smith and his fellow criminals within Fedex management were involved in a criminal conspiracy to commit fraud against our military. I had already known that Fred

Smith and Fedex was involved in a conspiracy to steal millions of dollars from the private and business customers … but now I was to find out that they were also involved in a conspiracy to commit fraud against the military and other branches of the government. This was betraying our brave men and women in the service.

This was NOT going to happen.

It was Helen Wilson who trained me in Dover and showed me how Fred Smith and Fedex committed the fraud against the military. And put our soldiers and civilians lives on the line, even elementary school children…while stealing millions of dollars. Fred Smith was currently stealing millions and he and other criminals within Fedex were planning even a greater conspiracy of fraud to steal more than a Billion dollars from our military and government, even the CIA and various government enforcement groups.

Fred Smith Was Stealing Millions Of Dollars From The Military And Government.

While Helen was training me on my new route in Dover I learned it was also to include the Dover Air Force Base which shipped a lot of classified sensitive military shipments through Fedex using Fedex's Phony C.S.S. "Constant Surveillance Service" service. Fred Smith and his high paid liars/thieves had convinced the military that Fedex did in fact have this C.S.S. service that would give complete safety to and accountability for these classified military shipments. Maybe with some money and help from friends in Washington? We know we just can't say it.

Helen and I were at the Dover Air Force Base in building 505. And there were CSS (Constant Surveillance Service) secret shipments of classified sensitive military equipment that needed to be shipped. By their classified status they needed constant surveillance and individual accountability from everyone who had possession of these shipments. Meaning they were not allowed to be out of eyesight at any time.

It was the Federal law.

After we signed the paperwork for them and loaded them into the truck (which was like a big bread truck) we left the base and headed away from our station. I asked Helen why we weren't taking the military CSS shipments back to the station like we were supposed to? She replied that "we never do, and that no one ever does."

I was truly shocked...this was a U.S. Military shipment of classified sensitive military equipment.

"What if we get caught." I asked, "isn't that a federal offense?"

Helen replied, "look, Fedex does it all over the country, don't you think Fred (Fedex CEO Fred Smith) has it covered. Those Fucking idiots in the military don't have a clue of what's going on. You see how stupid they are at the base, it's that way all across America," Helen said. For a dumb woman...she had it right on.

"Besides" she said, "that's the way I was trained to do it and I've even done it with managers and that's the way they want it done."

I soon learned that she would drive around while wasted on drugs all the time...probably most of the time ... while carrying secret "classified sensitive military equipment" some of it very explosive and dangerous. I remember some of the warnings stating that in case of fire all personnel had to remain at least 1500 feet away.

<u>And she's driving around with it while wasted on drugs and going into neighborhoods, schools, and shopping centers. Well so much for America's security and safety</u>

And Fred Smith was laughing all the way to the bank...

In the days that followed Helen would tell me many things. Sometimes just because she liked to talk and other times because she was "cranking or high on Pot, pills or cocaine " it didn't matter to her....as long as she was on her drugs. She was what I considered a typical Fedex employee.

She told me how she regularly stole drugs and valuables from shipments and how she would ship stuff for free using phony account numbers on the air bills. She said couriers all over America were doing it.

So she did it too.....as I said..."Typical."

She told me about her first performance review with her manager. She had been with Fedex about (4-5) months and it was time for her performance review. Her manager was Jerry Salomone and they were out on her route doing deliveries. They were in Newark, Delaware when she pulls up to this apartment house. She reaches into the back seat of her truck and pulls out an Overnight Letter. This is Pot she says to Jerry, I deliver it all of the time.

She says the next thing she knows ...Jerry Salomone is ripping the Overnight Letter apart to get to the Pot. She says there is only two ounces of Pot in the Overnight Letter and Jerry takes about an ounce and a half and tells her to go upstairs and deliver the rest to the drug dealer and she does. Then she and Jerry leave her delivery route and drive over to her apartment and get her Pot pipe. And they spend the rest of the day doing her route while they are stoned out of their minds.

To top it off … she only got a 4.0 on her performance review and she was pissed. She thought she would get a 7.0 for stealing Drugs with her manager. She said something like … "Boy did I get Fucked … I should have gotten a 7.0."

Maybe she really was "fucked" and only rated a 4.0?

Little did she know that Jerry had already told me that story and others awhile back when he was trying to convince me also to bring him drugs shipped on my route thru Fedex mail. I had been doing the pickups in north Wilmington and had customers that were sending out drugs in Overnight Letters and courier pak envelopes and boxes. I hadn't personally seen the drugs but I knew there were drugs in the shipments. I was a new guy and so I went to Jerry and asked him what to do. His response was to bring him the drugs so that he could try them out. And maybe I should even take him out on my route so that he could see if there were others out there. He told me how he and Helen had stolen the Pot while he was doing her evaluation. That it was good Pot and that they had stolen it and other drugs a number of times.

She would do the drugs right in front of me. Sometimes right in the Dover station, in shopping malls, even in the Delaware Department of Transportation parking lot.

Once she was going to cut out a line of coke while we were in the Dover Air Force Base…I said ohh no…NOT HERE… Not on a military base. Put the shit away…or I will stop an M.P. and turn you in. "You're out of your mind."

She just smiled and called me a wimp. Then she said, okay I can wait. I think my blood pressure went up about a hundred points. WTF

She did wait until we got to the Blue Hen Mall in Dover…then she snorted up the cocaine.

I was nearly finished training with her and I couldn't wait to be done. When I first started training with her I saw her start going thru the Overnight Letters and Envelopes looking for drugs and valuables and who knows what else.

"What are you doing," I asked.

"Oh, just looking," she replied.

When I asked her what she was looking for she said ..."drugs what else".

"Not while you're with me"...I have enough shit going on. Do it when I'm not with you or not in the same truck as you're driving. But not with me, understand? Most times it was me signing off the airbills and Fedex would have loved to fire "me" for stealing.

"No big deal," she said. But she did stop when I was with her...I think.

I finished my training with Helen and took over the run and did it just exactly as I was instructed to.

But I would come up with a plan to stop the fraud.

I just needed to figure out exactly how to do it and not let Fred Smith and Fedex get away with it. They had stolen tens of millions of dollars from the military. And would continue unless somebody stopped them.

But even worse...they had betrayed our soldiers trust and possibly put them in danger. If you read about something like this in the newspapers it makes you mad. If you are involved in it...you have to do something about it. Those guys are my hero's. You don't betray and screw my hero's. Not if I can stop it.

A CSS (Constant Surveillance Service) Shipment Works Like This

1) The person who picks it up signs for it.
2) He takes it "directly back" to the station where a 'CSS specialist' person' signs for it and locks it up.
3) The courier who takes it to the airport signs for it
4) The 'CSS person' at the airport signs for it and secures it.
5) The 'CSS person' at the Memphis Hub signs for it before it gets shipped out.
6) Upon arrival at the destination airport the 'CSS person signs for it.
7) The person who drives it from the airport to the destination station signs for it.
8) The 'CSS person' at the destination station signs for it and gives it to the delivery courier.
9) That delivery courier signs for it and takes it to the delivery recipient.
10) The recipient must sign off on it.

Every military CSS shipment has a DD1907 form attached to it. It must have all of these signatures on it. "DD" stands for Department of Defense.

The "CSS" means that the shipment is NEVER to be out of eyesight of the courier that has possession and responsibility for it. "Constant Surveillance Service"

The 1907 is a number for the military form. These are serious forms. That's ten (10) signatures that should be on every DD1907 Form that is with every CSS shipment. As little as one (1) signature was sometimes on a military CSS shipment. Most times two or three (2-3) and one of those might be mine. There was absolutely no accountability or security of these shipments. A courier could be selling these shipments to Terrorists or anyone and no one would ever know.

The honest truth is...all over America hundreds of Fedex couriers were driving around with these classified and sometimes dangerous military shipments and they treated them like "common freight" because they were ordered to, just as I was ordered to. Do what management says or get fired. Commit fraud or lose your job.

Betray your country or you won't work here.

Thanks Fred Smith...you traitor BASTARD.

Sometimes a CSS shipment that was Classified "sensitive" was thrown into my truck by another courier and that courier and I never even knew it was a "CSS" military shipment until I got to the Dover Air Force Base.

Many times I was carrying explosives in my truck that said "in case of fire persons are to remain 1500 feet away, (that's more than a quarter mile)." I unknowingly took many of these explosives into shopping centers, residential neighborhoods even schools. I later found out that I had taken (79) pounds of military explosives into an elementary school yard where children were present and never even knew it. Just what the parents want for their children. I never even knew it till later when I delivered it to the Dover Air Force Base.

And what would I say or how would I feel if children were hurt or killed because of a fire and explosion from a truck I drove onto their school grounds?

And that LYING THIEVING TRAITOR Fred Smith and his CRIMINALS at Fedex were laughing all the way to the bank.

There were a lot of times that the classified sensitive military CSS shipments would come up missing. More times than I could count.

What happened to them? Who had them last? They absolutely could not be found. And despite what lies Fedex tells it's customers it's tracking system is also a sham. There are so many thousands of times that customers have had lost and stolen shipments and Fedex lies about them as to what happened to them.

I will show you later in the book what I mean when the FBI calls me for help.

Catching Your Fedex Manager Doing Drugs

And as all of this was going on a manager who was my previous manager "Jim Herestofa" when I was in the Wilmington station was now the manager at the Dover station.

I have no idea why he was suddenly the Dover manager. Unless he was sent down to snoop on me. Maybe to find out what I might have said to other couriers down there?

He called down one day to say that he was coming down to give me a performance review. Why he was coming down at that time to do it I will never know. But I ran my route well and did well on it so I had no real concerns. My route had nearly doubled in size since I had taken it over and I still handled it and I was doing nearly twice as many stops as anybody ever did before me.

Still, I was surprised he even gave me a warning that he was coming.

That morning I got my truck loaded and I said to Jim, "time to roll". As we started out along my route doing deliveries it was obvious that he wasn't into it. He wasn't even paying attention to what I was doing . He talked very little at first and then he began rambling and he couldn't keep his thoughts straight. He started going from one subject to another.

I drove into the parking lot of the Delaware Dept. of Transportation building in Dover. After I parked I went to the back of my van to get my packages. I deliver to a number of different offices there so I always have to make sure I don't miss anyone. When I was ready I grabbed my clipboard and said to Jim ..." I'm ready." Jim just sat there and said to go ahead that he knew that I knew my job.

It was a very unusual thing to say. Before, when I had performance reviews the manager always stayed right by my side and never left it. Especially when I was with customers. Riding with a courier and them going with him while he interacts with his customers is a basic function when doing a performance review.

I went in and did my deliveries and said a quick "hi" to the girls in the office. When I came out of the building I went by the back of the truck and saw that I had left the back door open just a crack. It was a overhead pull down door and either I didn't pull it down tight or possibly it just didn't grab as it sometimes did.

Instead of pulling it down, I just pulled it open to go in thru the rear.

Herestofa was standing there in the back of the truck. Obviously I had startled him because he had a very surprised and awkward look on his face. I stepped up into the truck very quickly ... it was a conditioned reflex.

And there was my manager with a short straw in his hand and a small mirror on one of the shelves next to the packages. There were still traces of a white lines of powder left on it. I looked at the mirror and at Herestofa.

"Having fun," I asked him while looking at his face. He didn't even look up at me. He just put the mirror and straw back into his briefcase. Then went up front and sat in his seat looking very embarrassed. I was not that courier who thought it was okay to do drugs. And Herestofa knew it.

I started up the truck and headed back out onto the highway.

Several times that day he would try to explain to me how depressed he was. His wife was divorcing him or something like that and he was having other family problems. He said that he was having a hard time dealing with it all and that he was talking with counselors or whatever at Fedex. He rambled on about how everything was hitting him at once and how hard it was for him. He sounded like a typical drug addict that was hitting bottom to me. He just rambled on and on throughout the day. My thoughts at the time were simple ...straighten yourself out on the drug problems and then deal with your issues with a clear head. I tried to explain that thought to him. But he wasn't buying it. I guess to him the drugs helped him cope. .Yeah Right.

I also thought ...Look you Asshole Bastard, you and the other Druggie managers fucked me over royal up in the Wilmington station when your druggie dealing buddy jumped me in the station. And now you want me to be sympathetic to your personal problems? Fuck You, I hope your life goes to Hell slowly so you suffer ... and they find you dead in the gutter with a Drug Overdose.

And he was a manager for the GREAT Fedex company. What leadership !!!

Later that day we went to the Dover Air Base to do my pickups and deliveries. I drove my truck into Bldg. 505 and over by the shipping area. There were about a dozen packages to pick up and a few of them were CSS Classified shipments. Herestofa knew what they were. They were "classified sensitive military shipments". He knew this very well. He knew that the U.S. government was paying Fedex tens of millions of dollars for Fedex to provide full security and protection for these classified shipments. He knew that Fred Smith had told many big lies to convince the government to let Fedex handle them. He also knew that the CSS service was just a scam…it was a conspiracy to commit felony fraud and betray the U.S. government.

And he couldn't care less. He was happy snorting his coke.

He saw that there were a number of CSS shipments mixed in with the common freight and he grabbed a few packages and started signing off on them. Soon we were heading out of bldg 505 and off the base.

After we left I asked Jim Herestofa straight up… why wasn't Fedex afraid that the government would catch them?

His response was …"those ASSHOLES at the base were too stupid to know what was happening.

FUCK THEM," he said, "get all you can get."

I was expecting some kind of excuse or dumb explanation…almost anything but that. I guess it may have been that I had never heard an American, actually anyone for that matter, say something like that about our military and soldiers. He caught me totally off guard with that answer.

I said something about defrauding the government and how it was a serious thing.

Herestofa just said, " just do what you're told to do like everybody else." And he let me know that …that was the end of the conversation about the CSS service.

And so we continued on my route and numerous times we left the classified military shipment alone and out of sight with no security at all. Anyone could have taken them with no problems.

Meanwhile…

I continued to gather every piece of evidence of fraud against the military / government that I could get my hands on. Every time I handled a CSS military shipment I made a copy of it. Not once did I ever come across one that was handled even half way of what it was supposed to be. Even I never once had to sign for a CSS shipment ever. I was told to just drive around with it all day like it was common freight. It was ALWAYS handled just like common freight by every Fedex courier and employee all across America. And when it was lost or stolen it was treated the same way with no concern what so ever.

As my Fedex manager Jim Herestofa said quite clearly ...FUCK The military.

Wrong guy. Screw me, you might get away with it .... "Screw our soldiers"...no way.

I began collecting DD 1907 Tally Sheets and every CSS shipment airbill I handled. I made copies of every one. They showed clearly that there was NO CSS service in existence and never was. It was FRAUD...plain and simple. I would save every piece of evidence I could get me hands on. Then I would contact authorities.

LOST...HIGH SECURITY COMPUTERS PROGRAMED FOR SECRET NATO DEFENSE SYSTEM

For instance, and there are literally tens of thousands of times this has happened.

On my route there was a shipment of secret 'classified sensitive military computers' they were specially set up and programmed to run "a high security defense system" for NATO in Europe. There were supposed to be five (5) pieces of a complex computer system. I only received two (2) pieces of the shipment. They were just thrown in with the common freight as they always were. There were to be taken to the Dover Air Force Base for an immediate flight to NATO defense, in Germany I think.

NATO needed these computers for their defense systems ...RIGHT NOW.

I called everybody I could within Fedex's system... Nobody had a clue as to when they were all together last or even where they came from? And they were very nonchalant about it. So what if it was Classified Sensitive military equipment....so what if they were a very important part of our NATO defense system...

I tried to explain to Fedex management that it was a military ship-ment…a CSS shipment with almost no signatures on the DD 1907 form. And no way to track who had the shipment last. DAFB would be pissed and I would have to answer all kinds of questions about the shipment.

Find those parts I said….

"Yeah, we'll look but we have no idea where they are. And we're pretty busy. Just tell the General that they will turn up sometime"…the woman on the other end said. Obviously it was too much of a bother to her…and it showed.

I told my manager Jim Herestofa that we were missing three parts of a five part Classified 'Sensitive' military shipment. "Yeah well, just hold them in the station to see if the others show up," he said, "Don't worry about it, they probably don't even know they are supposed to be there."

"What about if they are stolen or lost forever," I asked him, "shouldn't we be putting a trace on them or have someone trying to find them."

"No don't draw attention to it," he said, " it might cause questions."

Then he just walked away. Probably to do a line of Cocaine with other management.

WTF … these were lost (maybe stolen) classified military shipments.

When I got to the DAFB I went to the officer in charge of Bldg. 505 and I explained to him the real situation about the missing shipments and that we were looking for them but haven't found them yet.

He was pissed and did question me in depth about them. When he was finished he said that he would not accept the few pieces I did have and to take them all back immediately and to put them in the CSS secure cages at our station and find the other missing ones fast.

The truth was we never did have a secure cage or storage area of any kind like we were required to in the hundreds of military contracts Fedex had signed with the military. All we had was a old garage type building with no security at all. No fire alarm system, no burglar alarms system, no bright lights at night. And you could easily get into our building without a key, I and other couriers had done it numerous times. There was no security of any kind on the building. So I just kept them in my truck rather than leave them in a deserted building all day long with no security at all. That night I left the military shipments in that station that had no security. I had no choice.

To my knowledge they never did find the missing computer defense systems. I finally had to deliver the only two parts of the shipment I had.

I have no idea what really happened to the rest of them. My wheels were turning I had to come up with a plan to stop this.

Contacting Federal Agents / Investigators

When I felt that I had collected enough evidence to prove fraud without a doubt I contacted the Office of Special Investigations of the Air Force aka .. "A.F.O.S.I. and O.S.I." at the DAFB.

There I met with special agent Paul Ackerman who was a government investigator. I showed him what evidence I had and explained how the fraud was being committed. He was very interested and made copies of the documents I had brought with me. Then he set up a meeting with his supervisor so we could all sit down together and discuss the details of the fraud.

I requested that I get back copies of all documents that I gave them and agent Ackerman agreed to it. So as I collected more evidence I would always make copies of every document I gave him and then he would make another copy and give it back to me. He never knew that I had already made the same copies of the documents I gave him, and that by me having him make another copy and give them back to me did two things. One it insured to me that they weren't hiding anything. Two it was my way of letting them know for sure that there were "always" extra copies of the evidence floating around somewhere.

* Even today I have more than a half dozen copies of everything in this book (including taped recordings both known by all parties and ones secretly recorded). That I keep in safe places away from my house with trusted friends and relatives. Maybe even in a church haha. It wasn't really that difficult to do, and it's a good idea just in case my house should 'mysteriously' catch fire or blow up.

I knew that Fred Smith and his Fedex Plantation was both powerful and corrupt and I trusted no one. I still don't when it comes to either one of them.

We soon had that meeting between agent Ackerman, his boss and myself. And after his boss questioned me thoroughly he said he felt we had a case and that OSI was going to open an official investigation.

What agent Ackerman or his boss never knew was that I secretly tape recorded nearly every one of our conversations from day one. And in case you wonder it is legal to do that in Delaware. They look at it in the same way as if I were writing a report of a meeting or conversation whether in the presence of someone or even on the phone. In essence I am/was making exact notes of the meetings. <u>Then NO ONE can lie</u>.

About two thirds thru the investigation and when he felt comfortable with me he told me something that I had already heard. But which did surprise me that he knew. After all he was an Air Force Investigator. An Air Force ...OSI agent.

He told me that the OSI, DEA, NSA, FBI, U.S. Marshalls and other Federal agencies ... some of which he couldn't mention were also involved in a secret government task force on "ILLEGAL DRUGS" and that they met monthly in Washington D.C. There were ten different Federal agencies in these meetings he said. He told me that the different agencies combined and pooled their information and knowledge concerning illegal drugs and drug smugglers. He then went on to explain to me that Fred Smith was involved in smuggling illegal drugs into the country but that they were having a tough time catching him. He told me that they knew Fred Smith was sometimes using Fedex planes and different airports and Fedex airports ramps to hide the shipments. He was not talking about the small time drug dealers shipping a few pounds of drugs here and there thru Fedex. He was talking huge shipments of thousands of pounds of illegal drugs being smuggled into and around America by Fred Smith. I hadn't realized just how large a smuggling operation Smith was involved in.

Apparently he was big. Very Big.

Ackerman then asked me about any strange or unusual large containers that I might have seen coming into or going out of the Philadelphia airport ramp. Had I seen any strange or different type trucks not driven by Fedex couriers, other than Fedex trucks, coming to pick up or drop off large containers? Anything unusual? I told him what I knew and also told him I was sorry I didn't get to work the ramp any more so that I might have been able to ask questions there. Maybe find something out. There were some unusual things I had seen there but at the time hadn't really thought about it too much. If you're not looking for something it can be right in front of you and you won't see it.

I remember once or twice seeing an "extra plane" at the Fedex airport ramp in Philadelphia and wondering why there were two planes there? I had never seen more than one before. I remember asking one of the supervisors at the ramp if the second plane was because we were expecting an extra heavy load of shipments going out that night to Memphis. To me it meant that we'd be working faster and longer if it did. At the time it was my only concern. He replied that it was none of my business what Fedex was doing. And that no, we would be shipping our normal loads out tonight. He was short and abrupt with his answer. I didn't know at the time if he was busy or just didn't want to talk about it.

Agent Ackerman also wanted to know about the flights coming and going into and out of Fedex's Philadelphia Airport ramp that were not part of their regular schedules and that were maybe not traveling their normal routes back and forth to and from Memphis. He said he had Fedex's regular flight schedules...he was looking for "something different". I thought about it but didn't know of any.

Later on I thought back and realized that was "why Mike Mitchell knew so much about Fred Smith smuggling drugs" Damm what a small world. The Wilmington station was just (20) minutes from the Philadelphia Airport. And for reasons we may never truly know...Fred Smith made personal stops at the Philadelphia and Wilmington stations in the early days of Fedex. ...hmmm. Those visits were "after" he went to Vegas?

I guess I'll never know.

But I'm sure that is how Mike Mitchell came to find out about Fred's Drug Smuggling. Mike was there from almost day one of Fedex. He had seen things no one else had seen and knew things that few others knew. I wonder what ALL he had seen?

I did have knowledge about the couriers and other Fedex employee's that would take a "jump seat" to Memphis on the Fedex jets and then to Florida to buy a Kilo or two of cocaine or any drug of choice to sell when they returned to the home station. It could any place in the country where Fedex had a Fedex airport ramp. It was simple to do. Fred Smith didn't allow law enforcement to enter his airport ramps for any reason unless he called them in. So if a Fedex employee wanted to fly to any place and buy illegal drug they could with complete impunity.

Unlike a real commercial airport flight where you and your bags are checked ... at a Fedex ramp there is NO ONE to check anything. So a Fedex employee flying "jump seat" on their airplanes carrying freight could pickup anything in the world. They could carry and put in a box or bag or suitcase (even a hundred kilos of it) and bring it home with them. It's done all the time.

Management knew it....and many times they were involved in the drug smuggling.

To be honest, I'm surprised that the Islamic Terrorists haven't gotten jobs at Fedex and used this "out of control" Fedex perk to transport their explosive, poisons gases or anything else that they could never take on a public commercial airplane. It's that easy.

Then again...maybe they already have or are?

But agent Ackerman was interested in the BIG drug shipments that Fred Smith was personally involved with and not the small time stuff the employees were doing.

I was later to see on the official DEA website a picture of one of Fred Smiths' "Fedex planes" flying illegal drugs into the United States from Mexico. It was traveling to Boston the picture and map showed.

Send an FOIA to the DEA and "maybe" they'll send you a copy of it. I actually sent out a few hundred copies of it to Fedex employees and others. Yes I STILL Have it.

Many people would find it hard to believe. Here is a rich successful CEO of a major corporation ...why in the world would he take such a chance and smuggle illegal drugs? Wouldn't somebody know? Or was "somebody" in Washington taking care of him? John McCain maybe?

Today we've had sitting in the white house....Bill Clinton and Hillary (both from Little Rock Arkansas too) they were involved in a LOT of Crimes, criminal acts and far more than any of us will ever know. If justice was true and fair both of them would have spent many years in the jailhouse instead of the White House. And we even have Hillary Clinton the "Secretary of State" of the United States. Makes you think. Or should.

Today there is Fred Smith CEO of Fedex Corporation ... RACIST, THIEF, TRAITOR, FELONY FORGER, DRUG SMUGGLER, FRAUD MASTER. And a Billionaire.

So far he's gotten away with some of those things too. And the media writes and says great things about him. And all the politicians run to him for money.

Well Bernie Madoff also gave politicians a LOT of dollars, had dinners with them and had them do "favors" for him. He also had the media write great things about him too.

The CEO and corporate heads of Enron is the same story. They also gave politicians lots of money, had dinners with them just so Washington would do "favors" for them.

And we don't even have to get into Freddie Mac and Fannie Mae and the mess that's happened to the banking and mortgage industry. It's really simple, Washington's politicians can be bought quite easily for the right money. Even Hitler would probably do well in America "today" if his pockets were deep enough.

People miss the most obvious truths.

Fred Smith has told that LIE about winning that money in Las Vegas when he was flat broke. I'm surprised his nose doesn't reach from New York to California. Just on that one LIE alone. The rest of his lies might take him to the moon.

<u>Did he ever show anybody his "Federal or State Tax forms that proved it...NO.</u> When you win that much money gambling you have to fill out a Fedex tax form at the casino before leaving with your money. Did Fred? NO.

But it is possible the "BOYS" you know...the connected "BOYS" in Reno might have given him any paper he wanted or needed.

BUT, FRED SMITH DID NOT "WIN" ANY MONEY IN RENO LIKE HE SAID...END OF STORY.

STOP THE LIES FRED.

Though it is possible he did use Fedex to "<u>launder a lot of money</u>" in the early years of Fedex's struggles.

Probably few have thought ...what did Fred Smith do with the money he got from Smuggling illegal drugs? There would be a lot of illegal money to hide. Maybe if the feds looked for an offshore acct. aka Swiss acct. or one of those in the islands? They might find a couple hundred million dollars or more. Money that Smith can't account for. But no one will look. Or they might already know?

In the year 2010 the U.S. Attorney's office is covering up for hundreds of well connected politicians, corporate and big business leaders that are heavy campaign contributors to both parties and other privileged ones. Their crimes will stay hidden as long as they pay.

Many will ask how Fred Smith has and can get away with the smuggling of illegal drugs into America?

I ask, how can John McCain even consider having him as a "running mate' when he KNOWS Fred Smith STOLE millions from the military and other government branches.   If the privileged few are committing "money laundering" and hiding their money in offshore accounts and the Internal Revenue Investigators and Prosecutors have their names and accounts with their money and where it is?   Why are these people NOT being prosecuted?   They ALL are committing very serious "Felonies' of both State and Federal laws.

They ALL are involved in crimes so serious that many fall under R.I.C.O.'s Federal Crime violations Act.

Just as Fred Smith has broken so many State and Federal Laws... Realize that without the newspaper stories and ABC's 20-20, Fred Smith would be stealing fifty million dollars plus a year from the government. And No One in government would have stopped him.   But instead, would have actually been "helping him" as I'm sure they were before 20-20.

And someone in government "possibly John McCain" did somehow stop the criminal prosecution.   Even though AFOSI and DCIS said it was a solid case with easy prosecution.

He's crimes fall under: **R.I.C.O.   Racketeering Influenced Crime Organizations**

But how much money has he given politicians in Washington?

Just like Bernie Madoff and Enron.   And how much was given to them "under the table"?

Big meeting of AFOSI agents at the Dover Air Force Base in Dover.

I was told by Ackerman that they were having a big meeting to co-ordinate nationwide investigations of CSS shipments.   That it would involve CSS military shipments shipped somewhere on the east coast and the shipment would be followed on it's way to the west coast to it's final delivery.

This would prove that the fraud was nationwide.   And the investigation did prove exactly that.   My presence was requested at the meeting so I could help coordinate the tracking of the shipment since I knew exactly how the shipments were handled and what to look for.   It was a big meeting with AFOSI agents from different parts of the country there.

I had just purchased a new pack of one hour cassette tapes for my tape recorder.   I also had a phone jack that I attached to my recorder when Ackerman and I talked on the phone.   But when I met Ackerman face to face I usually turned it on just before exiting my vehicle.   And left it running throughout the meeting as we talked. In this instance I had to go to the DAFB and then into an office in what I already assumed would be a long meeting. So I waited until I was getting ready to go thru the office door and into the meeting before I turned on my recorder.

When I entered the room I set my gray bag that was holding the recorder on the table in front of me so it would record clearly. My bag also held some of my Fedex paperwork, my pager, extra pens, backup maps, and misc. materials, even chewing gum. I always tried to disguise the bag as a utility bag that I used for work.

I was introduced to the other OSI agents in the room and we soon began working out a strategy to maintain surveillance of the shipment as it traveled across the country. I was informed that I was not to know the origin or destination of the shipment. So that it would not contaminate the investigation and that it would ensure the surveillance was sterile. Which was fine with me.

The meeting was a long one and at approximately one hour the tape recorder clicked as it shut itself off.

Oh Boy!!! .... Every agent in the room looked at the bag with a puzzled expression. Thinking real fast...I said, " it's just my pager, it's a pain in the ass."

I'm not usually that good at quick responses like that...I just got lucky that day.

After hesitating for a moment they turned their attention back to the investigation. There were about six agents there and they were into it hot and heavy.

Whew!!! That was close. When I think about it now I laugh. But at the time...it wasn't a laughing matter. Here I was secretly tape recording a meeting of a group of U.S. military OSI agents "Criminal Investigators" from different parts of the U.S. They had come together in Delaware to substantiate what they already knew was a solid case of "conspiracy to commit fraud against the military and the U.S. government" by Fred Smith and Fedex. And I was there to help them coordinate how they were going to do it. What to look for and the actual way the shipments were going to be handled, rather than the way Fedex had contracted to do.

I nearly got caught secretly recording the meeting.

WOW!

I'm sure they would have been pissed if they found out. And I don't want to know what might have happened.

They were going to be watching when the CSS military shipment was picked up and then follow it to the origin station and then the airport where it would be flown to Memphis. Then they would be at the destination airport ramp when it arrived from Memphis. And then follow it from there to the destination station and then follow the courier who delivered it to the recipient which would be a military base. I explained the entire procedure of how it was going to happen including how to determine what courier to follow to the recipient. (the military base)

At that time I also informed them that I had just gotten another CSS shipment that was missing two parts of a five part shipment. It was from the RAYTHEON CORPORATION and it was a Classified Sensitive CSS military equipment that was VERY EXPENSIVE. I told them how our dispatcher and tracking people didn't even seem to care about the missing pieces. The agents just shook their heads in disbelief.

When the meeting ended I wished them luck. But I already knew what they would find. There was absolutely no such thing as a CSS service. (their investigations proved that) Agent Ackerman told me that after the investigation had been completed.

Now we are certain that Fedex's CSS service is a "Conspiracy to Defraud the Government" and does not exist he said.

It was a conspiracy to defraud the U.S. Military and numerous other Government branches out of more than a BILLION DOLLARS. And Fedex was getting away with it because Fred Smith had paid BIG MONEY to Washington politicians to keep the fraud going. "America's highest paid "Prostitutes".

And who knows what harm may have come to our soldiers, our government or maybe even civilians?

* Is a Billion Dollar loss enough to make Fred Smith try to kill me at my home ?

The Phony Fraudulent CSS service was a Federal Felony conspiracy that was headed by and initiated by FRED SMITH.

In some countries they either shoot or hang men for what he has done. Too bad America isn't one of them.

Fred Smith created his Fedex Corporation and made it a RICO Organization.

And in The Meantime.

They had gotten a new Senior Station Manager at the Wilmington station. The first time I saw her was when she came to the Dover station to introduce herself.

The Wilmington station was kind of an umbrella station over the Dover station which was smaller.

Her name was Stephanie Seberg. She was attractive, pleasant and seemed very intelligent. She didn't have that druggie look so many Fedex managers had. And she seemed like a straight up individual. Somehow I didn't think it was going to go well for her. I knew she wouldn't understand the drugs and thieving games they play at so many Fedex stations. Unfortunately others in the Wilmington station knew that too.

After the introductions and formalities were over she casually mentioned that Al Ferrier was stepping down as one of the managers in the Wilmington station. She said it as politically correct as possible. She told us that Al was having an abuse problem and that he was seeking help for it.

YEAH RIGHT …what she didn't say was …Al had been working the evening shift and was so drunk that he could barely stand. That he had jumped into another couriers personal vehicle (a pickup truck) and ran through a red light just a few hundred yards from the station and nearly killed a girl that worked for a big customer of ours. And That his blood alcohol level was .19 and according to witnesses including the girl he hit, he was totally incoherent and stumbling around.

Doesn't he sound like just the …best and brightest Fedex manager ever !!!

We had already heard the story...we were just surprised that he wasn't still a manager. It wasn't anything new to us. I had personally seen Al drive into the station in his company van so drunk and wasted on drugs so many times. And his drug buddies in management knew it and never tried to stop him even once. Hell, they were doing the drugs with him … so who cared.

So we all held our tongue as Stephanie gave a vanilla explanation of why Al was stepping down. No sense embarrassing her...we didn't know her that well.

<u>Memories of Al as a Fedex manager</u>

I remember one night when I was first working the Wilmington station on the second shift. My car wasn't running well so my wife drove me to work that day. Al, found out about it and offered me a lift home. I declined at first but he insisted so I finally said okay. It would save my wife a trip into Wilmington at night.

On the way to my house he explained that he was months behind on his electric bill. And that just today he had stopped the electric guys who had come to shut off his power. He said that he begged them and finally got them to accept a post dated check for part of the bill. But that he didn't have any money in the bank to cover it.

Al, wanted to know if I could lend him the money until Friday and then he would pay me back...all of it. There was no way I was ever going to lend a "drug addict / alcoholic" a couple hundred dollars. So I told him that things were tight. Then he reaches into his pocket and pulls out an eight-ball of cocaine that he said he had stolen out of a Courier Pak envelope just that day. Could I lend him the money and hold the eight-ball till Friday. He said that he already owed the guys in the station money and if he gave it to them to hold...they would just use it themselves.

He went on to say that since he became a manager he couldn't go into the shipments as much as before. That when he was a courier he could make an extra $500 - $1000 and more a week stealing from Fedex shipments. Both in drugs and valuables which he sold.

I told him that if I had it I would lend it to him, but that I didn't. That I was broke till Friday and even then that money was going to pay my bills. I had the money easily. But I would never lend money to someone like him and I had no need or desire to hold the eight-ball of cocaine. And that was Al Ferrier.

Drug Dealers Threaten to MURDER Stephanie Seberg

I had called up to the Wilmington station for just "one more" missing parts of shipments and Stephanie answered the phone. After I asked a few questions about the freight that we never did find and was probably stolen.

Stephanie got all emotional on the phone and blurted out, " Gary, you've had problems with these guys up here, why are they threatening to KILL ME?"

We in the Dover had already heard that there had been threats to her life. And about her bodyguard. So it really came as no surprise when she told me that.

Bad news ... Always travels fast.

I had an idea what she was going through mentally. I knew what it was like being all alone and surrounded by a bunch of druggies and thieves who wanted you out. I also knew that because of her position... she really was in serious danger. She said that she was getting threats against her life, that they were going thru her office looking for stuff and even her mail. She said that at first she didn't take them too seriously, but that certain events (she wouldn't mention) made her realize that the threats were real and very serious. I believe she said they had followed her home.

She said that she went to Liberty District headquarters in King of Prussia, Pennsylvania and asked for and received a personal bodyguard. She was afraid.

She believed it was more than one person and I did too. In fact I was sure it was. There was quite a drug connection going on up there that involved big money and they wanted her out at any cost.

"Gary, could you please help me?" Stephanie almost begged.

I wasn't really too sympathetic to anybody in Fedex management, but still I agreed to meet with her and her bodyguard in a discreet location away from the station.

At the least, I could let her know what she was up against. After that it was up to her.

We met in a restaurant away from both stations. It was just Stephanie, her bodyguard and me. Her bodyguard had that big pro lineman look of a football player. He looked me over REAL GOOD then sat nest to Stephanie. She looked scared as hell and she was obviously under a lot of stress. It must have been very hard on her.

She started out by saying that she knew of the troubles I had had in the station and felt that because of that, maybe I could explain to her exactly what was going on There.   Why did they want her out?

I asked her what kinds of threats she was receiving?

Stephanie hesitated for moment then started... She said that they would leave notes in her office and in her mail to get out of the station or they would kill her. That they then trashed her office and were going thru her mail. She now realized that they were serious and they might actually kill her. They even made threatening phone calls saying they were going to get her.

Why did they want her out...she asked.

I knew exactly why they wanted her out. The problem was making her realize and understand it.   So I asked her a few questions to help eliminate other thoughts.

"Have you written up anyone since you've been there, " I asked.
"No," she replied.

"Maybe you gave someone a warning either written or verbal," I asked.
"No," she replied again.

"And to the best of your knowledge …you have done nothing to offend anyone in the station," I asked.

She thought about the question for a minute then answered, "no, not to my knowledge, I haven't," she replied.

"Do you do illegal drugs or steal from shipments," I asked "you know, do you get high?"
"No, I don't do any of that stuff," she said.

"Then I suggest you leave the station before they kill you or cause you serious injury, because they will," I said.   And I was dead serious. She didn't stand a chance.

She obviously didn't know what she was up against. Maybe she was new to Fedex…I have no idea.   But she didn't know a thing about everyday crimes committed there daily. Not just in the Wilmington, Delaware station but all across America.

She just sat there for a minute trying to comprehend what I had just said to her.   And whether I was right or not. But I knew she realized I was right…it was obvious. Even to her. I worked there for a long time and I saw it and heard it everyday. She and her body guard had spent many hours trying to figure out why anyone would want her dead. He was big and strong but he was "dumb as a post". She had to be told point blank.

And now she understood. I told her that it was not only the couriers that she had to fear, but also her managers that she was probably confiding it.

Think about it I said to her,   why are you the only one getting the death threats and not any of your managers?

She asked me more questions about the station. My experiences there and how strong the drugs and thefts were?   Then she asked me if I would go to the Liberty District headquarters with her.

I didn't know about that one.   I wasn't too thrilled with District Headquarters.

When I went there about my problems with the drug dealers and the druggies in management they did nothing.   And they still upheld a warning letter that they absolutely knew I should have never gotten. I knew the Liberty District was no good.

As we parted I told her to keep her bodyguard with her at all times. That they were watching her always and would find an opening when they were ready.

She responded that she did . That he picked her up at her house in the morning and never left her side all day. Even when she went to the bathroom he would go in first and check it out and then wait outside while she went in afterwards.   At the end of the day he drove her back to her door at home.

As I drove home that day I thought about Stephanie and all the things I had seen at Fedex.   How could such a big company be so corrupt and so screwed up. The threats, the assaults, the fraud and thefts, the lying to and cheating of the customers …all of the drugs and thefts of drugs. It just seemed unbelievable.

Then I thought about Fred Smith, his "beloved confederate Slave Flag," how he killed a black man and left him to die in the streets, his forgery to steal millions of dollars from his own sisters.   How he trained his couriers to cheat his customers, the CSS conspiracy to commit fraud. And how AFOSI had said he was a big time drug smuggler.   The intentional and knowingly shipping tens of millions of dollars of illegal drugs everyday just for greed.   It all fit in.   This was NOT a regular business company,   it was a company founded by a criminal.

A man who was evil.

I wondered if Stephanie would be smart enough to resign before they killed her?

Then…After They Screw Me…They Ask For My Help …Yeah Right
Several days later I got that phone call
District Direct Director Julio Columbo … wanted me in his office in King of Prussia, Pennsylvania the following Friday at 9:00

am sharp. They didn't say why, just to be there. I knew it was coming. Stephanie was scared and desperate. She was in Danger, Serious Danger

When I arrived that Friday at district headquarters I was asked to wait till they were ready. Then they ushered me into a conference room that already had about a half dozen people in it. Julio was there, my personnel representative (what a sick joke she was) , Stephanie and her bodyguard were there, as were two of Fedex's private investigators...a Thomas Sullivan and a Ed Picarella. They were out of New York and Julio introduced then to me saying they were his "Best men".

As I sat down Ed Picarella began setting up a tape recorder for the meeting. I too had brought my briefcase to the meeting and fortunately I had put my own tape recorder in it before I left my house. Seeing this I began getting out my tape recorder and I said to Julio that since they had a tape recorder to record anything I might say, I just happened to bring my own recorder and I was going to use it too.

I think Julio almost shit himself.

It obviously never occurred to Julio that a courier would be smart enough to also bring his own recorder to protect himself. He at first objected, but I told him if I could not use mine ... there would be no meeting.

Tom Sullivan finally convinced him to let me use it to record the meeting too. I've since made five additional copies of that tape recording. Thank You Tom Sullivan.

<u>I like at least six copies of everything dealing with Fred Smith and or Fedex. And since I have six great places to keep them it all works.</u>

As I sat my briefcase up on the big table Julio looked at it for a moment then he asked me what was in it. I had already set up my recorder and the briefcase was empty. I thought to myself, these guys have been screwing me around for some time. It's time to have a little fun with them.

So I said to Julio. **"Today I only have my tape recorder in it. But there has been some very important stuff in this case. I know you won't believe this Julio but this case has held stuff that will put Fedex in the Newspapers and on national TV. And it will cost this company millions of dollars."**

I knew I was being bold but what the hell. This was my turn. They wanted me here...they had to Pay.

I looked at the faces around the tables and saw the unbelieving smirks that I knew I would. The kind of looks that said…I was just a little nobody that had no chance to ever do any harm to a company as big and powerful as Fedex.

Julio just looked at me and said, "very funny Gary, very funny," then he laughed.

I laughed too because I knew what he didn't know. I knew that my briefcase had held many copies of military documents and shipping airbills that proved fraud by Fedex against the U. S. military and the government. It had held Fedex documents which clearly show violations of hundreds of U.S. military contracts with Fedex.

Some of which I had received from Paul Ackerman.

I just smiled and thought "Go ahead and laugh now you assholes …I will laugh louder later on."

After my recorder was set up Julio again introduced everyone around the table. Then he explained to me why he wanted me there today. That someone was threatening Stephanie and they feared that she was in serious danger. And that he wanted me to give him the name of that person who was doing it.

While I couldn't laugh at that time…I certainly thought that it was very funny.

So I instead asked him just why he thought it was only "one person." And Julio responded that they were pretty sure it was only one person but that if I had any evidence that it was in fact more than one …would I please tell them who they were.

Which meant that they had no clue what so ever of who or how many people were threatening to murder Stephanie.

Well now isn't this just great I thought to myself. When I had a drug dealing courier who was threatening me and actually assaulted me in their station … they did nothing about it. When I complained that their managers in the Wilmington station were druggies… they did "nothing."

And they gave me a "letter of "disruptive behavior even when they knew I had done nothing wrong.

Even when I went all the way to Corporate headquarters in Memphis they ignored it. When one of their "druggie Fedex couriers" nearly ran over me in a Fedex van while I had my three year old son with me…they hired a big money lawyer to get him off. And who knows how much they paid the Judge?

Now they have a senior station manager who's life is on the line ... and they have the balls to ask for my help. Let anyone go through the hell they put me through ...and see if they help them.

To me it was like asking the Jews to help put out a fire in the buildings where they poisoned them with gas.

The point is...they had no interest at all in cleaning up drugs and thefts in the station.   That would take out 95% of the people there. They were only interested in taking out one person...and they hoped that would scare the others into letting Stephanie alone.   And "maybe" she might be safe for awhile.   And it would be business as usual.

But taking out only one person might also make them mad enough to kill Stephanie too.

I had to think about what I wanted to do, and how I wanted to say it. I told them straight out, if they wanted Stephanie safe they would have to do a station wide drug test and that would include management. But I already knew that wouldn't happen.

While they may not have wanted to see Stephanie murdered,   she wasn't that important in the scheme of things within Fedex. She was after all just (1) station manager. And they weren't going to jeopardize the company's reputation and do a drug test just to save one person.

One of the investigators starting talking to me real serious like. He was trying to get me to help Stephanie ...hey Gary, you don't want to see Stephanie get hurt kind of talk.   Come on help us out here kind of stuff, give us something. Just a few names he was "begging me."

I'm thinking, Wow ... all this begging from a top Fedex investigator from New York and I'm just a little courier type guy.

It was tempting, real tempting for Stephanie's sake. But to be honest...I just could not play into their games.

If they had been honest with me and did what was right when I had problems with the druggies in the station, I would have gladly done what was right. But when I was the one being threatened , attacked etc. ... the station managers fucked me, district headquarters fucked me, and headquarters in Memphis fucked me.

So fuck them ALL now.

Management was never going to think I was a good guy who just wanted to do his job and go home to his family. They were never going to forget that I tried to get Druggies with management fired. They had already showed me what kind of company they were.

<u>I don't forget and I don't forgive. That's God's Job.</u>

I very calmly but honestly told them what I felt.   As Stephanie and her bodyguard sat there and listened.   I told them that they didn't really give a damm about Stephanie or they would clean out the station.

Then I looked at Stephanie and told her not to expect any help from the company because they wouldn't do anything that might cause bad publicity.

I told Stephanie that she would end up in a steel drum floating in the Delaware River before Fedex would take a chance of tainting their name.

<u>Yeah, I got ot ALL on Tape… Just ask Julio.</u>

It would have been easy to get rid of the people threatening to kill her. All it would take was a station wide drug test, but they wouldn't do that. And soon she would be on her own because soon they would take away her bodyguard and she would be an easy target…and they would kill her.

It was obvious that Julio was upset. He was hoping that I would give him a name so that he could just take out that one person and leave the rest of the station intact. Fact was …I could have given him names… would it have been ALL of them? I don't know.   He had gone to a lot of trouble bringing everybody together that day including his two top investigators from N.Y.   But he hadn't previously talked to me or even asked me for my help. And I certainly didn't ask for that meeting, didn't even want it to happen.   I showed up because I was told to.

I left the meeting feeling sorry for Stephanie. I knew she was in trouble and in danger.   But I wasn't going to get involved, I had more important stuff going on in Dover with AFOSI investigators.   I didn't need the druggies coming down there after me. Not now.   And there were just too many people doing too much bad stuff that I had seen up there in the Wilmington station and Philadelphia too.   Evidently a lot more and a lot bigger of an operation than even I had realized.   And Fedex management didn't want to disrupt it … no matter what.

I think Stephanie realized it too.   It just took her a little time.

And yet, I wonder if…maybe …something else happened to her. Something that I and many other don't know about.

Was there an attempt on her life ?

Did she get that, "<u>offer that she couldn't refuse.</u>" they show on the Mafia movies?

Something happened...because   SENIOR STATION MANAGER RESIGNS IMMEDIATELY

Stephanie Seberg ...quits Fedex immediately. No two week notice, no coming back and trying to hang in there. She fled Fedex, even fled Delaware. She went to another area of the country where she prayed she would be safe and out of danger.

Or did something happen to her? Did they harm her? Welcome to the world of Fedex Druggies and Thieves.

*As a side note...The meeting was supposed to be a "secret meeting" held in King of Prussia, PA. approximately fifty miles from the Wilmington station and no one was supposed to know about it. Yet the very next morning a courier from the Wilmington station told me that everybody in the station knew about it and they wanted to know what I said. I had told no one about the meeting.

Never underestimate Drug connections.

Vinnie's Pizza shop...
Mafia Connection goes down

Remember Vinnie's Pizza....the drug dealer ?

Since I was now working in Dover and wasn't doing Vinnie's pickups anymore I had lost track of him. And had actually forgotten about him. Then one day I was reading the newspaper and there was Vinnie's name on the front page. The FBI had busted him for trafficking in Cocaine. And then he implicated his Mafia buddies and got them busted too. I figured he was in big trouble.

Evidently the time when I had seen him at his Pizza shop and asked about his health was shortly after the FBI had busted him. I have no idea why they went after him in the first place but I can say with total honesty ...it wasn't me. I never said a word.

And Back in the Dover Station

There was a new job position posted on the bulletin board. It was for a CTV truck driver for the Dover station. A CTV truck is a "Container Truck Vehicle" it holds freight containers. The job consisted of driving the freight from the Philadelphia ramp to the Dover station. The driver would get the CTV truck parked at the Wilmington station and drive to the Philadelphia ramp and pick up the freight and deliver it to the Dover station. Where the driver would unload the freight and do a delivery and pickup route. Then he would take the shipments picked up that day back to the Wilmington station where it would be driven up to the Philadelphia airport ramp for the flight to Memphis.

It would mean I started work just ten minutes from my house again. It would also mean extra hours.

NOT a chance.

The other couriers were talking about it but none of them were qualified to drive a CTV truck. And actually none of them wanted the job because they all lived in Dover. I had already taken and passed the CTV driving course and was the only person in the station that was qualified. And I did want the job but I was pretty sure that the druggies and drug dealers in management wouldn't let me have the job anyway. They knew I had to travel nearly an hour to work in Dover and they hoped I would grow tired of it and quit.

But I signed up for it anyway...Just to see what would happen. After the job had been posted for two weeks and no one else besides me wanted it management decided to throw away the posting.

Oh well I expected it anyway.

Funny thing was ...all of the couriers in the Dover station had all said to a man that they (management) wouldn't let me have it and they were right.

When I asked one of the managers about it...he told me to just forget about it.

And instead management waited for awhile and then they finally did hire and train a CTV driver. No one was told about it, he just showed up one morning. His name was Del and he seemed nice enough. Surprising though was that he was a Black man and he was assigned to the Dover station. Del was to be FedEx's "token Black" in the Dover station for the books to show they were an equal employment company.

Dover stations first Black regular courier ever. My My.

I didn't hold it against him that he got the job I couldn't. If it wasn't him it would have been someone else. But It would have never been me.

The others in the station, who were all white, didn't like it at all. A few of them remarked ..."why did they have to hire in a Nigger, we don't need a Nigger down here." And they all stated that they wouldn't help him and were hopeful he would fail or just leave because he wasn't welcome. They didn't want no dammed Niggers down here in Fedex's Dover station.

I had been getting along with the couriers there pretty good. They really weren't a bad group. But I knew he would be in for a hard time. But not from me, I gave him all of the help I could. Even did some of his stops to help his delivery times. He was a good guy. Just trying to do his job. And he had a family who counted on him.

When Helen came down from the Wilmington station to fill in for a courier who was on vacation she couldn't call him Nigger enough. Whenever something was said about him or his route they never once used his name which was Del. They always referred to him as "that stupid Nigger, or "lazy Nigger", and sometimes …"that stupid fucking Nigger". He had it tough…and he knew they didn't want him there, yet somehow he hung in there and made it.

Dover Gets a New Manager… This Will Be Fun

We got a new station manager for our Dover station. And boy what an asshole he was. His name was Tim Keyser and he was from the Philadelphia area. He was that kind of guy who was always right no matter what. I guess they trained him well in managers school.

None of the couriers in the Dover station liked him.

They nicknamed him "Maggot." And they meant it.

When he first came to Dover he would constantly question me about the Wilmington station. The truth was he had already been filled in about my history there by upper management. He was sent to Dover with an "Agenda" and it involved "Me".

He already knew what was going on up there, he just wanted to know what I knew and what I was telling others. He asked me about the guys up there and what had happened. wanted me to tell him about the drugs and thefts and more. He was steadily trying to pick my brain about what I knew or would tell him about them.

To try to win my confidence he was always telling me about the bigger drug deals and thefts etc. in the other stations in Philly. In the beginning I wasn't sure if he was just making talk, was curious or what. But after a while I realized that he was only pumping me for information. I have no idea if it was for upper management in district (which I seriously doubt because they really didn't care). Or was he trying to find out what I knew so that he could let the drug dealers in that station know? To be honest, at that time I really couldn't care less what they were doing as long as they left me alone.

Tim didn't like having a Black man working in the station. But I never met a Fedex manager who did so it was nothing new. He told me that he had complained to upper management about it and was basically told that "to have a few Blacks around made it easier for Fedex to get government contracts" and it made the company look good. And to just keep them on a short lease... like they were a dog I guess. Several times he would go off on a rant and say something like..." that Nigger better jump when I say jump, better run when I say run.   First time he fucks up... that Nigger is history here."   And..."he better not start any of that Nigger shit in my station."

I'll fire him the first time I hear him complain."

Del probably never knew what Tim was saying about him. And it was probably better that he didn't.   But I do think he had some idea of Tim's thoughts.

The signs and were pretty obvious.

Sometimes Tim would begin a conversation with me by saying something nasty about Black couriers. He would begin with the, "the stupid Niggers in this Philadelphia station did this or said that."

How they would teach Niggers to just do what they were told, and how they fucked them or got rid of them if they tried to argue about it. Or he would start in about how Blacks weren't wanted in management because they aren't smart enough. So they kept the number of Blacks in management to the absolute minimum or else the company might fall. Tim said he would make sure there was "only the one token Nigger" in the Dover station if he had anything to say about it.

Then he would veer off to illegal drugs and how much he had seen in Philadelphia, about some guy who was a courier stealing $10,000 worth of cocaine from a shipment etc. And then laugh and say..."and now he's a manager."   Then he made sure to steer the conversation back to the drugs in the Wilmington station and "who was doing what?"   It's was just old tired rhetoric to me. I'd heard all of the racist stuff from about every manager there. That and the drug talk were just him planting seeds that he hoped I would help grow. And it didn't.

It bothered me to hear the Blacks called Niggers, and when he started in that direction I usually just walked away.   And I wasn't about to talk about what I knew about the drugs in the Wilmington station and or the Philadelphia ramp.   Let him go fish in another pond.

I also began to think that possibly he may have been instructed by Julio Columbo to find out what I meant when I was in Julio's office and said I was going to put Fedex in the newspapers and on TV. I had never once mentioned anything about the CSS investigation to anyone and I never would until the investigation was finished and was being prosecuted. I hadn't even told my wife. After he realized that I had shut down any out going information of any kind to him he changed tactics.

He began harassing me and pressuring me nearly every day on my job. He was coming after me every way he could.

Oh well, just when you think you might be forgotten about and might just and only be expected to do your job … the way it's supposed to be.

I had always done my job as best as I could both up in Wilmington, the airport ramp and now in Dover. And had always before, even well before I began at Fedex. No big deal …you have a job, you just do it the best that you can. That's the way it's supposed to be I have always thought.

It was how I was raised.

Many of my customers appreciated that and some of them had sent letters of appreciation to my manager in Dover. Some had called him on the phone to personally compliment me. <u>I never knew because he never told me</u>.

Some had told me they did.

One day while I was at the station and everyone else had left for the day, I was in the office making copies of the CSS tally sheets. And I came across two letters of expressing appreciation for great service to them. They were on the corner of his desk. They told of how I had gone well above and beyond my duty to give them superior service. And how much they appreciated it.

Normally within a day or two of receiving these letters a manager would make a copy for the couriers personnel files and give the originals to the courier along with a "good job" sort of acknowledgement. The letters on Tim Keyser's desk were more than a month old. I read them and made copies of them in case he destroyed them.

The next day I made a point of going into his office while he sat there at his desk and asked several questions on unrelated matters. As we spoke I casually let me gaze drift over to the letters that I had left in a manner so that my name was clearly visible. Acting as though I had never seen the letters before, I asked …"oh are these for me?"

Tim looked at the letters and realized that he got caught holding them. He stuttered a few times then said something like ..."yeah here," then he got up quickly and rushed out of the office. I just smiled...I knew he didn't like it that I got praise, and I did enjoy watching him get upset about being caught with the letters...after all the date was on them.

The Dover station kept getting busier and all of the couriers were getting pushed hard to somehow make it work. The other couriers were complaining that we were overstretched but I wasn't going to complain. I was working with AFOSI agents and they were my main focus.

Beides I figured it wouldn't do any good.

We just, as a whole just kept speeding faster and faster to try to make it work. I think everyone had to put radar detectors in our trucks by that time...and I think we thought of ourselves more as race car drivers than as couriers. I very rarely took a lunch break from start to finish and I once went three months without a lunch break.

Even with the increased number of pickups and deliveries Tim Keyser would still pressure me to get back earlier than I possibly could and he knew it. And I believe my route covered the greatest amount of miles of anyone in the station. It was certainly the busiest.

We finally did get another courier to help us with our routes. Well all of the other couriers did...but me. Their routes had increased by about twenty-five percent. My route had been fairly busy when I got it and soon it had nearly doubled since I took it over. Part of the reason was that Tim kept taking stops from other courier's routes as they got busier and added them to my route which was already very busy.

Tim took some stops from every other courier's route in the station and put them on the new couriers route. Except for my route, he didn't take a single stop from my route. Even the other couriers couldn't believe that he wouldn't give me any help at all on my route as it was the busiest one in the station.

In all honesty, I never expected it. His agenda was to get rid of me, not help me. He was going to push me to make a mistake so he could fire me. And he knew that if he just stayed on me and never let up I would screw up. Or I would just quit. It was a common management tool Fedex management used to get rid of those they wanted out.

If a Black employee said something about discrimination, or not being treated fairly, maybe he files a GFT complaint... next thing that Black employee knows is that his or her manager is all over everything they do on their job. And before they know it, that manager is joking at how He fired that Stupid Nigger, and how they fired him or her because they made a simple little mistake that many of their white co-workers made every day with no consequence. "Shouldn't have started that Nigger talk" they'll say and laugh. I had heard it several times.

Heard about it a number times. Nothing new.

And the discrimination complaint disappears and management at Fedex's Plantation comes out smelling like a rose.

No disgruntled Blacks here they say.

Of course not...they fired them all.   Every one that opened his mouth. They may not be able to whip them with a whip but the pen works well there.

Then Tim Keyser did honestly surprise me a few weeks after the new courier came to the station. He had taken stops from all the of the other couriers.   But just to have some fun with me ... he actually "added" a couple more stops to my route. A route that NO ONE else could do in the time I did it in every day.   Day after day I loaded my truck, raced around Dover like a NASCAR driver and made my deliveries on time. Lunch wasn't a dream, hell it wasn't even a fantasy.   If I couldn't eat or drink it at sixty plus miles an hour I wasn't having it. Pure and simple. And all that with an asshole manager looking at everything I did every morning, day and evening when I got back to the station.   Double checking every piece of paper work, every delivery and always trying to provoke me into an argument so that I would slip up and say something that could get me fired. Maybe even get me mad enough to punch the shit out of him.

He was such a Maggot.   And he just kept tightening the screws.

Even the other couriers tried to talk to him about it and he refused to listen to them and still just kept adding more stops to my routes.

By this time I came to realize that upper management had been orchestrating his actions all along. Yes, he was an asshole on his own, but he was dancing to the upper managements strings. It was okay, the investigations with AFOSI were not that far from being completed. When they were finished I would turn in my resignation and be gone.

I could handle anything they threw at me. If you pay attention to life you will learn many things. One of those things you will learn is that if you encounter a lot of adversity you have two choices. You can surrender to the adversity and run away. Or you can fight against the adversity and you will grow stronger. Whether or not you will win is not always certain …but you will grow stronger. I had grown stronger in my determination to not let them beat me and as hard as it may seem to believe…and Tim Keyser was growing weaker.

Another Performance Review…
Lets Play Screw Gary Rullo One More Time
One night after we had gotten the CTV loaded and ready for the trip to the Philadelphia ramp Tim came up to me and told me that he would be riding with me the next day for "performance review / check ride". I actually looked forward to it because he had been pushing me to get back into the station earlier for months. And I always challenged him to go out with me and show me a way to make better times on my route. I knew my route, I was fast and very efficient….it couldn't be done in the times he was trying to make me do it in. I knew he was just harassing me and pressuring me. This was my chance to put it in his face and shut him up.

I always kept my truck cleaned out and properly stocked and I did it everyday without fail. It was just a part of my routine. That night before I went home I did extra work in my truck to make sure he could find no fault with it. When I left for home my truck was well stocked and spotless.

The next morning we were busy unloading freight from the CTV truck to the conveyor belt, sorting freight and mail for our routes and then loading it into our trucks for delivery.

When that was all done Tim came up to me and said okay lets go. So I jumped into my truck and began writing down the mileage on the odometer. As I was doing that Tim began looking thru my truck and commented about how dirty it was. He found candy bar wrappers, coffee cups, and a pastry wrapper in my truck. He talked about how sloppy my shelves were. I looked over and sure enough there were all those things in my truck and my shelves did look sloppy.

"Wait a minute," I said, "you saw me clean out my truck last night. I completely cleaned and stocked it before I left and everything was neat and put away."

"I wasn't paying attention," was all he said.

"I'll have to mark you down for a dirty truck," he added.

"This is a bunch of shit, somebody was in my truck, " I said, " and you know that I don't even drink coffee," I was pissed. Yet I knew there was nothing I could do about it. I started my truck and headed out on my route.

It was an average day except that I had a few less deliveries than normal. That day I wasn't going to speed and fortunately I didn't have to like I normally did to make my route work. Normally we ALL had to speed just to make the routes work. I wanted him to see what my route was like if I didn't speed around like a race car driver. Because I'm sure he would have lowered my score if I sped while he was doing the check ride evaluation. I guess it could even been grounds to fire me.

I ran my route flawlessly and did my deliveries and pickups as efficiently as was possible. After all I ran it everyday. I was supposed to be good at it. We got back to the station late as usual. I knew we would because I didn't play Nascar Driver that day.

When we pulled into the station I said to him that I was late as usual. And I reminded him that we had five (5) less stops than normal that day. I had driven the speed limit that day which added the time difference for the five less stops.

Now you tell me how I can run this route faster than I do. He never said a word. He just got out of the truck and then told me to hurry and get my freight on the belt for loading into the CTV.

Then he walked away.

After the freight was loaded and the CTV had left and we were doing our paperwork I asked the other drivers if they had seen anybody in my truck after I left last night.

A couple of them told me that Tim had taken my truck up to the Wilmington station the night before. I realized that the coffee cups and wrappers were his. He had intentionally left them in my truck so he could lower my score on my evaluation.

When I confronted him about it the next day he said…"so what that's no excuse."

Like I said…TIM KEYSER WAS AN ASSHOLE.

Later that winter we had a nasty snowstorm that started on Wednesday and continued all day into the night and was still snowing come Thursday. I had gotten up at 4:00 am because I knew the roads were bad and I normally had at least a 45 minute ride to the station in good weather.

With all the snow I would be lucky just to make it to work. I was the first one to the station and somehow most of the other couriers also made it. Even though the Governor's office declared a snow emergency later that morning and only essential personnel were supposed to be out on the roads. We were going to try to get some deliveries in anyway if the CTV made it thru. The state highway department was steadily working on the main roads and somehow the CTV truck finally made it even though it was a couple hours late and the snow was still falling. Tim lived only a couple blocks away from the station and he also made it in. I believe he walked.

He decided that only the closest deliveries of about a couple miles would be attempted and so we sorted out only those packages to deliver.

And then we (the couriers) went thru and started distributing those deliveries equally between us.

After we divided them up fairly evenly ...Tim went over to the conveyor belt picked thru the rest of the freight and put in a lot of extra deliveries in my truck that nearly doubled my deliveries Then he told me that he wanted me to get them delivered. I looked at them and saw that a number of them were on the other couriers routes. When I said something to him about it, he said ..."just do what I say and deliver the freight."

While the other couriers deliveries that day were in central Dover where the roads were better, mine and especially the ones he added to my deliveries were out in the country where there were little if any snow plows.

I had dressed for the blizzard so I figured what the hell. If it can be done I'll do it. The other couriers came over to me and said that it really sucked what he was doing...I appreciated that. They had no love for him either. But there was nothing they could do, they needed their jobs too.

It was nasty out there and cars were stranded all over the place. Dispatch kept checking on all of the couriers and me too. When he found out how many deliveries Tim had given me he kept saying he couldn't believe I was sent out with so many stops when a statewide snow emergency had been declared, but he couldn't say anything either.

I made every one of my stops even though many of the customers weren't even there. I did double the deliveries and covered three times the miles the other couriers did. They were good drivers too so they may have been able to do my stops that day too. But Tim ONLY wanted to have me doing that many stops. I came in later than them. But as they were heading back to the station ahead of me they were calling me and checking on me and giving me an update on the roads which were really bad. It was early afternoon when I got in. I had kept in touch with the dispatcher and he was also giving me the "great job and the thank you for doing such a great job" stuff as I headed back to the station.

Yet when I came thru the station doors my manager Tim walked over to my truck and began giving me hell because I came in an hour later then the others. It was a little past noon. I let him get it all out. Then I looked him directly in the eyes and said …you gave me the packages and told me to deliver them, and I did. You gave me nearly double the deliveries of everybody else and with many more miles …and I made it. You had access to a radio and could have called me to tell me to come back earlier at any time…and you didn't.

If you wanted me back earlier why didn't you call me on the radio and say so?

He had no answer and just walked away.

Maybe some of the other couriers had said something to him ?

I went over and did my paper work and went home. I knew I had done a great job under very difficult conditions… and it just ruined his day that I did.

I barely made it home… but I felt good.

I look back now and I realize that all of the harassment, nasty games and pressure he used against me…only made me stronger. I realize now that it was my convictions of doing what was right and my belief in myself not only kept me strong, they actually made me grow stronger. My wife had always supported me and believed in me, and I also had so many good friends and family that encouraged and supported me too. Tim was an asshole, but he was just a little asshole and never was a match for a good and strong man. I think even he realized that when it was all over.

Then We Tried Vacation Fedex Style

It's hard to plan your vacation with your family when you have an asshole for a manager. Or was it possible that he was just following orders from upper management?

(1) I put in a written request for a week of vacation with the family a month ahead of the vacation date. Tim Keyser told me that yes it was okay and approved but he didn't sign the request or give me a written notice that it was okay. As the vacation drew closer several times I reminded him of it and he always replied, "sure no problem," I got it covered." But it was company policy that you had to have a written okay for vacations.

On the day before I was to start vacation he told me two minutes before I clocked out that I could not have the vacation he had already verbally approved. It was very upsetting to my wife as we had reservations at the beach etc. The family was ready … but no vacation.

(2) So after some time passed I again put in a written request for vacation with two weeks advance notice. Tim said, "probably … let me make sure." When I didn't get an okay in writing a week later I asked again and he said he didn't know for sure. But that he was working on it. Finally on the very day I had requested off I had to come to work because he had not given me a written okay. That morning he told me I couldn't have it.

It was pretty obvious by then.

Hey Tim you asshole, fuck me but don't fuck my family. Burn in hell you Nazi bastard.

(3) Once more I put in for just one day off with two weeks notice. Tim said, "probably." Then he kept putting me off until the day I asked off for came.

Then he said I couldn't have that day off either.

None of the other couriers ever had their vacation requests denied while I was there.   Not even once.

So yeah I filed the "GFT" grievance that Fedex has it's employees use when they think they have been treated unfairly.

Tim trashed it.

Fedex calls the (GFT) "Guaranteed Fair Treatment" grievance.

It's actually the (GFT)….."Guaranteed you're getting Fucked Treatment" grievance.

Lets Play Screw Gary Again …
<u>First Time Late Ever and I get a "Written Warning."</u>

One day on the way to work I had a fan belt problem and had to get it fixed on the way to work. I called the station a half hour before start time and told them what happened and that I would be there as soon as possible. I wound up being about two hours late. The next day Tim gave me a written notice for being late.

I had been with the company for four years and had never ever been late. And now I get a written warning for being late, for the first time ever.

Posted on our company bulletin board in the station there was a notice. It was the official company policy and procedures for being late or missing time.

The memo was from Personnel Headquarters in Memphis
It stated:....

First time late in a six month period................no action Second time late in a six months period ...verbal reminder Third time late in a six month period ......written warning

This was my first time late in four years and Tim the ASSHOLE MANAGER hands me a written warning for it.

I went over to Tim and asked him to walk over to the bulletin board with me. And I pointed to the posted company policy regarding lateness. I said, "according to this I don't get a written warning until I am late three times in a six month period." I asked him, "How can you give me this letter after I was only late once in four years?"

Tim just looked at me and smiled and said, "that's the way I see it."

Later that day I handed Tim a GFT grievance complaint letter. I told him I wanted to take the issue to the District Headquarters in King of Prussia. I told him calmly but straight up that I didn't think he was mentally capable of properly addressing the issue. It was nice to say that to him face to face. He was supposed to be a station manager but he had become that "little boy" that did stupid things that irritated me, and that only showed me that he was way over his head. Maybe he was just too indulgent in drugs and had lost his focus. He certainly did seem to have that "brain dead" type demeanor that you see with Pot heads when they've ... smoked far too much pot.

How he could give me a written warning for being late once in four years when it was clearly posted on the company bulletin board that I was to receive nothing ...surely the official company policy would force them to remove the letter ?

The other couriers in the station couldn't believe it.

They honestly believed that district headquarters would remove the letter. I wasn't so sure.

As for their thoughts about Tim Keyser and what he was doing to me... they had him down as an asshole. And when ever he wasn't around they called him "MAGGOT" Which did make me feel good. But it didn't take away the heat... only soothed it. I could handle his bullshit.

And yet I knew my time to leave wasn't that far away.

In The meantime: <u>The investigation by OSI was proceeding forward and nearly wrapped up.</u>

They had decided to do more surveillance on more CSS shipments. But this time in eight different locations across America. When I asked where they would be I was told again that they would rather that I did not know where or even what states they would do these investigations in. The best they could tell me was to think of it as an East, West, North, South investigation. That way there was no chance I could influence the surveillance. I understood that fully. But I did insist that I be kept informed after the surveillance was finished of how they came out. And agent Ackerman agreed to that. I told him I felt it was only fair and he agreed. What he didn't know was that every time I called him on the phone or even when he called me, I was secretly tape recording our conversations. I knew what the results of the investigations were going to be. And it sure was nice to record him saying ... that there was no CSS service on any of the shipments they investigated.

And when I said to him, " then it is fraud?" And to record him saying, "yes it is Fraud."

And I did call him often.

<u>Meanwhile I do Have Fun in The District Office</u>

I did finally get my GFT hearing at District headquarter in King of Prussia, PA. And what a joke it was. But I'd already suspected it would be. My personnel representative (aka. Company spy) was there. District Director Julio Columbo was there in his four hundred dollar suit and was sitting at his big fancy desk. He just had that look of a grease ball New Yorker about him.

Julio sat at his desk and says, " what is the problem Gary?"

I showed him the written warning Tim Keyser had given me about being late. I then explained to him that I had never been late since I came to Fedex, and that was about four years. I told him that Fedex had a written company policy that was posted on the company bulletin board that stated there was no action to be taken for the first time an employee was late.

Then I showed him a copy of the written company policy regarding lateness. I had made a copy of it just in case.

Julio looked at the papers and looked at the woman who was pretending to be my personnel representative. Then he got a BIG SMILE on his face and said, "that's the way we see it, the warning stands."

"Even though I have only been late once in four years, "I asked.

"Yes," he replied. And he gave me a big smiling smirk.

As I looked at Julio and the Bitch pretending to be my personnel representative who never once opened her mouth but only smiled, I got a perfectly clear picture of what Fedex management and the company was all about. I realized exactly why I had never gotten any real fairness and honesty from Fedex's management. All the way from the Wilmington and Dover stations, the District headquarters, Regional operations, and Corporate headquarters in Memphis, Fred Smith and Fedex didn't hire management people because of their honesty or integrity or fairness. On the contrary, I don't believe Fred Smith would EVER knowingly hire an honest person if he knew that the person was really honest and had integrity. I was a rare mistake.

Fred Smith only wanted SLICK LIARS, who would do anything they were told to do with no qualms. People who espoused honesty, character and integrity ... yet had none of their own and didn't want anyone in the company that did. Fedex's philosophy was simple ...hire only those people who had a "drone mentality" that would do whatever they were told to do without question. It didn't matter if it was immoral or illegal. That's why hundreds maybe thousands of Fedex management and couriers alike all across America would knowingly and intentionally commit fraud against and betray our men and women in the military and America.

That is why their management can easily train their couriers to cheat and steal from their customers from one end of this country to another everyday.

If someone should say or think ...hey there's a lot of good people that work at Fedex. Well I'm sure there is, and if left on their own these people would probably do the right thing most times. But not with Fred Smith Fedex Plantation leading them.

Try to realize this …many of the Germans who rounded up the Jews and hauled them off to concentration camps to the gas chambers through the week …often went to church on Sunday after doing it. And they considered themselves "good Christians". They too had that "drone mentality."

It's a Fedex requirement for employment there.

The three of them were looking at me. They had just said "we are fucking you Gary Rullo and you can't do anything about it. We will continue to fuck you until you quit or fuck up. This was the time when I was supposed to stand up and say something like "fuck you assholes, I quit. Or maybe I was supposed to threaten one or both of them. Or maybe just lose it and start cussing. Any of the above …so that they could fire me.

Their problem was…it wasn't my "First Rodeo with these Assholes."

I looked at Julio with the Big Smirk on his face.. I thought about it for a moment.

Then I decided …I'm going to leave Julio with something that "some day" he will remember "this day" … for the rest of his life.

I looked at Julio and said, Let me show you something Julio. Stand up for a minute please." I said it very calmly without anger or emotion.

Julio looked at me dumbfounded.

"Come on Julio, let me play you for just a minute. I'm going to show you something that you will never forget ever. I promise."

He hesitated for a moment, I could see that he thought I might hit him. But that was not my intention. Oh he probably would have loved to have me knock the shit out of him so he could fire me. And it would have been enjoyable to be honest.

But I didn't have to resort to violence to beat these assholes.

"I'm not going to hurt you Julio," I said, "just stand up."

He must have believed me because just like a trained dog, he slowly stood up from his chair at my command. He might have sucked at his current position as District Director, but damm he would have made a great dog. And who knows what tricks you might be able to teach him … with proper training?

And I have trained retrievers before.

I walked over close to him and asked him to move to the front of his desk and he did. Just like that. It was obvious that he felt awkward and uncomfortable. Julio was used to being the BIG SHOT and in control while having others kow tow down to him. Here I was just a lowly courier and I had taken over both his office and his desk in just a matter of seconds. All without violence or force but only with the mental power of "suggestion". Julio was that Big New York City greasy scumbag.

In reality Julio wasn't that smart after all. And in truth he was probably dumber than most others under him especially the couriers who had to think quickly on their feet every day. But he did have that "$400 suit" that fit Fedex's image.

I sat down in his chair …at his big expensive and fancy oak desk.

I remarked to him how nice it was as I slowly ran my hands over it while they watched. To this day, I would love to know what they were thinking.

Then … I looked him in the eyes and I smiled at him … <u>like he was a nothing</u>" just so he would know what it felt like.

I said to him, "now this is you Julio, sitting at your desk not too far in the future. The phone rings and you hesitantly pick it up. I picked up his phone acting all hesitant and very nervous and scared.

As I put his phone to my ear and I said to Julio, " you sound nervous and scared…you say yes…yes … yes…. Fred …yes he told me …yes Fred I know Fred. I'm sorry? Fred ? …Fred ?… sighing …ohhhhh.

Then you hang up the phone like a "condemned man,"

Then I put his phone back on it's receiver and hung my head like a man condemned to death while still sitting at his desk.

I looked up at Julio and smiled…"that will be you someday soon Julio."

They all looked at each other trying to figure out if I was serious. They were totally confused and dumbfounded. Then the old look of … nobody can hurt Fedex came over them.

Except for Julio who still looked a little dumbfounded and a little unsure. I had shaken him like he had never been shaken before. Whether he believed me or not I don't know for sure. But he had never let someone take over not only his office but also his own desk….he will remember that day forever. I PROMISE YOU.

<u>Ohh yes…that day did come…exactly as I said it would. It's later in the book.</u>

The experience at District headquarters only made me more determined not to let them fire me or force me to quit. Not until it was time. I was not leaving until my work with AFOSI investigators was wrapped up. And I was not going to let some dumb assed piece of shit manager like Tim Keyser think that it was him who pressured me enough to make me quit or to make a mistake so he could fire me. I had important work with the A.F.O.S.I. agents to get finished. I would stay until the investigations were fully completed and ready for prosecution. And I didn't want management to know when or why I would resign. I would give them a two week resignation when I was ready and they least expected it, when things were quiet. I could handle Tim, I had grown well above him. And to be honest, it was him who began wearing down in this contest not me. It was Tim who failed to get me out in any way he could. He was weak. Or as I said before, maybe he was just too caught up in drugs to be able to come after me successfully?

I waited about a week then I called special agent Ackerman at OSI headquarters and he informed me that the surveillance of the CSS shipments were in motion. The other OSI agents had begun sending the shipments and were secretly following the couriers who had made the pickups and deliveries to see just where the fraud began. He said that he hadn't talked to them yet and hadn't seen any reports so he couldn't give me any information yet. But he did ask me to call him the next day in case he needed more information, and he said he would be able to tell me more at that time.

He also added, "and please Gary, be sure not to mention this investigation to anyone." And I never did, not even my wife. I never wanted her involved in any way. I knew she would be proud of me for what I had done. I just didn't want her involved.

Ackerman also informed me that he and another agent had conducted surveillance on another courier who was handling CSS shipments. It was the courier who drove the freight from Dover up to the Wilmington station, then the courier who drove it from the Wilmington station to the Philadelphia ramp. He wouldn't say what day it was or which courier they followed to the Philadelphia ramp but he wanted to see for himself how it was handled from the Dover Air Force Base to the Philadelphia airport ramp. And then he would compare the CSS tally sheet to see if it was signed. And it wasn't signed by either courier from Dover or Wilmington…or even the Philadelphia ramp. I'm certain they both also saw the CSS shipments left unprotected a number of times before it got back even to the Dover station in violation of hundreds of government and military contracts Fedex had signed.

But Fedex did bill the military for the CSS service it never gave them.
It was Money Fred Smith STOLE from the military.

Agent Ackerman had repeatedly stressed to me that he wanted me to stay on until the investigation was completed and was in the prosecutors hands in Washington. He also explained that it was crucial that I was not fired by Fedex. So I made sure that I wasn't. Besides, after the last meeting in Julio's office in the King of Prussia I think Tim Keyser may have been warned to back off. Or maybe he just plain gave up. Whatever it was…he wasn't in my face a whole lot lately.

Agent Ackerman said the investigation was going very well and everything I had told him was proving true. Every CSS shipment they investigated and followed all across America was and act of "FRAUD." Fedex was handling CSS shipment like common freight and doing nothing to protect them. Yet they were making millions of dollars for lying and saying they were. Fred Smith was involved in a conspiracy to betray and defraud the military and the government. He and his fellow criminals at Fedex were also committing the same fraud against thousands of business and private individuals with his phony C.S.S. service too.

Every time a Fedex customer had a lost or stolen valuable shipments, a Fedex sales representative or courier would encourage them to use the more costly C.S.S. service to better insure it safety. When in fact there was "no difference" in it's security or safety. So in fact…if your shipment were being stolen by thieves within Fedex, they would entice you to pay even more to ship it the next time with a non-existent service. And there was a good chance the very same Thieves would steal it again.

Talk about a "win-win" situation for Fedex and a "lose-lose" situation for their customers… this was it.

It's called R.I.C.O.

Racketeering Influenced Crime Organization.

The best part was… the more shipments Fedex employees stole… the more PHONY CSS service they sold.

I was secretly tape recording the conversation with agent Ackerman … and I asked him again, "was it fraud.?

And he responded, "**yes it was fraud, we clearly observed Fedex couriers violating the CSS contracts...In every CSS shipment we followed they violated military regulations.**"

I always knew the answer ...I wanted it on tape

And they had followed them all across America.

Ackerman went on to say that he had been told by Federal Prosecutors in Washington to contact the Justice Department in Wilmington, Delaware and to coordinate with them for prosecution. That the case was "solid."

I wondered at the time.

How could they do this with 'Classified Sensitive" Military Defense Equipment, Explosives and documents.

Fred Smith and his band of GREEDY THIEVES and TRAITORS are betraying our men and women in uniform and compromising their very safety along with the safety of Americans. Our soldiers depend on that equipment not only to protect America, but also for their own personal safety. And Fred Smith and Fedex couldn't care less.

We don't need "Terrorists"...We have Fred Smith.

I have obtained an "internal Fedex office memo" (yes Fred Smith knows I have it) that put the projected potential of a non existent ... fraudulent CSS service at $50,000,000.00 Dollars annually.

Fifty million dollars annually is a lot of money for a fraudulent service that doesn't even exist.

If the "fraud" had only involved private citizens and didn't endanger our soldiers or the safety and security of America's citizens it wouldn't be near as serious. But it did involve the military and the government and the safety our soldiers.

How would you like to get fifty million dollars a year for doing absolutely nothing?

On the next two pages is an actual Fedex interoffice memo detailing the amount of money Fedex was planning to "Steal" from the government with this Phoney Non- Existent Service.

When you look at this memo realize that Fedex treated these shipments like they were no more important than a sack of potatoes. Some of this equipment was for Air Force jet plane parts, Secret Programmed NATO computers going to Germany that were lost or stolen by Fedex employees. Electronics used by our military, both military and government documents and technology that were classified sensitive that I believe was from the CIA, FBI, NORAD and other government agencies.

Included were military explosives that were so dangerous that on the shipments were warnings that stated "in case of fire, firemen were to stay 1500 feet away." That's a quarter mile away, and yet I was ordered to park it on school grounds within fifty feet of an elementary school building while elementary school children were inside and or playing outside within feet of my truck.

Imagine (79) pounds of military explosives within fifty feet of little school children.

Thanks Fred Smith you ASSHOLE.

Fedex management knew they were supposed to have their trucks carrying these explosives "Placarded" with signs that warned that they were carrying explosives. But that if they "Placarded" those trucks Fedex would not be allowed to drive through neighborhoods, into shopping centers and onto school grounds.

And the "security, safety and surveillance" of these shipments was …"Non-Existent." There was NONE.

This is just one of Fred Smith's acts of "Conspiracy to Commit Felony Fraud Against the U.S. Government."

The memo covers two pages.

John IM, Turner   **INNER OFFICE MEMORANDUM**
    managing Director ….Government Sales

To: William P. Henrickson
cc: Henry Autry
Richard Metzler
Staff'
SUBJECT: CSS/High Value Potentials in the Government Market
The purpose of this note is to provide estimates of Actual
CSS and High Value Potential in the Government.

The potential in the Government for High Value is very
limited. I have no reason to believe that there is any
slgnlflcant amount of -High Value- (Gold - Diamonds. etc.)
traffic avallable.
Basic CSS Service is not only critical to our role in
the Government Marketplace but has exceptional potential.
Our basic CSS Product utilizing the Signature and Tally
Record (1907) has a minimum potential in the Defense Market
of 5000 ADP and in the Non-Defense Market of 12,000 ADP
(Intelligence Community).
**It is my best guess that we are looking at an annual op-
portunity of $50 million.**
NSA continues to evaluate Electronic CSS as a substitute
for the DD1907. this is a painfully slow process but we <u>have
General Stanford's support</u> and we are making progress.
In addltion to "Vanilla CSS" we have a requirement for a
<u>Dual driver- CSS. This service would allow us to expand our
movement of weapons and certain classes of explosives that
we currently move in limited quantities.</u>
This "dual driver" requirement is already in place everywhere except on the initial pick up and final delivery

leg. We are being met with positive feedback from Station management when we discuss the feaslblllty of doing this service and are advised that the break even on the extra body is (100) pcs/day. Bill, we Should do thls one now. We could easily charge a S200 surcharge for this service without any question.

    Secret level Clearance - presently the super hub is the only fleld location that is approved by the intelligence community for "**Secret**· Clearance". We are working wlth them on gaining clearance throughout our system to handle this classification of traffic.

<u>From:</u> **John Turner**
    That is fifty Million Annually for a service that doesn't even exist.

    And it puts America and our brave soldiers at risk.

    Many Times Fedex Drivers are high or wasted on Illegal Drugs and or Drug Addicts.

    That's great...Fedex management is trying to get the military to use "Fedex Courier Druggies" to move military weapons and explosives through our neighborhoods and into our schools.
    I have honestly seen this happen.

I later found out that while doing other deliveries I had unknowingly taken 79lbs. Of military explosives to a local elementary school while hundreds of school children were in the playground and within (50) feet of my truck.

    We don't need Terrorists to kill our children ...we have Fred Smith and

"Intelligence Community" ... does that sound like NSA   and CIA documents?

What kind or rotten traitor bastards would contract with the CIA and NSA and who knows what other government agencies to handle " secret documents that contain classified information that completely endangers the national security of our government, our soldiers and America?"

Fred Smith and his corrupt Fedex management created this "Fraudulent Service." They never intended for it to exist and they knew that many times the couriers responsible for the security of these documents were high on drugs while transporting them?

Fred Smith and his fellow criminals at Fedex are lucky they are NOT in China…they would be hanging from a rope.

And Good ole General Stanford, Commander of MTMC is going to help them STEAL $50 million dollars a year from the military and government.
Fred's SLAVE BOY. …He'd be on a rope too.

Fred Smith is a CRIMINAL ……… I can HONESTLY say that because he is.
Fred Smith is a TRAITOR Against America and our soldiers … I can HONESTLY say that too.

Of course it might make Fred Smith send someone to kill me at my home.

Something else I was doing while working in the Dover station was to check the computer in the Dover station in the morning. I was looking at it one day and realized all of the locally stolen shipments on it. Even CSS shipments were stolen. You cannot begin to imagine the thousands of shipments of cash, valuables and illegal drugs stolen from Fedex everyday. It would take a library to list all of them but here are a few so you get the idea.

"trace agent says she was desperate, the client was ready to eat her alive"

Missing :
ZIRCONIA SYNTHETIC DIAMONDS …1 PKG.
$314.00 CASH AND $750.00 CHECK
$2000.00 WATER PAINTING
ONE POUND OF (ahem) WHITE POWDER AND OPELS $8000.00
CASH FROM KENNY TO SUSAN

PLATINUM GOLD PLATES

Ohh and here's one to think about:
MISSING: RADIO ACTIVE SHIPMENT FOR "PATIENT ON OP-
ERATING TABLE" ... <u>PATIENT WAITING FOR SHIPMENT FOR
BRAIN SURGERY</u>.

**I'm not kidding ALL of those and many thousands more were stolen
and ...ahem and or missing.**

There are literally tens of thousands like this. If you think your Fedex shipment is safe and ... Think Again.

And that doesn't even include the tens of thousands of shipments
of illegal drugs that are completely stolen and never reported at all. Or
where there is only some of the drugs taken and the rest is then delivered
to the drug dealers.   The drug dealers accept the partially stolen shipments of drugs as a "tax" paid to Fedex couriers and members of Fedex
management for the safe delivery of their drugs.   That way the drugs
continue to flow and the police are not contacted.

Meanwhile,   agent Ackerman and his OSI team of investigators
were nearly finished the investigations and they were forwarding there
reports to Washington and Wilmington, Delaware for prosecution.
Ackerman told me he knew the investigation was a solid one and that
there should be criminal charges and prosecution against Fred Smith
and Fedex.   He also expressed a concern that Fred Smith had many
government contacts, senators and congressmen etc. that he had to be
concerned with.

Politicians are easily bought he said, and Fred Smith and Fedex has
a lot of money so it would be tough to get past Smith's "bought and paid
for corrupt politicians in Washington."

Maybe like (R) Sen. John McCain for one , who has certainly gotten a LOT of money from Fred Smith and Fedex.   Maybe just a little
"high paid whore"?

I put out hints that I might go to the newspapers when everything
was done. But I wasn't exactly sure if he caught them or was even concerned about them. I would later find out that he wanted the newspapers involved to offset the corrupt politicians Fred Smith had in his back

pocket (well maybe inside his front zipper of his pants) that would be in Washington trying to stop the prosecution.

Meanwhile Back at The Station ....
It was a rare time but Tim Keyser had not been messing with me for awhile. Actually he had been kind of quiet since our last go around in the District Headquarters.

I'm not sure if he had been told to back off or if possibly he had given up. For some reason I had felt pretty relaxed at the meeting and I'm not sure but thought it was possible all of his efforts at harassing and battling with me was putting a strain on him.

The investigation was pretty much wrapped up and had been forwarded to Federal Prosecutors in Washington and Wilmington for prosecution. So I began putting in applications for a job elsewhere.

Looking back, it should have been quite clear to me the day back in the Wilmington station when I first refused that first letter for "disruptive behavior" that my days at Fedex were numbered. I wasn't going to be that guy who let them stick it up my ass and smile about it and go on about my business. I wasn't raised that way. While I wasn't one to look for trouble, I wouldn't back down, and I wouldn't run away as so many others have. The druggies ruled Fedex and the honest guys never stood a chance. That might sound impossible, but you have to realize that many of the "Druggies and Drug dealers" were in management. From founder and CEO Fred Smith on down.

Stephanie Seberg realized that and ran away. I hope?

The fact that I survived there that long is just a testimonial that a man can withstand a great deal of adversity if his convictions are strong. And mine are and always have been. Just do what's right, do what you're supposed to do. It's simple and basic.

And everything else is in God's hands.

I owe an awful lot to my wife for her support in a difficult time. Our wedding song was by Kenny Rogers and it was "Lady, I'm your Knight in shining armor."

As corny as that sounds...I've always believed that.

I still do today. Fortunately for me, she believes that too.

There were a number of times I laid in bed at night and tried to figure out just why they did what they did. And why they wouldn't do what was right? Not only with me and many of their employees, but against the government and their customers and especially to the Blacks who worked so hard there, and even the military and our soldiers.

The simple truth is… as long as Fred Smith is in control of Fedex … Racism, Thefts, Fraud, Illegal Drugs and Lies will rule. Because that is all that he understands. He has no morals, no decency and no honesty and he never will.

And now it was time to leave Fedex. I've stopped the betrayal of our brave soldiers. Fred Smith and his corrupt Fedex plantation / corporation would not get to steal that billion plus dollars from the government he and his gang of criminals at Fedex had planned.

I did what I could. And I knew that when the story hit the papers I would be fired. So I would leave on my terms because I would make sure it did hit the papers.

But before I do
Fellow Couriers at Dover Station Put Manager in His Place
But before I turned in my resignation, there was going to be a Christmas party for the Dover station. It was going to be my last time with the couriers in Dover.

As I look back I realize that they were pretty good guys. They were pretty much just trying to do their jobs and keep them. They weren't into the Drugs and Stealing from Fedex shipments. Would they have went along with the CSS Fraud stuff? Yeah.

It was what Fedex management would make them do or they would lose their jobs. In Dover good paying jobs were hard to come by and they would have had little choice.

But to be honest, I don't know if I could have made it without them. They never did anything against me, and I think they had come to respect me and what I did everyday in my duties as a courier. All while putting up with Fedex management.

And I had come to respect them also.

And one thing was certain…after seeing what Tim Keyser put me through day after day, they absolutely had no love or respect for that Bastard. And they never will.

It was so sweet to see it at the company Christmas party. I was going to be leaving soon but they didn't know it at the time.

Our dates or spouses attended the party with us as it should be. The other couriers had gotten together on their own and presented me with an award. It was a wall plaque. On it was an award for courier with "Most Effort". It was really nice of them and I greatly appreciated it. It showed my wife and me that my co-workers actually did respect just how hard I had worked especially with what I had to put up with everyday.

Tim Keyser had brought a very young looking girl that many thought was maybe still in High School. While Tim was about thirty-ish. We never did get her real age but we were all really curious. Several people even commented that maybe she had to be "home by ten." Because she really did look too young to be at an adult party. I just figured that a woman around Tim's biological age would have been too mature for him.

At any rate the other couriers, without my knowledge, also presented Tim with an award too.

It was a T shirt…with the word "MAGGOT" stenciled on the front of it. It was what they thought of him and his treatment of me and even the rest of the station. And when he opened it in front of everybody … We all laughed "at Him". …Not with him.

Merry Christmas "ASSHOLE."

It totally ruined his night with his date , who I'm sure he was trying to impress. And it didn't happen. He was pissed the whole night and was the first to leave.

Maybe the young girl did have to be home by ten?

Time To Leave.

One of the companies I had put an application in with had called and wanted to interview me. It was a national company with good pay and benefits. After the interview they hired me and I told them I wanted to give Fedex two weeks notice which they respected. I couldn't have cared less about Fedex, but I wanted to leave in a formal way.

No hectic …fuck you I quit stuff.

I wanted to leave my way.

When I gave Tim Keyser a written two week notice… I think he almost shit himself. He was honestly shocked….surprised. I had withstood all of his harassment and bullying bullshit and survived it. It was he who grew weaker and he who wore down. He and the others in Fedex management had tried so many times in many different ways to intimidate me and put fear in me. They had used their positions of power and numbers to try to break the spirit of a common working man …and they had failed.

And I had only grown stronger. In the end the couriers in the station saw him for the little man he really was. They had come to realize that he was not even close to being a man or a real manager who leads by example and discipline but rather more like the "village idiot" who had no real focus and who switched ideas and procedures daily.

And they had come to respect me as I learned to respect them also.

When they heard about my two week notice of resignation they came up to me and expressed amazement that I had withstood the harassment and abuse that I did nearly everyday and had not lost it or screwed up.

And they wished me well. They had ALL expected me to last less than two months.

I couldn't tell them the true reason of why I was leaving, only that it was time.

And I left them to imagine why.

After I turned in my resignation I worked one week, and then management offered my second week's pay without coming in to work.   I kind of figured they would. Management was afraid that I would tell my customers about all of the bad things within Fedex. I thought about the offer and decided …sure why not.

Management was already too late.

I had already guessed management would do that and I had already told my customers what assholes Fedex management was. And to look in the newspapers because soon Fedex was going to be in them and it would involve a major scandal.

And I began to enjoy working again

Some time later agent Ackerman called me to ask how the new job was going. He seemed genuinely concerned and after we talked for awhile he said that he wanted to meet with me.

He said that he just wanted to bring me up to speed on the investigation and where it was going. But there was more to it than that.

He also said that his career would get a big boost after this major investigation and that it was in large part due to all the documentation I had collected and the information and help I had given him and the other investigators.

CHAPTER 3 FRAUD AGAINST THE MILITARY AND GOVERNMENT

After some more talk we decided to meet at a Denny's restaurant in New Castle. It was the same one that I had met Stephanie Seberg and her bodyguard at. In a way it seemed ironic that shortly after I met Stephanie there she fled from Fedex. Now I was meeting Agent Ackerman there and it was shortly after I resigned from Fedex.

Gotta be careful about those Denny's.

Ackerman brought another AFOSI agent with him to the meeting. They seemed to be good guys, just doing their jobs. As we talked I explained to them that even though I had a lot of bad experiences at Fedex, even if things had been great there.

I would have still gone to AFOSI.

Because regardless of the situation ... it was and always will be wrong to betray our soldiers and the American people. Our soldiers protect us with their lives everyday and to betray them was unforgivable.

One of the sickest and saddest things I had come to realize was that all across America, hundreds probably thousands of Fedex employees were knowingly and intentionally involved in the fraud against and betrayal of our soldiers and our country.

And they did it for just a few dollars. How sad.

It wasn't just wrong ...it was despicable.

How could they do that, I asked both agents?

They had no answer.

They were military...I'm sure it bothered them.

Ackerman did say that I would have to look at the person who ran Fedex. Because that man is the one who started the fraudulent CSS scam, smuggling illegal drugs into America, and all of the other evil that goes on within Fedex everyday.

He is the Evil One. That man is Fred Smith.

Ackerman informed me that the investigation was in the second level for prosecution in the justice department in Washington. He said that the report he got back was that the investigation was good and solid. And to expect the government to proceed with criminal prosecution against Fred Smith and Fedex soon. They had done their jobs well and were confident that the facts would support a Strong Criminal Prosecution. It was "Felony Fraud"...

But he also cautioned me again that Fred Smith had bought and owned a lot of powerful Senators and congressmen, and that they had to be careful they didn't try to water down the case. By putting improper influence on the prosecutors.

They casually let it be known that if the media got a hold of the story it would help with the prosecution a lot. The media stops a lot more crime than people think they said. It puts pressure on the government to do what's right. It's a spotlight that highlights crime and puts it out front for everyone to see. That stops a lot of "Politicians pressure" and helps the case get prosecuted to a higher degree.

They reminded me that I had all of the paperwork that would be needed to get the newspapers to do a story. What they didn't know was that I also had the secret tape recordings too.

Then Agent Ackerman again expressed concern for my safety again and to be careful of Fred Smith.

"Remember … Fred Smith is a Drug Smuggler and dangerous," he said …"be careful."

He is going to be very mad at you …and he might come after you. You have stopped him from stealing hundreds of millions of dollars and will be responsible for Fedex losing hundreds of government and military contracts.

Fred Smith will never forget that. He may send someone to harm you physically.

I was somewhat surprised at how concerned Agent Ackerman was for my safety. It was the second time he had expressed that concern to me. The first time I didn't give it too much thought. But now I wonder what other information had he found out about Fred Smith during the "fraud and the drug smuggling" investigation that would cause him so much concern for my safety?

It wasn't Smiths money or his attorneys he was concerned about. It was my physical safety and my life he was worried about.

He was in AFOSI agent, a government criminal investigator so he had access to federal information data bases and resources that civilians don't. He met in Washington in monthly meetings with DEA, FBI, NSA, Federal Marshalls, the Justice Department and a number of other government law enforcement agencies where they shared information about criminals in on going investigations. About ten government enforcement agencies he had said. Had he found out something more in one of those meetings about Fred Smith that made him realize just how dangerous Smith was? Something specific that he couldn't tell me about but could only warn me?

How much danger was I in?

His previous warnings to me had been only the normal expected warnings of caution a law enforcement agent would give to an informant or witness when the investigations had just began.   Now they were a much more very deep and serious concern for my safety, by now he had done a LOT of research on Fred Smith through government data banks and other government agencies.   Had spoken with other government agents and had gained more evidence and information about Smith and his criminal activities and connections.

What had he found out about Fred Smith that worried him so much?   And what made him so concerned for my safety now?   He was sincerely worried for me.

Had Fred Smith been involved in the murder of other men?   Had the founder and CEO of Fedex murdered others before?

What more had he found that he couldn't tell me?

I told him I would be careful.   And I had every intention to be so. But at that time I didn't really think Fred Smith would actually come after me to cause me physical harm or death.

He has too much to lose…I thought.

But Then…

Sometimes when you re-visit events you remember or see things that you didn't see clearly or understand fully the first time.   I guess it's like watching a movie the second time, when you realize more and even different events in that movie the second time around that you missed the first time.   It's why we many times re-read important documents.

I realize now… that he wanted to meet with me not really to see how I was doing or to bring me up to speed on the investigation.   He could have done that over the phone.

He was seriously concerned for my life.   He knew then and I didn't… that I was in more serious danger than I had realized.

I had gone to and worked undercover with , and given evidence to Federal Criminal Investigators that might and should have put Fred Smith and others within Fedex management in Jail for many years. Would certainly cost him hundreds of military contracts and a billion dollars or more.   He was not just a "white collar criminal" committing white collar crimes.   He was much more and far more dangerous.   He was a "HARDENED Criminal."

It was only a short time after drug smuggler and FBI informant Barry Seal was murdered by drug smugglers in the Medellin Drug Cartel.

Fred Smith was a drug smuggler too. And he and Barry Seal were both located in Arkansas. Was there a "connection"?

Both Barry Seal and Fred Smith were based in Arkansas. Had they worked together in drug smuggling operations? Was Fred Smith connected to that same "Medellin Drug Cartel" that Barry Seal was? I don't know.

Had Fred Smith done business with them? Maybe?

Was Fred Smith…the CEO of the Fedex corporation involved in the Death of Barry Seal?

Either way… there was something that agent Ackerman learned about Fred Smith in his investigation with the other Federal investigators in Washington. There was more to Smith's CSS fraud and his drug smuggling activities that gave him added concern and fear … for my safety and my life. You could see it in his eyes because he looked me directly in the eyes while warning me to be careful. He was afraid for Me.

He wanted me to take these warning seriously VERY SERIOUSLY.

Was he thinking that I would probably be dead soon too?

I can't speak for others in law enforcement. But I think it would be difficult for most investigators, if they had a regular civilian with a family, come to them with evidence against a dangerous criminal. To work with that person undercover against this criminal …knowing for certain that when the investigation was finished that individual would be exposed as the man who started the investigation and provided the evidence and the information that stopped the criminal. Maybe put him in jail.

I was going to be exposed and I knew that when I first contacted AFOSI. I had done serious damage to a criminal and drug smuggler. But when you're just a regular working class guy you can't always see the end of the road. You don't always realize the possible ramifications of just "doing what is right."

I didn't actually think at that time …that Fred Smith would send someone to Murder me at my home.

Meanwhile ….

Things were going well with my new job. Management seemed okay and the guys were just regular guys. Most had a wife, a home and kids. The American dream. There were no drugs or thefts in the work place, and no talk about drugs by the workers.

But I had more work to do. I knew what Agent Ackerman wanted me to do. I knew that it was important that I did it. Nothing had been in the news about Fedex and it's fraudulent C.S.S. service. That only indicated to me that the investigation was being slowed by corrupt politicians in Washington. They were trying to get Fedex off the hook. It's sad to really know just how easily a senator or congressman can be bought. This is a Great Country with a Lot of Great People in it. It's sad that we have so much corruption in Washington. There's soldiers out there everyday giving up their lives to protect this great country and our people. And there's elected politicians that will compromise America's security and the safety of the American people for a pocket full of money.

Sad…

I knew it was time to hit the newspapers

Through research I determined that the Philadelphia Inquirer would be a good bet to do the story. And it was.

I called a reporter at the Inquirer and talked to him for awhile. I'm sure he had some doubts that a major company would commit fraud against the military, the government and American citizens and businesses. And how could I even begin to prove what I was saying so that he could write a story about it even if it were true?

For a newspaper or any major media source to actually put out in writing something so damming against a major nationwide corporation there must be overwhelming evidence to prove it. I explained to him that I did in fact have all of the evidence to prove it including tape recordings of a government investigator stating it was fraud. He asked a lot of questions over the phone and I answered them to the best of my knowledge. At the conclusion of the call he asked me to come into his office and bring some of the documents so that I could better explain the fraud.

His name was Mack Reed and his office was in downtown Wilmington in Delaware. His office was a branch office of the big and powerful Philadelphia Inquirer located in Philadelphia. And he had some time to think about the fraud by Fedex and the possible headlines of reporting such a major story. I'm also sure that between our phone conversation and our meeting he had talked with his bosses about it. And that he was told to examine the information very closely.

I had taken along some CSS DD1907 tally sheets and some delivery records so that I could lay out and explain just how the fraud worked. <u>Even copies of the military contracts</u> <u>Agent Ackerman had given me</u>.

It took a few minutes of explaining just exactly how the CSS "Constant Surveillance Service" was supposed to work according to the government contracts. And then I showed him the DD 1907 tally sheets with the delivery records and he got it. I then showed him military contracts that detailed the regulations for handling classified military equipment shipments. Agent Ackerman had given them to me during the investigation. And I realized at that time why he had given them to me. I worked with him and other OSI agents for some time. I'm sure he had thoughts "maybe hopes" that I would some day be sitting in the office of a major newspaper with their reporter showing him the contracts and other documents and explaining just how the fraud worked. I don't know to this day if agent Ackerman knew he and other agents were being secretly tape recorded. But it was important at that time to secretly record exactly what was said about Fedex's fraud by a government investigator.

It was actually funny to see Mack Reed's face as he realized I was telling the truth and that I could prove it. He got a "I can't believe Fedex would do this kind of thing," look on his face. But I had all the documents, even the tapes with OSI agents telling me it was fraud, to back me up and prove it.

I had made many copies of these documents and I left him with some of them. Mack and some of the top Philadelphia Inquirer editors went over the military contract regulations and the DD 1907's for a day or two then he called Helen Wilson at her home.

Helen was the courier who had trained me in Dover and showed me how to commit fraud against our military ...she told me I had to or else I would be fired. It was through her that I learned that hundreds probably thousands of Fedex employees all across America were also doing it. It was nationwide and company wide fraud and betrayal against our soldiers by a very un-patriotic bunch of Fedex employees. They didn't care about the safety or lives of our brave soldiers one bit.

I later found out through lawyers that by Federal law, they were actually criminals guilty of Felony Fraud against the United States too. Every one of them, and they knew exactly what they were doing. He also explained that Fred Smith and his Fedex plantation / corporation were a R. I.C.O. organization. R.I.C.O. means Racketeering Influenced Corrupt Organization. Boy that is Fedex to a "T".

Actually in the same group as the Mafia, Drug Cartels etc.

To be honest I would have thought that Helen would have lied and told him that the CSS shipments were always handled properly. But as I said earlier, Helen was stupid. Or possibly ...she was high at the time or maybe she just didn't care.

Because when Mack Reed called Helen to question her about the handling of CSS shipments she told him that yes the CSS classified military shipments were left alone and unguarded many times when she went into the Blue Hen Mall and many other places while she did deliveries or just plain went shopping for herself. She said that everybody handled them like that all across America.

Mack Reed must have realized he had a big story because he made a special appointment with a top editor at The Philadelphia Inquirer. The Inquirer did some preliminary investigations on their own. Then the big guys held meetings with their legal staff to go over legal aspects of the story. It took a few days but Mack Reed assured me that they were in fact going to do the story.

Fedex Finds Out About the AFOSI Investigation

They found out (probably because they were contacted by the Philadelphia Inquirer) that AFOSI was charging them with FRAUD.

And now I had gone to the Philadelphia Inquirer.

So Fred Smith ... had one of Fedex's big shot corporate (asshole) lawyers call my little small town lawyer.

Fred's Fedex lawyer told my lawyer to, "tell Gary Rullo to keep his mouth shut about the "CSS Fraud stuff" or they would take away our home and put my family out in the streets forever and he will never ever be able to work again."

I look back now and realize that may have been a threat to kill me. Read all of the book and you'll know why.

My lawyer called my wife and asked for both of us to come in to his office. When we arrived at his office he sat us both down and told us what Fedex's lawyers had said. He told us that we had to be careful, that Fedex had a lot of money and power. And that they could make it very bad for us and our family. He said something like, "these are not nice people, they will do whatever it takes to shut you up."

I wonder now if he meant that Fred Smith would try to murder me at my home?

Before he finished speaking with us my wife began crying and got hysterical. She said that she didn't want to lose our home.

She said to him, "these bastards have been screwing my husband for years. They put him thru hell and made our life miserable. All he wants is to tell the truth and do what's right, and these bastards are going to take our home away?

She was hysterical now and scared. She is just a regular housewife and mother, A PTA mom, she didn't know about the CSS stuff or anything about it. And she was afraid we would lose our home. She was afraid for our family. Afraid of what Fred Smith and Fedex would do to me and our family for going to the government and telling them the truth about the fraud. I felt so bad for her, here I was trying to do the right thing and it might wind up costing my family our home and more.

As I held her and tried to reassure her that everything would be okay, that somehow we would survive ... I began to get angry, very angry. So many times they had forced me to put up with their shit. They knew I had two small kids and mortgage payments to make no matter what. And they held that over me. I thought about the snobbish attitude that was so common among Fedex management and how they loved to throw their weight around. Fairness, honesty and decency was never in their mentality. Only Power and Greed.

I thought to myself, this is still America. These bastards will have to kill me to shut me up. I will go to every state in America if I have to ... to tell The Truth.

So Fuck Fred Smith and Fuck Fedex.

As for Fred Smith and his Asshole Lawyers...I pray to God that their children and their grandchildren...ALL BURN IN HELL FOR ETERNITY.

Yeah I don't like those Bastards one dammed bit.

I then told my lawyer that I had many documents to prove the fraud, and that I had tape recorded the conversations with the AFOSI investigators and that on the tapes AFOSI investigators had stated that Fedex was committing Fraud against the military. And not to worry because I had a number of copies that were not even in my home. So even with a search warrant they could never get even one third of them. He again cautioned me and repeated that I had to be careful as Fred Smith was a bad person and he might try to hurt me in a number of ways.

Did he mean that Fred Smith was dangerous and might send someone to kill me?

What had Smith's lawyers actually said to him? Was there more threats made than to just put my family out in the streets? What was said to mean that "I would never work again? Were threats of physical harm insinuated ?

When we left my lawyers office my wife was still upset and crying hysterically. She had no idea what I knew from AFOSI nor what I had in documents and tapes. I knew she was shaken, she had every reason to be. We're just regular working class people. We work hard, try to do the right things and try to take care of our family. Just trying to live a normal life. And through events that happened within Fedex we were now caught up in a situation that I'm not sure we totally understood.

I had grown up as a "New Castle Boy" we were never known to be that smart. But we were known to NEVER run away from a fight. It didn't matter how many or how big they were, we never ran away. If you ran away ... you were branded a "coward" forever. If you stayed and fought at least you were respected as a "fighter who had heart and character." The bruises and the wounds would heal but being branded as a coward would stick with you a lifetime.

If you look back in history you will see that the early colonialist who were mostly just farmers, shop keepers and tradesmen fought against the most powerful army and navy at that time. They were out gunned. out numbered and had a serious lack of military knowledge. And they suffered a lot. But they did have "heart and character" and they continued on until they were victorious.

That story is true throughout history.

I told her to have faith in me and also that I had to see Mack Reed a reporter for the Philadelphia Inquirer.

Mack Reed's office was in Wilmington so it was a short walk to his office. The Inquirer's investigators had been working hard on the story and through their investigation and contacts they had come to know for certain that everything I had told them was true.

As we walked into his office Mack Reed got up from his desk with a big smile on his face. He shook my hand and I introduced him to my wife.

He said, "Gary, I have to be honest with you, when you first came into my office I thought you might be exaggerating somewhat but everything that you told me is right on the money. We have done quite a bit of investigating on our own. And everything that you said about the CSS Service being Fraud is true."

I looked at my wife and for the first time in awhile she had a smile on her face. I had never told her about the particulars of the CSS stuff. Only that I was working with government investigators. So she never had any real knowledge about CSS and had never been involved with it in any way. But she loved me and believed in my judgment and my honesty. So she had always stood by my side.

"So, is there going to be a story," I asked.

Mack never even hesitated as he replied that "yes there most certainly will be a story. It will take a few weeks to finish and schedule, but yes there will be a story for sure."

I told him that we had just left our lawyers office and what my attorney had told us about Fred Smith's threats to put our family out in the streets forever because I had gone to government investigators and told the truth about their fraud. I told him that everything I had said about the CSS service being fraud was 100% true and I wasn't going to back down.

Mack's response was that the top editors and the legal department of the Philadelphia Inquirer already knew that everything I had told him was true, and that they were going forward with the story. So if Fedex was going to sue me, they would have to go thru the Inquirer first. And that the Inquirer also had big lawyers.

It was a big relief to have someone stand behind me for a change. It was a good feeling to have someone big stand up to Fred Smith and Fedex and say... what's you're doing is wrong and illegal and your not going to get away with it.

Mack told us to have faith and that things would be okay, that the Inquirer would not back down from doing the story.

I cannot print the exact newspaper article because of copy write laws

However…the story went like this…

Last July 18, Fedex charged the government for Constant Surveil-lance Service for shipping classified military computers to the Air Force Base in Dover, Delaware. Once in Dover, a military cargo plane was to airlift the computers to Germany for use in developing a **Classified Secret NATO Weapons Systems**. Records show, that while in Fedex custody surveillance was anything but constant.

Two of the eleven packages were lost for two days and company re-cords show that the rest were left temporarily in an unguarded truck … in violation of defense Department regulations.

The Air Force is now investigating allegations that the fraudulent service which was also available to the public and is estimated to bring Fedex $ 8.5 million a year in defense contracts alone is a FRAUD.

Dangerous and sensitive military cargo sent through Fedex's CSS service is sometimes left unattended and is treated no better than com-mon freight . In violation of government regulations according to Fedex documents, former Fedex couriers and CSS customers.

Fedex officials deny the allegations but have declined requests to be interviewed.

"Constant Surveillance means exactly that," said Jim Crawford, branch manager for the General Services Administration (GSA). It does not mean you leave it somewhere and just walk off and leave it un-attended."

Fedex's response

"Our only response is that Fedex has not been notified by the U.S. Air Force of an investigation and should the Air Force have a concern, we would expect them to contact us directly." Said Fedex Spokeswoman Shirlee Finley.

My Response to Fedex

Of course the U.S. Air Force didn't notify you. They were in-vestigating you undercover so you couldn't hide your criminal activ-ity. You IDIOTS. Since when does a law enforcement agency notify criminals that they are investigating them as they continue to commit their crimes.

The Inquirer story continues…

a) The NATO computers arrived with only one (1) signature on the CSS 1907 tally sheet. (which would mean that the courier who made the original pickup in the U.S. must have delivered it in person in Germany too).

b) Part of the NATO defense computer system was lost. It was a specifically programmed system designed to work with NATO's secret defense operations that was in place.

c) Paul Goodman, a formal Fedex courier who also serviced the Dover Air Force Base, said the CSS service was a "JOKE". No Paul it was FRAUD…

d) Helen Wilson, another Fedex courier who serviced the Dover Air Force Base said she was never told to drive the CSS shipment back to the station from the shipper. And that she sometimes took hour long breaks away from the truck. "It's handled like a 'normal package' in the way we drive around with it," she said.

e) One time (79) pounds of a military explosives shipment were left unguarded in the Fedex depot for a whole weekend. The depot had no burglar alarm or fire alarm, no containment cages for the CSS freight as required by the Defense Department and only a plate glass front door with a simple three button combination lock.

That same (79) pounds of explosives were driven into a elementary school in session with hundreds of small children and parked right at the front door by the main office.

* The driver was ordered to do this by Fedex management or be fired.

There were many more violations listed in the news account and references to statements by members of congress calling for a broader investigation of the fraudulent CSS service. Obviously those were ones that Fred Smith hadn't yet given any money too.

Oh Yes…Remember Julio Columbo District Director for Fedex

If you remember from earlier in the book. When I had been given a warning for being late for the first time in four years. And Julio upheld the warning even after I showed him the company policy that stated a warning was only to be given out after an employee had been late three (3) times in a six month period. Remember how I talked him into letting me sit in his chair at his big desk and told him a phone call would be coming to him from Fred Smith?

Well shortly after the Philadelphia Inquirer broke the story on the CSS Fraud I gave Julio Columbo a phone call. It may or may not have been the thing to do, but I had to know if that call came up from Fred Smith as I said it would.

When I called the District Office, I asked to speak to "Julio Columbo". There was a few minutes before he finally came to the phone. I figured they were hooking up a tape recorder to record what I was going to say. I had hooked up mine before I called too. Just so those bastards couldn't lie about what I said to him.

When he finally came on the phone, God it was so funny. His voice was so shaky, he sounded very nervous and he seemed like a little puppy that had been bitten by a big bad wolf.

"What, what what … do you want Gary," he asked. He sounded so pathetic….none of that "Fedex confidence, obnoxious New York bullshit" was in his voice now.

Just a scared nervous little voice …like a scared Condemned man."

"Well Julio, did you get that call," I asked him.

"What…what…what is it you want," was all he could say with a very, "scared and nervous little voice".

Yes it was obvious that Julio did get that call from Memphis. Fred Smith must have reamed his Greasy Ass big enough to drive an eighteen wheel tractor trailer thru it without even touching the sides.

Because he certainly sounded like Fred had…Julio sounded just like a "scared little man"

I hung up the phone. How does it feel you asshole I wondered.

Did he lose his job? I have no idea.

And I thought, of how many times Julio played a big tough guy with some little hard working courier who was doing his or her job as best they could? Only to be treated like shit by this big greasy New York asshole in his $400.00 suit.

Yeah Julio, you probably enjoyed sticking it up enough couriers asses…how did it feel when Fred Smith drove it up yours? Was he gentle with you or did he drive it up yours like a 100 mph Mack Truck

Were you on ALL fours when he stuck it UP YOUR ASS Julio?

Ha Ha Julio you asshole…. here I was just a little courier, a common family man. Nothing special. And I called that shot months before it happened …exactly the way it happened.

I bet you don't have that Big Obnoxious Smirk on your face now do you?

Is your asshole still BLEEDING Julio?

You Big Greasy Obnoxious New York Slime Bag.

Burn in hell you Bastard.

After the story broke I received a lot of phone calls at home about it. They came at all hours of the day and night.

One came from a Fedex employee who worked at the Philadelphia airport ramp. **He told me that 'after the newspaper story broke' Fedex management came in and held a class at the ramp to explain what a CSS shipment was.**

He said that he had never even heard of the word CSS and neither had anyone else at the ramp. He said that Fedex management told them to keep quiet about it and NOT to talk about the CSS class to anyone.

That should prove to anyone...it was FRAUD. Not sloppy handling. But an Intentional Planned " Conspiracy To Commit Fraud" against the Military and the U.S. Government.

He also told me about all the drugs 'white powder etc.' at the ramp, how everybody there was doing them. Isn't it great to have a huge jet plane being loaded by a bunch of drug addicts wasted on drugs...I wonder what the pilots were doing?

He told me that the guys who bought and used it at the ramp were treated better by Fedex management than the few who didn't. (I swear he honestly told me that)

I told him to just do like I did when I worked there...'just do your job and try not to get involved or else he might get hurt or lose his job," which he said he needed.

<u>Been there done that.</u>

There were many other calls (many I recorded) from people who said they were Fedex couriers. They said that they had always known that the CSS service was a way to get people to pay extra money for a service that never existed. They said it was a Ripoff.

Some said to be careful because Fred Smith would send someone after me.

Then there were some callers who didn't want to discuss the particulars of CSS service. They called just to tell me that Fred Smith and Fedex would give me what I deserved, "for ratting on Fedex".

Some callers called to complain that because I had exposed the phony CSS service it was going to hurt their profit sharing and they were upset about that. That was the same reason I had been given by 'Colin Baines' when he told me to cheat the customers all I could because once Fred Smith's pockets were full whatever fell out would come to us in the way of profit sharing.

I would ask those callers, "so you're saying it's okay to commit fraud against your country and betray our soldiers and our country for a few dollars in profit sharing?" And they mostly responded something like "Fuck You asshole."

A number of them did say it was okay to betray their country for money. WOW !!! They will do well at Fedex.

Some of the calls were just pure harassment calls of hanging up the phone when I or my wife answered it, and sometimes a 'fuck you', or a 'asshole', along with a number of 'You're Gonna Die' threats followed by a quick hang up.

Yep these were the kind of Fedex people I knew. Rather than being honest and saying, "yes we were screwing the hell out of our military and America and we were wrong to do it." They instead chose to harass the only man in the whole company who was honest enough to stand up and tell the truth.

They reminded me of the German Nazi's who after the war was over and they were being tried for killing millions of Jews in the gas chambers ... they cried and pleaded that they were only following orders. Like they didn't know it was wrong. And for all I know that is why Fedex hires and promotes only certain people with certain character traits. White people who mostly know how to think of and treat Blacks like they are less than human, people who will cheat customers for all they can get, and betray America for just a few dollars, people who think nothing of lying or telling lies to get whatever Fedex management wants. You want to work for FedEx ... well how low can your morals go? If they go low enough, well maybe they will hire you. If you lie well and will cheat your customers...you'll make even more.

Some of the calls came from people who said they worked at Fedex in Memphis which is Fedex's headquarters. They said that they knew Fred Smith and they knew he would send someone to get me. That Fred Smith would not let me get away with ratting on him, exposing him and costing him money.

<u>That my days were numbered</u>.   They may still be?

Some of the threatening callers said that I didn't know Fred Smith and what he was capable of. That one morning I would start my car and I'd be blown to pieces. "It's coming," they said, "you wont know where or when but it's coming … Fred won't let you go."

Well Drug Smugglers and Serious Criminals do kill a lot of people in retaliation …

I had a wife and kids, it does make you think …a lot.   For a long time every morning when I started my car I stood outside and turned the key to start it. I can still remember thinking that I was glad I didn't have a stick shift. Every morning without fail for some time I started my wife's car the same way. She sometimes drove the kids in the mornings and I was afraid they might mistake her car for mine.

Sometimes doing what's right can put you thru a lot more hell than you would ever imagine. Come at me straight up…like a man.   I'm afraid of no one. Threaten or harm my family   Don't let me catch you.

One man who called, said that I didn't have any idea what Fred Smith was involved in … and that I was in serious danger. He said he wasn't calling to harass me, but to warn me and not to hang up on him. He said not to think of Fred Smith as a regular businessman<u>, but to understand that Fred Smith was a dangerous person and he had done bad things to people who had done a lot less against him than I had.</u>

When I asked him why he thought Fred was dangerous, he said …. <u>"I'm just trying to warn you to help you, I've been here a long time."</u> He went on to say how he understood why I did what I did and that he didn't think it (the phony CSS) was right either.   But Fred's done a whole lot worse things than the CSS stuff.

Fred's not the man most people think he is, or the man he pretends to be,

<u>"Fred's involved in things you don't know about"</u>.

And very few people do… he said.

I felt like he wanted to tell me more but couldn't. So I asked him straight out,   "are you trying to tell me Fred is involved in smuggling illegal drugs? Because I was already told that by others." His only reply to that question was,   "I'm in management here (Memphis headquarters) and I have family too and we're not going to talk about that, I just called to warn you that…you don't know who you're dealing with here, be careful."

Of all the calls I had received and all the warnings and threats, somehow I knew that this one was real and too dammed serious. The man sounded like he was late forties maybe late fifties, he sounded like a good man, a sincere man, and he was very calm. He didn't sound like a man who talked small talk or dumb talk. He sounded like he had even been hesitant to even call me, but that maybe he thought he should because it was the right thing to do. He probably knew I was in way over my head.

I had pretty much been concerned about Fred Smith coming at me with his army of asshole lawyers with lawsuits etc., Maybe my concerns were looking in the wrong direction?

<u>Maybe the man did know what he was talking about, and maybe he was right</u>.

<u>Maybe Fred Smith was going to send someone to kill me?</u>

The fact is … four different people in four different areas who don't have any connection to each other and don't know one another, had all told me that Fred Smith was involved in smuggling illegal drugs into the U.S. Surely all four can't be wrong or lying. Two were federal investigators and two were in Fedex management. Plus, I found out later, the DEA had posted a picture of one of Fred Smith's cargo planes flying illegal drugs from Mexico to Boston. The plane was over a map and DEA had stamped the words "illegal drugs" on the fuselage of the plane. I've seen flight patterns of Fedex cargo planes and none ever showed one flying from Mexico to anywhere else in America. ALL cargo was routed directly to Memphis first, then sorted … then flown to the destination city air port. That was exactly what agent Ackerman was asking me about in Dover.

And we all have heard and read many times about drug smugglers killing people.

After the story broke I had an interesting conversation with Tony Giamboy who was a former courier for Fedex. He had just been fired from Fedex for stealing from City Bank in New Castle, DE. He was not a close friend just a co-worker when I worked at the Wilmington station.

Evidently the couriers and or management were hitting City Bank pretty hard and they realized they had to fire someone to at least slow it down.

Tony said, "they (Fedex) really railroaded me, they set me up like a bowling pin. They put an ultra violet dye all over my records and did an illegal search and seizure at my house."

According to Tony they upset his wife so bad that she got hysterical and he had to take her to the hospital for treatment.

He said that a Fedex investigator by the name of Hubble "shook" his hand and put the ultra violet dye on his hand. Then the Hubble guy put Tony's right hand under the light and there were little specks of dust on it, but none on his left hand. Tony said the Hubble guy told Tony there was dye on his face but he looked in the mirror with the light and couldn't see any. Tony said there was a an awful lot of thefts in the Wilmington station and they needed a fall guy. (Flash back to Julio Columbo and Stephanie Seberg)

Tony said that Fedex investigators knocked on his door and said to his wife, "do you mind if we come in?" …as they walked right thru the door. His wife said she guessed not … since they were already inside his house.

Tony said the investigators then 'ran upstairs to his bedroom' and began looking for his Fedex uniform he had worn that day.

They checked it and there was no dye on the uniform Tony said.

Tony said he had talked to an attorney and the attorney said there was little he could do.

Well, that was Tony's version of how he got fired.

* During the conversation I asked Tony if he had handled CSS shipments and he said he had numerous times and they were never handled properly, they were just another way of many that Fred Smith stole money from his customers. (Yes … I recorded that conversation too)

Another former courier of Fedex I talked to was Paul Oberg. Paul had been a courier at the Wilmington station for eight years and had left shortly before I was hired there. He told me several things that I found very interesting.

After I had been attacked in the Wilmington station and had gotten a letter for 'disruptive behavior' I filed a GFT letter at the station and gave it to my manager . Fedex touts the GFT program as a 'Guaranteed Fair

Treatment" program they have, but in truth it is a Fedex program that Guarantees they Fuck you Treatment' program.

Al Ferrier, my manager at the time, told me he tore it up and threw it in the trash can. So I wrote up another GFT letter and sent it directly to Liberty District Director Dave Bronzack who was the district director at that time, and asked for an investigation.

One of the things I put in the letter was that Mike Mitchell had a serious drinking problem and that I had seen him drunk in the station numerous times. Dave Bronzack said that he had never heard anything about Mike's drinking problem. And had no idea what I was talking about.

Yet in my conversation with Paul Oberg, Paul said that he had filed similar charges against Mike Mitchell when he was a courier and Dave Bronzack was at District Headquarters then too, and he was well aware of previous charges that Mike was an alcoholic and was always drunk on the job. Paul said that he even went all the way to the Regional Director Dave Spina about Mike's drunkenness and Spina told him he would look into it but never did anything to Mike or even admitted that Mike had a drinking problem.

Why?

Because Mike Mitchell had an ACE in the hole.

Mike was untouchable.

He at least had inside knowledge of Fred Smith's drug smuggling operation . Whether or not he was ever involved with it in any way I will never know, but he knew about it.

NO ONE could touch Mike Mitchell...he could do whatever he wanted...and he did.

Paul also said that if he would have pressed the issue of illegal drugs in the station they wouldn't have done anything either, because they would have taken out more than half the station including management. They actually would have taken out more than three quarters of the station. He said that management including Jerry Salomone and Al Ferrier were always using and dealing drugs everyday. And he saw drug use and thefts nearly everyday. And upper management knew it but didn't care.

Paul told me what I had told Wilmington station manager Stephanie Seberg when she requested bodyguard protection to keep her alive.

He said that, "if you messed with all the druggies in the station ... you're life wouldn't be worth a plugged nickel." They're ALL fucked up druggies, drug dealers and thieves and they'll come after you and you may not live to see your kids grown. He said they wouldn't stop at roughing you up, they would kill you and worry about it later.

Thank God Stephanie Seberg was smart enough to run away. Or did she?

Paul seemed like a good man who obviously didn't fit in with the Druggies and Thieves at Fedex. <u>Still I secretly tape recorded our conversation...just for the records.</u>

What he was telling me was nothing new to me. I had seen and known of so many thefts of valuables and drugs at Fedex. It would be hard for the average person or customer out there to imagine. And it wasn't just the couriers and cargo handlers, it was also Fedex management.

The word at Fedex was ..."you can do you're best shopping on the conveyor belts at Fedex". Gold, Jewelry, TV's Computers, Furs, Money, Drugs

ALL FREE AT FEDEX.

My managers were always trying to get me to bring them packages containing drugs and or other valuables. And not only in the stations but also at the airport ramp. It wasn't just those stations in Pennsylvania, New Jersey, New York, Atlanta, it was everywhere from coast to coast. You name a state and Fedex has tons of thefts there. You could buy anything at half price or less that was stolen from customers shipments. And you could sell it like that too because the couriers were always buying or selling.

There was a time when I was on vacation at a beach in New Jersey. I was sitting with my wife and kids on the beach. After a while a guy and his family came over near us and spread out a blanket. At first I didn't pay any attention to them but then I realized he was wearing a Fedex hat. After awhile I got up and went over to ask if he worked at Fedex and he replied that he did in New York. I believe he said he was involved with distributing supplies to the stations etc.

As we began to talk about Fedex he started talking about all of the thefts in the New York stations. And how it was impossible to stop. He told me that the furriers and jewelers were always the hardest hit. And that it was so bad that they (the furriers and jewelers) were having a hard time getting their valuables insured with their insurance companies because of so many thefts by the Fedex couriers. And the computers stores were the next best targets by the couriers. He said it was so unbelievably rampant and that the Fedex couriers were making huge amounts of money from all the thefts. You just can't stop Fedex couriers from stealing he said.

I couldn't have agreed with him more.

Time to Turn To ABC 20-20 and Chris Harper...

I had tried to find out if the Military Traffic Management Command (MTMC) had stopped Fedex from handling CSS shipments yet. I had figured the newspaper stories would bring their crimes to an end. But I couldn't get any up to date information either way. Some of the callers who were Fedex employees that said I had done the right thing suggested that I also take the story to ABC's 20-20. That Fred Smith owned so many politicians that only a major national TV show like 20-20 would guarantee the end of the CSS fraud.

Bear With Me On This... it does have Closure

I may have found out how Fred Smith got away with all the fraud for so long... how it was "allowed to continue."

Back in Colonial times when slavery was common and the slave boats traveled to Africa to get their slaves they sometimes offered African natives "potato cakes and sweets to get them to come on board their SLAVE ships. Then they would put them in slave quarters and brought them back to America. Upon arrival they sold them to work on the slave plantations in the south. Like the cotton slave plantation Fred Smith grew up on.

Well the Military Traffic Management Command had a General John Stanford. A Black African American" in charge at MTMC. Fred Smith and his gang of criminals knew that General Stanford was the top man at MTMC and that he was the man who oversaw ALL military shipments which included "Classified Sensitive Shipments" that Fedex had contracted to handle. Fred knew that Stanford would quickly see that there was NO Constant Surveillance Service (CSS). It was very obvious if you just looked at the 1907 Talley Records. General Stanford had seen and read the contract regulations. He was a veteran logistics army officer. It was his responsibility to make certain ALL paperwork was filled out properly. It was his responsibility to make certain that ALL military shipments were handled properly and correctly and transported within military specifications and regulations. And he certainly had sufficient officers below checking also. It had to be known.

So Fred Smith invited Stanford down to his Slave Plantation and offered him "barbecued Chicken" and who knows what other "gifts" and how much money they gave him. Maybe teased him with an offer of a position at Fedex when he retired, maybe just money?

And they got Stanford on board of "Fedex's slave ship." All at Fred Smith's southern slave plantation. Just like the good ole plantation days of old. What better place to lure just one more Black African into white servitude than at Fred Smith's "Fedex Plantation"

As one member of Fedex management told me "'<u>Fred Smith was raised on a cotton slave plantation ...he knows how to handle Blacks</u>'. Well I guess he did.

Because he had General Stanford all the way.

Probably made Stanford say.. "Yesum Master"

To All Blacks...Always REMEMBER, when you are talking to Fred Smith..."He is talking to a Nigger."

Never Forget That. Don't fool "yourself."

The only questions are ...After Smith dismissed Stanford and sent him back home to his job at MTMC did they make jokes about him? Did they say ...Blacks are easy to buy? Did they joke and say something like, "a white southern plantation owner just bought another Nigger.... Probably.

"Long live the confederacy"? Did Smith wave his confederate slave flag?

My guest is that they did.

Because there is no doubt that Fred Smith and Fedex owned General John Stanford of the United States Army. They made him into their very own "Fedex Slave" who did exactly what they told him to do. They made him a "<u>TRAITOR</u>" against his very own military...his fellow soldiers and America. The question is...how was he bought?

His job as commander of MTMC was to make sure that all shipping of military property and equipment, especially classified sensitive and dangerous equipment and military components such as explosives, Fighter jet components, weapons and secret classified computer systems (which Fedex LOST) were handled with complete security and safety.

Yet General Stanford did everything in his power as a general and commander of the U.S. Military at MTMC to provide a cover for Fred Smith and his gang of thieves so that they could continue to steal millions of dollars from the government while compromising America's security. He knew Fred Smith's ultimate goal was to steal more than a billion dollars from the military and government. And it was General Stanford's duty to Fred Smith to help him get away with it. He was "Fedex's ALLY"... NOT America's.

And they would have gotten away with it, if not for Air Force Special Agent Paul Ackerman and his fellow AFOSI agents all across the United States.

You have to wonder just what or how much Fred Smith gave to Stanford or paid him, or even promised him for Stanford to betray his fellow soldiers and his country.

What does it take to buy a Black U.S. General? How much do they cost?

More than a Plantation era slave I bet.

It seemed that everybody NSA, MTMC, the government shippers ... ALL knew that the CSS service was non existent. And they were all trying to stop it.

All except for Fred Smith's "Slave Boy" Stanford.

NSA, AFOSI, CIA, numerous military branches, government shippers all complained.

Yet General Stanford not only let Fred Smith and his criminals at Fedex continue to steal millions of dollars from the government while betraying our military and compromising their safety, he actually helped them to cover up their crimes. He knew about the missing computers system that were needed for a highly classified NATO Defense system and still tried to cover up for and protect Fedex. He would do ANYTHING including Committing Treason for Fred Smith and his corrupt Fedex company. He was that bought and paid for Traitor.

Owned by Fred Smith and his Fedex plantation.

He was that bought and paid for "Black Slave" just as so many other Black Africans were bought and paid for by rich White cotton plantation owners during the Colonial Era.

Even after AFOSI's investigation was completed and proved beyond a doubt that the CSS service was a fraudulent non existent service, even after the newspapers had reported on it … General Stanford still was trying to help Fedex continue the Fraud to steal millions.

He was still trying to convince the higher ups in the government and military that it was me who was lying and that AFOSI was wrong.

You have to wonder how a career army officer with so many years of service could betray his own soldiers and his country. How much did they give him or what did they promise him to commit such a despicable act?

On the following page is an actual "FEDEX inter office memo" detailing one of General Stanford's visits with Fedex Executives.

Isn't it interesting that they describe him as an, "<u>unswerving ally and supporter</u>" And that he has to maintain an "<u>extremely low profile for valid political reasons</u>".

Like signs of being a corrupt Traitor maybe? His job was commander of "MTMC".

Yet he was "Fedex's ally and supporter."

What's wrong with this picture?

Fred Smith owned General Stanford like a "Colonial Cotton Plantation" owned Slaves…

Southern Plantation owners …owned Slaves.

INTER-OFFICE MEMORANDUM

7518;4;(21493,0);(0,0);(0,21470);(21493,21470)0
FROM: John Turner
TO: Tom Oliver
SUBJECT: Executive Visit - Military Traffic Management Command

The purpose of this note is to request that in view of current events. the member of Executive Management at Federal Express extend the courtesy of meeting with General John Stanford, Commander of the Military Traffic Management Command, Falls Church, VA.

John Stanford has been an (**unswerving ally and supporter**) of Federal Express /FEDEX and has done much to help us make the right decisions in this marketplace over last 24 months. <u>Although John has maintained an extremely low profile for very valid political reasons during this entire CSS episode,</u> I think **it is** critical that we demonstrate our continued commitment at the highest **levels** this marketplace by arranging an Executive visit. I will be contacting you shortly after the Global Sales Rally to determine time when this visit would be convenient.

Thank you for your continued support.

Very truly yours, John M. Turner
Managing Director   Government Sales-Worldwide

DEPARTMENT OF THE ARMY
HEADQUARTERS MILITARY TRAFFIC MANAGEMENT COMMAND
5611 Columbia Pike ......Falls Church. V A 22041·5050

Office of the Staff Judge Advocate
Ms, Christine P. Richards Senior Attorney
Federal Express Corporation (FEDEX) Box 727 Memphis, TN
38194

Dear Ms. Richards:

In his letter of May 12, ----, Colonel Roger Maguire en-
closed a summary list of Federal Express (FEDEX) Corporation's
service failures reported to us by Department of Defense
(DOD) shippers.

As discussed in our phone conversation on June 12, 1989, I
am enclosing additional information on problems the National
security Agency (NSA), a DOD shipper, has experienced with
your company. This information consists of: (a) a letter
from NSA dated June 8,----; (b) a letter from AT&T dated
January 31, ----: and (C) copies of records forwarded from
NSA.

Please let me know if you have any questions concerning
this material or the General Freight Board scheduled for
June 22, ----.

Sincerely,

Daniel L. Rothlinsberger
Colonel, Judge Advocate
General's Corps Staff Judge Advocate

NATIONAL SECURITY AGENCY
FORT GEORGE G, MEADE. MARYLAND 20755-4000
Serial: S1/199-99

7518;4;(21489,0);(0,0);(0,21500);(21489,21500)00
7518;10;(21498,0);(0,0);(0,18015);(11975,18015);(11975,
14853);(16412,14853);(16412,21490);(18874,21490);(18874,18
015);(21498,18015)00
7518;4;(21483,0);(0,0);(0,21493);(21483,21493)00

very Important

MEMORANDUM FOR THE COMMANDER, MILITARY TRAFFIC
MANAGEMENT COMMAND, DEPARTMENT OF THE ARMY
SUBJECT: Non-Use Status of Federal Express (**FEDEX**)

Meeting Between Mr. Bob Jones, MTMC, and NSA
Representatives CDRMTMC message, DTG 121900Z ,
Subject: Carrier Performance
Action - FEDEX / Federal Express

1. This memorandum is in response to your action placing FEDEX/Federal Express into non-use status for DOD css (Ref. b.) pending a Freight Board review. During Reference a., we provided Mr. Jones with approximately 19-20 case reports evaluating transportation violations involving FEDEX. All electrically received messages describing DOD CSS violations by Fedex Express are being forwarded to your Security Office. Additionally, we have forwarded letters submitted by AT&T, Motorola, and the Office of the Sergeant of Arms, O.S. Senate, all three citing DOD CSS violations against FEDEX/Federal Express.

2. We support the suspension and any other necessary steps that need to be taken to ensure that violations of DOD CSS standards do not continue. DOD CSS was approved by this Agency for transporting Confidential COMSEC equipments, as well as controlled cryptographic items (CCI) based Pg.2 on the service's requirements to prevent unauthorized inspections, tampering, pilfering, or **sabotage** by providing for continuous surveillance and custody of a Shipment in transit.

3. Fedex/Federal Express is the largest, most widely used and available commercial carriers providing DOD CSS. But we cannot continue to ship our COMSEC equipments with a carrier that cannot ensure the accountability or access integrity of those equipments. Therefore, any action that can be taken to ensure that commercial carriers continue to provide the safeguards DOD **CSS** is designed to provide, is greatly appreciated.

O W. Chief Information Systems Security... International Policy

RICHARD DAY

DEPARTMENT OF THE ARMY
Military Traffic Management Command

Oakland California   Oakland Army Base
Reply To:
Attention of: Carrier Services Branch
Ms. Mary Ann Wagner,
Account Executive Federal Express (FEDEX)
4640 Forbes Boulevard, Maryland 20706

08 February

Dear Mrs. Wagner

We are again writing a letter of concern regarding **the
unsatisfactory handling of one more Department of Defense
(DOD)** freight shipment which was not afforded the special
service requested (CSS). The delivering driver did not present the DOD Form 1907 for signature with the shipment.

The shipment moved from Honeywell Incorporated Marine
Systems Division, Everett, Washington on you're A.B.
No. 2001-12383 to Naval Supply Center,
Norfolk, Virginia and consisted of one carton of classi-
fied cargo, weighing seven pounds.

**Of further concern is the report we received that your
driver tore the classified labels off the carton and oblit-
erated the Constant Surveillance Service {CSS} mark on the
freight bill.**

The incomplete Signature and Tally Record is a serious
violation of procedures and standards required for shipments
moving under Constant Surveillance Service (CSS). Our regu-
lation states "carriers providing this service must maintain

a DOD Form 1907 or Form AC-IO (Signature Service Record) and continuous surveillance and custody of shipment while in transit."

Your flagrant disregard for performing special services that were tendered to your firm is totally unacceptable for handling DOD freight shipments.

You are again requested to submit a written explanation concern ins the incident to this Headquarters within 15 calendar days of receipt of this letter.

Further, request you advise us of any other. corrective action taken, or contemplated to preclude recurrence of similar incidents. One more incident of failure to provide a DD Form 1907 upon delivery will cause the convening of the Area Command Freight Board to consider disqualifying your firm from participation in DOD traffic.

Address your response to: Commander, Military Traffic Management Command, Western Area,

Attention: Y.TW-INSC, Oakland Army Base, Oakland, California 94626-5000. Should you require any assistance please feel free to contact Warren Winters at

Colonel McCormick, U.S. Army Director

Sincerely,
Sincerely,

Sincerely,

DEPARTMENT OF THE AIR FORCE
WASHINGTON DC 20330-1000 NOV 2 0 1989

OFFICE OF THE SECRETARY
DEPARTMENT OF THE AIR FORCE

WASHINGTON DC 20330-1000

The Honorable Bill Bradley
United States Senate
Washington, D. C. 20510-0001

Dear Senator Bradley Bradley:

This is in response to your letter to the Department of Defense in behalf of Mr. Gary Rullo regarding Fedex /Federal Express Corporation's handling of classified shipments. The Air Force Office of Special Investigations (AFOSI) advised they have referred this matter to the Defense Criminal Investigative Service (DCIS) based on the potential victimization of multiple agencies within the Department of Defense (DOD). DCIS will evaluate this matter along with a companion DOD Fraud, Waste and Abuse Hotline report and advise AFOSI of their intentions as to further investigation.

We appreciate your interest in this matter and hope the information provided is helpful. A similar letter is being provided to Senators Roth and Biden and
Representative Weldon who also inquired on this subject.

Sincerely,
Eugene J. RONSICK Colonel, USAF Chief, Program Liaison Division Office

OFFICE OF THE SECRETARY

DEPARTMENT OF THE AIR FORCE

-

WASHINGTON DC 20330-1000

The Honorable William V. Roth, Jr.

United States Senate   Washington, DC 20510

Dear Senator Roth:

This is in response to your inquiry to the Secretary of the Air Force in behalf of Mr. Gary G. Rullo regarding allegations of improper handling of classified documents by FEDEX. The Air Force Office of Special Investigations (AFOSI) referred this matter to the Defense Criminal Investigations Service for further investigation, as they may deem appropriate. The violations appear to affect a service provided to several departments of the Department of Defense. Similar information has been sent to the Honorable Curt Weldon/ House of Representatives, in response to his inquiry.

We appreciate your interest in Air Force matters and trust this information is helpful.

Sincerely,

RICHARD GAMMON, Lt Col, USAF

Congressional Inquiry Division

Office of Legislative Liaison

Colonel Roger J. Hakola
Director of Inland Traffic
Management Support Branch Department of The Army
Military Traffic Management Command
Headquarters, Eastern Area
Bayonne,New Jersey 07002

Re: Fedex Corporation   ph.301-369-3600
Dear Colonel Hakola:
Board hearing originally had been postponed until _____

   we discussed this afternoon over the telephone, the Air Cargo Council of the Air Transport Association has proposed to General Small and his staff at the Military Traffic Management Command in Washington, D.C. a meeting, to be held in mid-January, for the review of Constant Surveillance Service Requirements and related government traffic issues. This letter is to confirm the agreement reached at our meeting of December, to the effect that the proposed disqualification hearing before the General Freight Board will be held in abeyance pending the outcome of the ATA-MTMC meeting. AS you know, the General Freight is scheduled for December I will contact you promptly following the conclusion of the ATA-MTMC meeting to further discuss this matter from a procedural and substantive standpoint. I appreciate your cooperation and that of Deputy Director Hicks. During the interim if you have any questions, please do not hesitate to contact me at. the address shown above or at telephone number (901)369-xxxx.(numbers x'd out by me)

Mark R. Allen
Associate Attorney

I had tried to find out if the Military Traffic Management Command (MTMC) had stopped Fedex from handling CSS shipments yet. I had figured the newspaper stories would bring their crimes to an end. But I couldn't get any up to date information either way. Some of the callers who were Fedex employees that said I had done the right thing suggested that I also take the story to ABC's 20-20. That Fred Smith owned so many politicians that only a major national TV show like 20-20 would guarantee the end of the CSS fraud.

So I wrote ABC's 20-20 network in N.Y. and told them about the fraud and illegal drugs at Fedex. It didn't take them long to get back to me.

The person who contacted me was Meredith White, she was the executive producer for 20-20 and she wanted me to tell her a little more about the fraud.

I talked to her for a few minutes while answering her questions, than I asked her if she had access to the Philadelphia Inquirer. And to my surprise she said that it was one of a half dozen papers they read everyday. So I told her to look up the article and get back to me if they wanted to do the story.

She called me the next day. She said they were very much interested in doing the story. She said she was going to have her top producer meet with me and we set up a date. His name was Chris Harper and he was coming down from New York. He was coming to my house and have dinner and then we would go over the documents I had.

The next day I made some phone calls to friends and relatives to pick up some of the documents I had stashed away. Out of concern for my family then, and even more so today I rarely keep even a small part of my documents at my house unless only for a few days. Call it being paranoid or whatever. I call it caution and discipline. there's no need to keep them close and I know that where they are they are safe. It's something a law enforcement officer told me to do a very long time ago, he'd seen a lot and knew a lot. And as he said ...why take chances when you don't have to. So I've always followed his advice on that and a few other things I can't mention.

He was an old friend from way back with great knowledge in security. He also was the one to tell me to make a number of copies of not only the paperwork but also all of the conversations I had recorded on tape recordings and to keep copies of everything in different locations. He warned me that Fedex was a large and powerful company and with Fred Smith's history there was no telling what he might do. He said that Fred Smith would send people to my house to get the evidence in whatever manner they had to, whether it was by theft or by force…"if they wanted it they would come and take it…make no mistake."

He did tell me he was impressed that I had secretly tape recorded so many conversations with the federal investigators. The Fedex employees that I secretly recorded ….he thought it was not so hard to do. He had done it many times.

GET IT INTO YOUR HEAD FRED … THERE'S NOTHING AT MY HOUSE

But there's plenty of copies of everything elsewhere……. Not That Stupid…

You may kill me but you will NEVER get all the documents.

Getting Ready to Have an ABC Producer Come to My House…

I had to get ready for Chris Harper and 20-20. It took nearly all day to get what I needed. After collecting the documents and sorting thru them I began organizing them in my dining room on the table. When I was finished I looked over them and said to myself, "I think this will show quite clearly the fraud." I not only had the DD1907 tally sheets which showed a lack of signatures and 'non-surveillance' and security, but also copies of the rules and regulations with some of the military contracts that were signed by Fedex management.

It was the DD 1907 tally sheets that proved without a doubt that Fedex was guilty of FRAUD. They were the proof that Fedex was billing the government and military branches for millions of dollars for a service that NEVER existed.

And Fred Smith and Fedex management always knew that. He just never figured that a Fedex courier would actually turn him in.

No wonder Fedex could grow so fast in size and revenue when so many millions in revenue was from 'stolen money' that stolen from the government, stolen from the military and even stolen from the civilian sector.

Wouldn't it be great to have a business where other people just gave you tens of millions of dollars every year for NOTHING. So easy to be successful that way.

At any rate…the documents were finally ready.

Chris Harper came to Delaware by way of train. He said he hated to fly and the only time he did was if he had no other choice. He arrived at my house in the early afternoon and after introductions and small talk he immediately wanted to see what documentation I had. So I showed him my dining room table. It had been opened up so it would seat fourteen people. And it was completely covered with documents and tapes. (all copies) I had arranged the documents in chronological order. The rules and regulations were separated along with some of the warnings that came with the shipments. I also had copies of taped recording which corroborated many of the things I had told him. I actually have three times that many now, not counting copies. The tapes contained conversations with OSI Investigators. Fedex employees talking about drugs and thefts at Fedex etc., shipments of illegal drugs within Fedex.

Chris was a very sharp individual, I would say even extremely sharp. He very quickly understood just exactly how the CSS shipments were supposed to be handled. And just as quickly learned how they were mishandled. He was a very quick study. You told him once and he got it the first time.

There was no need to repeat yourself with this guy. As he was going thru the documents my wife came into the room and announced that dinner was ready. So we put down the documents and went into the kitchen to eat a pot roast dinner my wife had cooked especially for him.

During dinner he asked about our family and how they were doing. We had left them with friends so they wouldn't disrupt Chris and I. I had figured that if 20-20 was going to send a producer to my house to do a story the least I could do would be to give him my undivided attention. And an atmosphere where we could concentrate on the documents and the story. He told me that he had been ABC's correspondent in Italy for a number of years and had just recently returned to the states. He was a pleasant man and not cocky or pretentious at all. He was there to do his job and it was obvious that he not only took it seriously but that he was very good at it.

After dinner he mentioned that he would like to take a walk around the neighborhood to stretch out a little. I lived in a typical suburban development. There are about sixty single family homes here. And a small cluster of townhouses close by. The homes are well cared for with neat well trimmed lawns and I was kind of proud to show Chris around.

We had bought our house brand new, actually we decided what kind of house we wanted and they built it. The homes are set up on cul de sac's with eight houses per street. It keeps it safe for the little ones as there is no thru traffic so the cars always drive very slow. The wife and I have walked those streets a thousand times and many times with our children. It's what we call home.

Once back at our house Chris began going over the documents again. He had given it a lot of thought and had pretty much made up his mind by now.

It became obvious when he began complimenting me on my ability at collecting data. He said that in all of the time he had been gathering information for news or shows he had never seen such a collection of documents. He stated that most times when he does research for a story he's lucky to have one tenth of what I have. And when that is the situation it can be difficult to make a decision as to whether or not they will do a story. But with what I have there is no doubt that 20-20 will do the story.

Chris said they never make a decision on a story without meeting to discuss it as a group. But 'this time he is certain that they will do this story.

He said, "I have <u>NEVER</u> seen such a complete job of collecting evidence …you have truly done a great job.

"And I have NEVER told anyone that before," he said."

My wife was in the kitchen cleaning up and was obviously listening to the conversation. She asked Chris, "did you really mean that Chris, did he really do that good of a job?"

And without hesitation Chris responded, **"yes Dot, your husband did great. He's going to be on 20-20 in front of thirty million people."**

Chris asked me if I had any copies that he could take back to New York with him. Hell, I had made a lot of copies of everything. And the ones I had sitting on my dining room table were just for him to take back to New York with him.

As I packaged them up for him we went over a few more details. **He said that since the story was so good and I had collected so much documentation, he felt that this might be a story for Tom Jerrial. Maybe even the feature story of the segment.**

I drove Chris back to the train station in Wilmington for the ride home.

It had been a good day.

My wife and I decided in the beginning that she could not and would not ever be involved in anything to do with Fedex. There were just too many druggies and thieves there and we figured that if someone came after me and somehow I got killed at least she would be left to raise our son. That may sound dumb or corny but it is something you have to accept. Realize that I didn't have twenty asshole lawyers to advise me. And I couldn't afford bodyguards.

I was and am just a regular common family man.

So even though this was entirely my project, my wife supported me, and trusted me and she was happy for me. She knew what they had put me thru and she knew that they were no good rotten bastards. But she also knew I wasn't a man to run away from things. And that I tried my best to always do what was right. Soldiers, firemen, policemen and others do it everyday. I wasn't special.

I had found an honest government investigator who worked hard and brought together a whole team of government investigators. They worked all across the country to collect enough evidence to prove that Fred Smith and his Fedex corporation was involved a felony conspiracy to steal many millions of dollars from the government. And they had planned to steal more than a billion dollars before they got caught.

I had found a newspaper reporter who brought in the best investigators that the Philadelphia Inquirer had so that they could do a factual story that told of the crimes Fred Smith was committing against the government while putting our soldiers and actually the safety and security of the whole United States in jeopardy. They actually were the first to bring to light the crimes and were the forerunners to end of the phony CSS service.

And now I had found ABC's 20-20… a national television show with thirty million viewers that would learn about the crimes against the United States military that were committed by Fred Smith. Who is no more than a traitor and a criminal.

A few days later Meredith White of 20-20 called to confirm that they definitely were going to do the story. They would begin getting things ready and could I manage to get off work for a few days while they were shooting? I told her that I could. And she said that she would get back to me about what days I would need off.

I talked to my boss at Air Products where I was employed and explained the situation to him. It was obvious that he didn't like what Fedex was doing by the comments he made and the questions he asked. He said sure no problem, just let him know what days I needed off.

Chris had asked me if I had any 'old courier uniforms I could wear for the interview. I remembered that when I resigned I had turned in my Fedex I.D. badge to my manager. I had also taken in my uniforms but he said I might as well keep them because they were mine. And that I could do with them as I pleased. He was only interested in my I.D. badge. I told Chris that I did have some old uniforms but wouldn't Fedex get pissed if I wore them? He said not to worry, ABC would take care of any problems if they came up. Fedex didn't scare ABC one bit.

The initial shooting took place in the Hotel Dupont in Wilmington, Delaware. When I arrived the crew was already setting up. Chris introduced me to Tom Jerrial.

I had though that Tom would be a man who kept his distance but he wasn't. He was a friendly and pleasant man. While he was very articulate and quite professional, he was also pleasant and fun to be around as he was very humorous.

His world was much bigger than mine and yet he made me feel comfortable and at ease. Chris said that it was because Tom truly enjoyed his work. I was introduced to the sound, camera and lighting crews. In no time they were ready to shoot. It was an education.

The first shooting consisted mostly of Tom and I sitting in chairs facing each other, each with cameras behind each of our chairs to record the conversation.

In the first part Tom asked me questions from a prepared script and I answered as best I could. It is a lot harder to respond to a question when there is a camera on you than you might think. After I finished answering the questions they turned the cameras on Tom and he again went through the questions. Then they would piece the questions and answers together. It was interesting.

That evening I went with Chris Harper to rent a van so they could begin filming in Dover while I drove around my old route. And the next day we went to Dover with the whole crew to shoot the next sequence for the show.

Once we were in Dover the camera crew set up the lighting in the van and put in microphones so that Tom and I could talk and be recorded as we drove around.

They took a lot of shots of areas where I normally drove around in Dover while carrying the CSS shipments and we even went to the elementary school where I delivered to while I was carrying a lot of explosives that were in the classified military shipments. I think back now and realize just how dangerous and stupid it was to do that. But at the time with management on your back to just do what you're told or be fired , you find that you do a lot of things that make no sense at all. In truth whether I was at a shopping center, neighborhood, or school, I should have just called the FBI and let them handle it from there. But that would have cost me my job. And I was not going to let them fire me. I had a job to do with OSI investigators and part of that job was to not get fired.

Finish the investigation and resign in a formal manner.

And I did my job.

While we were at the school Chris Harper went into the school to talk to the principal and notify him of why we were there and also to inform him that Fedex was sending couriers to his school while it was in session and full of children, with many pounds of explosives in their vans. They told him that at least once and probably more a Fedex courier had parked right at his front door of his office with nearly a hundred pounds of explosive in his Fedex van. The principal was extremely upset that they would do that. How could they do that he asked. I'm sure he made some calls.

One stop was the Blue Hen Mall. It had been a regular stop on my route and every time I did it the CSS shipments of classified military equipment was left unguarded in my van. And the vans don't even have a burglar alarm system in them. The deliveries were mostly on the second floor of the mall so every time I made a stop there I would be away from my truck for at least ten minutes and often more and hundreds of yards away from it. It was done exactly the way I was trained and ordered to do it or else.

They shot film as Tom and I walked across the parking lot with him asking me questions as we walked. How often did I come here, how long was I usually in the mall while the truck was left un-attended etc.

Then we traveled to the Department of Transportation which was also a regular stop and they shot more footage.

Then it was time for lunch.

After lunch we drove around on roads I normally traveled while doing my route.

Chris had decided to try to interview the manager at my Fedex station in Dover. He said he had gone through every channel he could to get an official interview with Fred Smith or Fedex management and they repeatedly put him off. So he was going to try to interview the manager in the local station instead. Chris went into the station to make sure someone was there and saw the manager and at least the CSA was in the building. He was also checking the place for the film crew. But when we came back just a few minutes later they had locked the doors and pulled the blinds.

So Tom Jerrial did a stand up outside the office. It was so funny to know that the station manager Tim Keyser was cringing in the office. I guess they didn't feel so big now did they?

I later learned that Fred Smith wrote letters to ABC's executives "CRYING AND WHINING" about how 20-20 was treating them.

While they were shooting in Dover they had lunch there. During lunch one day Chris Harper told us that **Fred Smith had called ABC and cancelled about twenty million dollars of advertisements on ABC in protest**. At that everybody at the table burst out laughing. They didn't care about and weren't afraid of Fred Smith and his corrupt Fedex company one bit. Chris said Fred was such an "IDIOT," that there were a whole bunch of sponsors standing in line to get their advertisements on 20-20. And they were going to pay even more that Fedex was now paying. So in effect Fred Smith was doing 20-20 and ABC a big favor by cancelling out his advertisements. He said that 20-20 and ABC will get up to four times more money for their air time than Fedex was paying.

At that, a few of the film crew asked with a laugh, "does that mean we all get raises"?

And everybody busted out laughing.

I had waited a long time for this. To tell the truth about Fedex to thirty million people. It wasn't that I wanted to be on television or be a big shot, that's not me. I just wanted Fedex stopped from stealing from and betraying our soldiers and our country. If even one soldier had been killed or injured because of their crimes and I hadn't done anything about it I would have felt bad about it till the day I died.

When Fedex management told me, "Fuck the military... get all you can get."

That's when I knew I had to do what I could to stop it.

Fred Smith had zero loyalty to America. And couldn't care less about our soldiers. Like a LOT of corrupt politicians...Fred Smith put son a big show. Just like John McCain.

Then stole every penny he could.

You don't molest or harm children, you don't rape or harm women and you DON'T betray your Country or our soldiers. Period.

Fred Smith needs to learn that

Later on I read the letters that Fred Smith had written to ABC I laughed my head off. Even today I laugh when I think about them.

After reading the them it was easy to see that he is a professional compulsive liar. He behaves like a spoiled little brat. He is that little rich boy on the street that is the only one who has a ball. And when the other kids insist that he play by the rules like everybody else ...he takes his ball and goes home.

He complained to John Sias the President of ABC and Victor Neufield the Executive Producer of 20-20 saying that the CSS segment was 'shallow, scurrilous and deceptive.'

Aww come on Fred you little CRYBABY ... 20- 20 just told the truth.

It was you Fred Smith who is the LYING THIEVING CRIMINAL.

If ABC's 20-20 lied why didn't you sue them Fred?

Because they told the truth.

* Just days before the story aired on 20-20 Fedex tried to put a spin on the AFOSI investigation and imply that their CSS service was a good one. But Tom Jerrial cornered Fedex vice President Tom Oliver and he was forced to say on 20-20 that Fedex NEVER had a CSS service.

He said that in front of (30) million people. Did you forget that Fred?

2) I have a memo which shows that "your friend and ally General Stanford" the commander of the Military Traffic management Command

(MTMC) stated that he knew (Fedex) didn't have a CSS service and never will. Yet he continued to help Fedex bill the government and steal millions of dollars from the military for a fraudulent service. And he says there is a lot more money to get from the military and government. He's a "Black army General" who had been down to "Fred Smith's cotton slave plantation" numerous times. He not only let Fedex steal from the military, he actually helped them continue to steal millions of dollars from the military.

How much did you pay him to BETRAY his fellow soldiers and his country Fred?

What did you promise him to get him to come on board your Fedex Plantation Slave Ship?

General Stanford should have been court martialed.

3) Fred Smith said that Fedex had a 99.1 successful service level on the CSS shipments. I have looked at thousands of CSS 1907 Tally sheets and I know Fedex had a 100% FAILURE rate on every CSS shipment. Also on every CSS shipment that AFOSI agents investigated all across America Fedex had a 100% violation of contract regulations. How can you have success on a program that doesn't exist?

That's why he hid the 1907 Talley sheets that proved the fraud. Or did Fred Smith have them burned ?

The 20-20 story on ABC was the final stopper of the phony CSS service forever. No matter how many lies General Stanford told to cover up the fraud and no matter how much Fred Smith and Fedex lied the phony CSS service was over forever.

Thank God for the media.

The OSI agents were right….the best way to stop crime was thru the media.

We'll never know just how many corrupt politician or just how many corrupt military officers were bought and paid for by Fred Smith and his corrupt Fedex plantation, but we do know that it took the media to stop them.

I do know that Senator John McCain who is on the "Armed Forces Commission" has gotten a lot of money from Fred Smith at least "after" the CSS was exposed and stopped. I wonder how much he got "before"?

How big a role did he play in stopping criminal prosecution of Fred Smith and the Fedex corporation? Was he afraid the evidence would lead BACK to him? How big a role did he play in Helping Fred Smith Commit Fraud against the military?

The media reported that McCain had Fred Smith on a "short list" to run with him as Vice President in the 2008 Presidential election. And that Smith had given McCain a lot of money. Some people still look at McCain as an patriotic American hero.

Any man who takes money from a criminal that stole millions from the military and our government, who betrayed our soldiers and jeopardized their lives and America's safety will be nothing but a SCUMBAG to me.

That McCain would consider Fred Smith as a running mate for Vice President after all he has done and all the millions he stole from the military…are you serious?

It only tells me that McCain is just another SLIME BAG politician.

I did learn that Smiths connections were stalling criminal prosecution against Fedex.

And I have a letter that says General Stanford recanted my story concerning the Fraud. Was he also afraid of being court martialed ?

Well he should have been. I believe they should have given him a trial and hung him. He's a no good "Traitor Bastard General."

I wrote several letters to senators and congressmen and others. They in turn wrote letter to the defense department and they got only generic responses from the military.

Between the politicians and the top military brass…there was a cover up in the works. Politicians are usually cheap to buy when you need to buy them. For a handful of money politicians will help anybody steal from the government.

And obviously army generals are a very well priced also.

But at least the CSS fraud was stopped …for now.

FBI Says Help…
Fedex Thieves Stole $100,000 in GOLD
Shortly after the 20-20 show aired, the FBI in Wilmington, Delaware called me and asked me to help them. When I went to their office Special Agent Adkins of the FBI asked me to explain to him what was going on with the CSS stuff.

I think the FBI was pissed because top military brass … aka Stanford etc. had somehow succeeded in stopping "criminal prosecution" of Fred Smith. There was easily enough evidence to prove "Felony Criminal Conspiracy to Commit Fraud" against the military and government. It was an "open and shut case." I believe that if the case had gone to Federal prosecution General Stanford and possibly more in the military would have been indicted of federal felony charges, or court martialed. So somebody in the top branches of the military or the defense department was covering for him.

And it didn't happen.

Agent Adkins wanted to know why I didn't come to the FBI and let them investigate it, instead of going to AFOSI which was military. Where it could be more easily covered up? Looking back, I wasn't knowledgeable enough to know that the military top brass and Washington would try to bury it to try to protect "their own."

As I look back, I wonder how I would have done "secretly" tape recording the FBI agents if I had gone to them. Would I have pulled it off …well I would certainly have tried.

After we discussed some of the details concerning the CSS service and the investigation he said he had a more pressing problem that he had to deal with now.

He asked if I would help him and of course I told him I would do all I could. He explained that part of his responsibilities as an FBI investigator was to protect money and other valuables in banks. Then he went on to say that the Bank of Delaware had shipped a $100,000 gold shipment through Fedex about a week before and it had come up missing. The package container it was shipped in had showed up in Atlanta but it was empty and the gold was no where to be found.

I explained to him that stealing from a shipment and then sending the empty package or envelope on to the destination station was a common trick that Fedex couriers and managers used when they stole valuables and drugs from shipments.

Then he said something that surprised me. He told me that the FBI was well aware of the thefts and the drug shipments and the thefts of drugs within Fedex. But that <u>Fedex management would NOT cooperate with the FBI. So they couldn't stop it.</u>   (interesting isn't it?) Then he said that even I had "no clue" of just how much illegal drugs were being shipped thru Fedex everyday. I already knew there was a LOT. I knew there was an "unwritten rule" at Fedex, that you NEVER called or told police about the illegal drugs that you saw or knew were being shipped and delivered thru Fedex. It could and most likely would cost you your job. Because there was so much money involved

If there was much more than I realized ...WOW.

Then it must be a enormous amount. Tens of millions of dollars worth ... in illegal drugs daily.

Then Adkins turned the conversation back to the missing gold shipment. He said the investigator that the bank had sent to the Philadelphia airport where they load and unload Fedex planes felt that he was being stonewalled. That when the bank first called Fedex and told them about the missing gold shipment Fedex management had promised all kinds of cooperation.

But that when the Investigator went to the airport and began asking questions they were being VERY vague and evasive. Even close mouthed about answering any questions at all. The bank investigator, who most likely had been former police or FBI investigator was pissed because he felt it was obvious they were withholding information. I wasn't surprised.

"And it was," Agent Adkins said, a"$100,000 gold shipment" which is a LOT of Gold to be stolen in one shot. And now it had been about a week and no sign of the gold and "no help or cooperation from Fedex management in recovering it."

Out of curiosity I asked him how big the box was that the gold was shipped in. He replied that it was about the size of a shoe box. I had never really thought how big a $100,000 worth of gold would be. And to be honest I was surprised. As I tried to visualize it, I realized the gold was gone forever. Fedex couriers have stolen shipments as big as TV's and computers.

A gold shipment worth $100,000 and that small size... well that's a "shipment from heaven" for a Fedex courier or member of Fedex management.

Adkins asked me to explain exactly how a package was handled from the time a courier picks it up from the shipper to the time it was delivered to the recipient. How many people had the opportunity to steal it and who had the best opportunities to steal it and get away with it. I explained the whole process step by step.

Then I asked him if he knew the name of the courier who made the initial pickup. He didn't have it at the time but said he would get back to me with it. But that they had already talked to him and checked him out.

He asked me if anyone at the airport could have taken it?

What, are you kidding me I thought to myself. Of course, absolutely yes. But so too could anyone from the Wilmington station including management. And that includes the people and management in Atlanta too. Most of Fedex was a haven for thefts and illegal drugs I told him.

I went on to tell him about the drugs and thefts in Atlanta. That because of so many thefts Fedex management did a first time ever station wide drug test that took out more than two thirds of the station including management. And how I was told that upper Management at Fedex vowed to NEVER again do a station wide drugs test. And that even reporting thefts of drugs or drug shipments were a no no.

We spoke a few more minutes about all of the drugs going thru Fedex and then he got real serious and looked directly at me. And he explained to me that I had cost Fred Smith and Fedex a lot of money in exposing their crimes. Then he said that, "besides the CSS fraud, Fred Smith was involved in other illegal activities."

"He is smuggling illegal drugs into the U.S. from below the border." Adkins said.

"We know, but haven't caught him at it yet," he said. He added that Fred Smith was considered by Federal Law Enforcement Agencies as a "Dangerous Man." That because of what I have done to Fedex and the problems I had caused Smith ..."I had to be very careful because he may send someone to harm me."

He seemed genuinely concerned for me.

It wasn't until I had gotten in my car and had started home that what he had said about Fred Smith being considered a "Dangerous man" and that he may send someone to harm me set in.

It did give me reason to think back to everything I'd learned about Fred Smith. The conversation with my manager Mike Mitchell who was the first to tell me Smith was smuggling illegal drugs. AFOSI agent Ackerman asking my help with information concerning flight patterns and routes of Fedex cargo planes and telling me that Smith was smuggling drugs. His warnings that Smith may send someone to harm me. The fact that his second warning was more serious and the worried look on his face the second time he had warned me. What additional information had he learned about Smith that he may not have known the first time he warned me?

The man who called from Memphis when he warned me about Smiths' vengeance against those who crossed him. That man worked for Fedex in Memphis headquarters, he knew a lot about Fred Smith. He seemed concerned for a little family man who was in way over his head …and didn't realize it.

It was an uneasy ride home that night.

As far as I know they never found the gold or caught the Fedex thieves who stole it. Whether he was a lone courier on his own or if he was working with members of Fedex management. How do you catch one thief when he's working within a group of thousands?

The truth is that millions of dollars worth of valuables, cash and illegal drugs are stolen from Fedex shipments annually, maybe even monthly.

I Did What I Could …

There is no question that politicians and others in government covered up and stopped the criminal prosecution of Fedex and Fred Smith. Not to mention all of the others involved in the fraud including General Stanford.

By going first to AFOSI and then to the newspapers and 20-20 I did stop the CSS fraud but there is only so much a little guy can do. I guess stopping someone from stealing more than a billion dollars from our government is a small victory at best. But I also know that I stopped Fred Smith from compromising the safety of our servicemen. And that is something.

It was just sad to realize that criminals have so much power over our politicians and justice system in America.

I realize now that when we do read in the newspapers or see on TV that a criminal prosecution of a major corporation or a very rich individual does happen, It is ONLY because that company or person isn't politically connected. They haven't paid enough money to our senators and congressmen in Washington to gain their protection.

It's not really that different than in the 30's and 40's when a small businessman, bar owner or shop keeper paid money to the mafia for protection. It's the same game, just a different kind of payment and a different level of protection.

We see it everyday in the media.

Fred Smith's Fedex Planes on DEA Website ...

I had gotten many comments and questions from current and past employees within Fedex. Both on the phone and online while on AOL. From the many conversation I had with them I collected a LOT more information. You'd be surprised just how many current and former employees feel the same about Fedex as I do.

It was a Fedex employee in Memphis (Fedex headquarters) directed me to the official DEA website which had an interesting picture. He said the picture showed one of Fred Smith's Fedex planes flying illegal drugs into the United States from Mexico.

Wow ...Right there on the official DEA website.

He said he had been a Fedex employee in Memphis for a long time and had heard the rumors about Fred's Drug Smuggling but nothing specific. Just the rumors. Someone had told him about the DEA website and picture and he was just letting me know about it.

I looked it up and sure enough on the "Official government DEA Website" there was a picture of one of Fred Smith's Fedex cargo planes as it crossed over the border. They showed it on a flight path from Mexico to Boston where organized drug trafficking was very, very strong. And on the fuselage of the plane DEA had stamped the words **"illegal drugs."**

I thought back to agent Ackerman asking me about Fedex's flight patterns for their cargo planes and realized that this was what he was talking about. There was also more information about the planes and the illegal drugs they were carrying on the site.

It all made sense. If you had "cargo planes" and access to airports both big commercial ones and the smaller private ones in America and various parts of the world including Mexico and South America where there was NO ONE to check or inspect your "cargo and freight" you could ship anything ...anywhere. No check in lines and no inspectors to inspect your cargo or planes like they do with passenger planes. That's how Fedex employees were moving their own drugs in a smaller capacity (kilos) . It was a common thing at the Philadelphia airport ramp. As I'm sure in many other Fedex airports ramps all across America. Couriers and management flies to Florida, buys a couple kilos of cocaine etc. and flies back to a Fedex airport ramp near their home. Walks out to his car that is parked on "private Fedex property" and drives away.

No one there to check what he brings back.

No cops, no DEA agents, and no FBI. There were NOT allowed on Fedex ramps or property.

No one asks...no one to check packages and no one tells. It's all totally safe. I understood why the AFOSI agents questioned me about "strange or different" planes at Fedex's airport ramp in Philadelphia. Did I notice any "different flight patterns by Fedex planes"? Did I see any unusual or different containers while at the ramp?

They were after "BIG" shipments of Illegal Drugs.

I copied and began sending out the "Official DEA" picture of the Fedex plane flying illegal drugs into the United States. And there was a lot of talk about it.

I soon received a letter from one of Fred Smith's ASSHOLE corporate lawyers. Fred was again threatening to take legal action against me if I didn't keep quiet about his and Fedex's wrong doings and illegal activities.

I replied back to go ahead and take this to court. Because the media will have a feast on their crimes. I think it's still true today.

And about (45-50) taped conversations. I never really counted them all. But I have a LOT.

Fred Smith didn't want any more of his crimes and illegal activities aired in public. Some of them might have to be shut down and could cost him hundreds of millions of dollars in illegal drugs, maybe a billion dollars? Maybe there would be criminal penalties like jail time?. Was he afraid ABC's 20-20 might do yet another story on his "Drug Smuggling" this time?

No Fred Smith wouldn't let that happen.

And he never responded. He knew I had amassed a lot of information on him and he didn't want it to come out.

Didn't want me to open "Pandora's Box."

Why was I doing all of this? Why was I taking it this far?

Well, as I stated earlier, I'm a "New Castle Boy." That bastard had done a lot of bad things, criminal things that I didn't like. But it was more personal too. While I worked there his Fedex management had lied about and screwed me a lot. But more personal to me, while they were screwing me over they were also making life a living hell for my wife. At the time I had just bought a new house and couldn't afford to quit my job and they knew that. I'm not the only man or woman they screwed over, I'm sure I was just one of many.

But for ANY bastard to threaten to take our home away and put my family out in the street forever, to threaten me that I would never be able to physically work again and make my wife cry like they did.

I NEVER forget. And I NEVER forgive.

God forgives …that's his job. Not mine.

If Fred Smith had been next to me when his lawyers first threatened me…I would have punched him in the face. But he is a COWARD. If he was any more of a "Sissy Girl" he'd have a menstrual period. He uses his corporate attorney's that have no morals or scruples to deal with men who he is afraid to meet face to face.

I'm not that dangerous violent guy, just a regular working guy. I would never go after him or anyone with guns or weapons. I'm better than that. But if he had been in the room that day when he made my wife cry… I'm sure he knows a good dentist. Or he would have found one.

Fred Smith's letters of threats didn't stop me from sending out the DEA Photos…

So Fred Smith went to PLAN B.

He couldn't scare me away… but he had another way to get rid of me.

About (6-8) months after I had begun sending out the DEA website picture of Fred's Fedex plane smuggling the illegal drugs into the U.S. I began getting <u>STRANGE</u> phone calls from blanked out ten digit phone numbers.

It started in December 2001.

I am a masonry contractor and I work a lot of hours from about late March to mid December. Then thru the winter months I spend my days at home re-organizing my tools and equipment, and getting ready for spring.

My wife was working in the daytime and leaves for work about 7:30 am and returns about 4:30pm. My son left for school about 7:00am and because of his sports and after school activities he wasn't normally home till about 6:00pm.

So I was basically home alone in the daytime thru the week from mid December until sometime in March.

We live on (22) secluded acres and our house is situated a quarter mile from the road. So while we very much enjoy the privacy and setting...we are also very vulnerable should someone come after us to cause us harm.

At first I would just get mad about the calls.

They only came In the middle of the day while my wife was working and I was home alone. I would get the phone calls. Only then. The callers' ten digit number was always blanked out and when I answered the phone I would say, "Hello."

But the caller on the other end wouldn't answer ... just hold the phone leaving the line open. After I said a few "hello's" I would hang up. Though I knew the caller was still on the phone and not answering. Sometimes I could hear him breathing or other noises he made. The caller never once hung up on me...just held the phone line open. "To listen to me talk."

The calls would come nearly every day once or twice a day around "mid day" and only while my wife was at work and I was home alone.

Telemarketer phone calls always came in the evening when both of us were home and they always gave you an answer and why they were calling. Unless there was a pre recorded message with a call back number.

These calls were different....

The calls continued thru the winter. Always when I was alone and never in the evenings or weekends when my wife was there. It was very annoying. The phone would ring, I would answer it and sometimes I could hear them breathing on the other end, but they NEVER answered.

It got to the point where I would answer the call ...hear them breathing but not answering ....and I would say "screw you bastard, stop calling me".

But they never answered or replied and they never stopped !!! Every week day Monday thru Friday they called in the middle of the day while I was alone. It was always one or two calls nearly everyday and no answer.

And the ten digit number was always blocked out.

Then…

On March 22, 2002 my son was going to pitch the opening game of his High School's baseball game. The game was to start about 3:30 pm. The wife had called from work to remind me to have the video camera ready and to bring the tripod for it.

To pitch the opening game of the season was a big deal. My son had worked hard for the honor and he was going to get it. And we were going to record the game.

Shortly after 12:00 noon (when the midday calls usually came) I started down to our basement to get the tripod where I had seen it several times, even that week.

I remember walking out of our bedroom past our TV on the way to the basement to get the tripod.

As I got to the basement door I saw a man coming thru it and into my dining room. He looked about (35-40) years old. About my size (5'10" - 6') medium build with light brown - blondish short hair. He was wearing khaki tan pants and a tan shirt. His left hand was on the door knob and I don't know what was in his right hand.

The next thing I remembered was that I was staggering back past my TV going in the opposite direction and back into my bedroom.

I was semi conscious and very dazed, I was pretty much out of it. My head was bleeding and covered in blood.

I was so out of it that I thought my ears were bleeding and never even wondered why I was covered in blood. I was losing consciousness quickly.

I fell on my bed where I lost unconscious.

The lucky thing was that I had fallen on the right side where my head was bleeding. It was an open head wound and falling with the wound down where I could bleed out probably saved my life. If I had not bled out the pressure from the trauma to my head could have swelled my head and caused my death.

I was very lucky to be alive.

For the next four to five hours I laid there slowly bleeding from a hole in my head and drifting into and out of consciousness a number of times. I was so dazed and in shock that I didn't realize what had happened to me and so out of it that I didn't even question why I was covered in blood. I had probably only made it back to my house and bedroom purely out of instinct. And nothing more.

My wife had called about 3:00 pm and somehow I came to and I answered the phone next to the bed and I told her I would be there at the game...but then I fell unconscious again right after I hung up the phone. I was still dazed and in shock.

I did know I was bleeding when she called me but I didn't want to alarm her. So I didn't say anything about the blood. In my foggy mind I was somehow going to try to get cleaned up and dressed and somehow try to make it to the game. I guess I just had it in my head that I had to get to my son's baseball game and little else. He had played sports since he was four years old and I had never missed a game.

I guess that thought was ingrained in my head.

Just get to my son's baseball game.

But I was in shock. And nearly dead.

I lost consciousness again ... I wasn't going to make it to his game. It just wasn't going to happen.

About 5:30 pm my wife called again and the phone ringing brought me back again. She couldn't understand why I didn't come to the game. I had never ever once missed a school or sporting event of my sons. And he was pitching on opening day, and I didn't come...why?

What's wrong, she asked.

I then told her that my "ears" were bleeding and I didn't feel good.

I still didn't realize at that time that I had a serious head injury. She began asking me questions on the phone as she rushed home.

She rushed into our bedroom and found me semi-conscious and covered with blood on our bed which was also covered in blood. The picture she saw when she walked into our bedroom must have been terrifying.

I'm sure it scared her ...a lot.

She asked me what had happened and I really couldn't respond too well to tell her. And to be honest at that time I didn't know. She immediately called our family doctor who I had just seen that morning for a routine check up and who had told me I was in great shape. Now my wife was telling her I was laying on our bed and covered in blood barely conscious and incoherent. My doctor told her to call an ambulance right away and she did.

The ambulance rushed me to the emergency room. It was the ambulance EMT who told me that I had a large hole in my head. It was on the top rear of my head and slightly to the right side.

At the hospital a whole team of doctors worked on me while I was unconscious.

The blow to the head should have killed me but somehow I survived.

That night as I lay in my hospital bed I awoke to my wife caressing me. When I looked up she was smiling at me.

You're going to be okay she said.

The doctors had told her that most people with a head injury as severe as mine usually die. And the few that do survive usually go into a coma. Somehow I had been lucky.

Very lucky.

I was not really clear headed yet and still in a lot of pain but I did understand what she was saying to me. I still had not yet on my own wondered or thought about what had happened to me or how.

I wasn't that conscious or clear headed.

Then she told me that my family doctor had questioned her about my injury. She said my doctor believed somebody..."whacked me on the head".

And had actually asked her if somebody had whacked me on the head.

My doctor had been my physician for about fifteen years and she knew me to be in great shape and very agile. The injury to my head didn't fit into any logical sense but that of someone striking me very hard on the top rear of my head. And I had no other visual injuries. Just the blow to the top back of the head.

My doctor had also apparently talked to the physicians in the emergency room. And she knew.

At any rate while I was still in pain from the injury and still not mentally right, and when my wife told me what my doctor had said to her, I immediately went into Post Traumatic Stress Disorder. (PTSD) syndrome.

I knew I had nearly been murdered...but I couldn't remember much of it. It's a really bad feeling. It's one thing to consciously know you're been in a battle for your life and being seriously injured. It's quite another when the attack comes from out of nowhere and you never even knew it was coming. Especially when it happens at your home where you would normally feel safe from your enemies.

I remembered the man coming up thru my basement door. I vaguely remembered being in my pole barn and someone standing behind me and striking me.

I remembered being struck very hard on the head from behind. But little else.

It was a very difficult time mentally. I was weak and my head hurt a lot and I couldn't even begin to sit or stand up. I was in a bad place both physically and mentally.

I've since learned that head injuries can be very bad for the mind as well as the body.

Today I still run a successful business, am an active member of a very large charitable organization, and active in our church, coach little league baseball and am blessed with a great wife, great family and many friends.

I am lucky and blessed to be alive and healthy in all ways.

And I am eternally thankful for all of that.

Several days after I returned home from the hospital and before I could walk very well, I still managed to get up from my bed and make it to the "pole barn" where it happened. I had to see. Maybe there was some clues in it that might help me.

There was a dried up pool of blood about two feet in diameter where I must have fallen to the ground after I was struck and laid there for some time bleeding out.

I'm guessing the person who struck me on the head saw that I was not moving and thought I was dead, or possibly, that since I was bleeding so heavily and there was no one around to help me they believed that I would bleed out and be dead in a matter of minutes.

It was close…very close.

There was a blood trail …drops of blood coming from the pool of blood in my pole barn and coming across my yard and into my basement. The blood trail from my outside basement door to my basement steps and up to my inside basement door was clear and easy to follow.

My wife had cleaned up the blood coming into our living room and then into the bedroom. The bed covers and sheets had to be washed as they were soaked in my blood.

I can only imagine the scene she saw as she came into our bedroom. The trauma it must have put her thru. We had been together since she was twenty years old. And I had almost bled out and died in our bed.

As I looked at the dried drops of blood on the basement floor I saw the "tripod" I was going to get. It was exactly where I had seen it several times previously in the weeks before.

There had been no reason at all for me to go out to the pole barn.

The tri-pod sat in clear sight against the wall about eight feet from the basement doors.   But there was no blood trail coming from or going to it.

I had not been near it while I was bleeding.

Someone had taken me out to the pole barn to kill me.

And they nearly did.

And the mysterious Phone calls ....

They stopped completely and forever the exact day I was nearly murdered. I didn't realize it until I had been home recuperating for a couple weeks and then one day it struck me. <u>**The "mysterious" phone calls had stopped exactly the day before my head injury.**</u>

And they never returned again...ever.

It doesn't take a rocket scientist to figure out that the phone calls were a way for someone to track my habits from long distance. And to find out just when I was home alone all day without even coming to Delaware.

They may have followed my wife to work a few times because obviously they knew my wife worked in the daytime Monday thru Friday and was only home on evenings and weekends when there were never any anonymous / mysterious calls.

It was a professional hit.

That I survived … was against the odds.

They figured out that during the winter months I would be home alone in the middle of the day.

They had clocked me perfectly.

And as I stated previously we live on 22 ½ acres.   And our home sits almost exactly one quarter mile from the road in a very private and secluded wooded cove.

Beautiful.....but also very vulnerable. It would be so easy for someone to walk into our woods from the backside and then sneak up to my house without anyone detecting them or knowing they were there. After the assault they could walk away undetected.

The FBI and OSI investigators and others had told me Fred Smith is a "Drug Smuggler" and very dangerous.

To be very careful because he might try to harm me.

He did, he sent someone to kill me.

About a month after the assault I had a scheduled follow up visit with a surgeon who had treated me in the emergency room. He was a middle aged doctor who had been around and seen a lot.

He told me point blank without me even asking him, that he had seen a lot of head injuries like the one I had. He said that he was certain my injuries were the result of someone hitting me on the head from behind.

And advised me to go to the police.

I had never asked him about the injury or what he thought caused it. He told me that on his own, apparently he thought I should know. He was the professional, he knew.

I had been thru a lot of physical and mental pain from the injury and as hard as it may seem to believe … it took awhile to actually go to the Delaware state police and talk to them.

I was afraid they wouldn't believe me. Try to realize how difficult it would be for a detective to believe that a very rich CEO of a major corporation would send a hit man to kill a common little working man like me. It would be hard not to laugh at a man saying that.

Even I realized that.

I live in Delaware and I didn't have any enemies and certainly none who would do me harm. And nothing was taken from me or from my property. Nothing had been moved around. It was clean…get in…kill me, and get out.

Except that I didn't die.

Did I think the police would even consider that a big corporate CEO like Fred Smith would send someone to kill a little guy like me?

They didn't.

Well actually, I believe it was a combination of things. It was just six months after 9/11/01 and every law enforcement agency across the country was busy working twenty-fours a day on leads etc. regarding terrorists. There were so many alerts, false alarms and all. They were all working extra hours and doing their best to stop further terrorists attacks.

They surely didn't have time for some little working class local guy claiming that a "Big Shot CEO " had tried to kill him.

That couldn't happen they thought.

But that's not what the FBI and AFOSI agents had said or thought when I was working with them.

Which was well before 911.

So I told the officer to put my name in a file. And if I came up dead in the near future … I didn't die of an accident, I didn't commit suicide, and I didn't accidentally drown in a river. So please investigate.

They said they would …but who knows.

After a few days to think it over I contacted the FBI in Wilmington, Delaware. The same office where they had asked for my help in dealing with the Gold theft from the bank of Delaware. The same office where an FBI agent had told me that Fred Smith was a drug smuggler and considered dangerous. And that he might try to harm me.

They too were very much wrapped up with all of the 9/11/01 terrorists stuff. They had received thousands of calls about possible terrorists and were checking them out as they made plans for security of building, schools, bridges etc. And they had little time for me. After all I was just a working class guy. It was a different agents in the FBI office then I had spoken with before, but I'm not sure it would have made a difference.

I soon began to realize …I was on my own. It was not a good feeling.

I wrote to AFOSI for help. I was after all a government witness and they had told me to contact them at the first signs of danger from Fred Smith.

The problem was…agent Paul Ackerman had left AFOSI and no one there even knew who I was. So I got no response from them. Terrorist were the "soup de jour".

Still on my own.

It was a difficult time.

I tried writing to several newspapers to possibly get my concerns out there.

The AFOSI had taught me that if someone is doing something wrong. Once the media gets a hold of it and does a story…the wrong doing will stop.

But like every law enforcement agency across America…the media too was obsessed with terrorism and the terrorists and they had no time for me.

Many will forget now or maybe just don't know or remember that much of 911... But there was a time when every single day the media focused on the terrorists.

And almost nothing more.

I knew what had happened, I knew there had been an attempt on my life.

And I knew who did it and why it happened.

But probably my main concern at the time… would they come back to finish … the job? Now that they realized I was still alive.

What did I remember of the assault?

And if they did come back…what if a member of my family came home while they had me in the pole barn?

What if a family member stumbled upon them as they were coming or leaving?

I don't believe that people who would make an attempt on someone's life and know that they failed …would want the victim walking around.   Especially since I had partial memory of what happened, and some memory of what the killer looked like and might recognize his face?

Maybe a realization of how it all unfolded, maybe things said to me either in my house or in my pole barn?

What if I regained total memory of the events that day?
Sound far fetched ?

Realize this …I had never for a second thought that Fred Smith would really send someone to kill me. Somehow I just never took the warnings that he was a "Dangerous Man" and the threats that seriously.

Fred Smith would never really send someone to harm or kill me. I was sure of it. He had too much to lose.

I was WRONG… and it nearly cost my life.

What Fred Smith really …had to lose was his "Drug Smuggling" operation. It could mean a loss of many millions of dollars…it could mean going to Jail.

Does it really sound too hard to believe?

Read This (You can find this story on the internet)

A Mr. John Wheeler of New Castle , Delaware was a decorated Vietnam war hero. He had served in Washington for Ronald Reagan and both the George Bush's Administrations.

He is the man responsible for the Vietnam War memorial. A graduate of West Point, Yale and Harvard, a pretty smart guy. He was at the time working with the Defense department in December of 2010. The Russian KBG knew all about him, he was that important.

It was in December of 2010 that they found his body in a landfill in Wilmington, Delaware.

The first stories that came out reported that he was going to Washington from New York by train to "expose" someone or something important the day before he was murdered. But evidently he never made it.

His body had been dumped in a dumpster in Newark, Delaware. Then loaded in a trash truck and disposed of in the landfill. He had been murdered.

The first news stories came out in totally different directions with information. A man I know told me at that time …we'll NEVER know what happed to him or who did it.

He was right.

Wheeler was still wearing a very valuable ring (I believe it was a West Point ring) on his finger. He was still wearing a Rolex watch and had his wallet and money in his pocket. Does that sound like a robbery?

Right away the FBI in Delaware whose office was less then three miles away from where Wheeler's body was found stated that they "were too busy" and didn't have the resources to investigate the case. The Delaware State police never got involved. The Wilmington Police Department where the body was found and had a good sized police force that had investigated a hundred murders yearly "nothing". Not a peep.

The case was handed over to the Newark police department. They are the "Mayberry cops" of Delaware. They write traffic tickets and arrest college students for being drunk and fighting. With not one hundredth the experience, skills or resources of the other law enforcement agencies mentioned above.

Why?

A man as big as John Wheeler, the positions he held. Served on three Presidential administrations, worked in the upper layers of the defense department, and they turn his murder over to a very small town police force? It's been more than a year since his murder and the Newark police have stopped the investigation. His case sits in a filing cabinet where it will stay for eternity.

Russian papers wrote about his death and the KBG followed it to see what happened. The truth is the Russians probably know.

It was a sanctioned "professional hit." He was murdered to keep him quiet.

It happens a LOT. Far more than we realize.

I am just a "little guy" a nobody who could easily be disposed of with no questions asked and no real interest from anybody but my family and friends.

I had done a lot to make Fred Smith pissed at me, hate me, I'm sure he wished me dead a thousand times. I had exposed his racism and his racist and discriminatory practices and programs against Blacks within Fedex. Probably have cost Fedex more than a hundred million dollars or more in discrimination and equal right's lawsuits by exposing the discrimination there. While the racism and discrimination still continue there today and ALWAYS will …Smith has had to be more discreet about it now. A little more "subtle". But it's still there and will be as long as he is CEO.

But It wasn't that. ……Well maybe it was part of it?

I had gone to authorities and worked undercover with AFOSI to prove the fraudulent CSS service was fraud and never existed. Exposed it in the newspapers and on ABC's 20-20 in front of thirty million people. Over the years that cost Smith and Fedex more than a billion dollars in government contracts etc.

That would have been part of the motive to have me killed.

But the one thing alone ….

That would make Fred Smith send someone to kill me. Was when I put the DEA picture of his Fedex planes smuggling illegal drugs into America from Mexico. It was raising a LOT of chatter about his drug trafficking.

I HONESTLY believe…He still is Today?

But he wants No One to know or talk about it. And he wasn't going to let some little blue collar working guy in Delaware… open Pandora's Box on his illegal drug activities.

He was too big, too powerful, too well connected and respected. (And VERY Vindictive and Dangerous) as I have found out first hand.

The OSI agents warned me, the FBI warned me and others too.
That he may send someone to Murder me.
If the media or other writers got wind of his drug smuggling and started digging ...well they have more resources and skills than I have ... there would be more stories.

The picture of Fred Smith's Fedex Plane loaded with "Illegal Drugs" on the next page is a simulated picture.
I am saving the original for the media in case Fred tries to stop or sue me. Or I may put it in a "second book?"
In 2012 Drug Trafficker Orlando Pride testified that Fred Smith's Fedex planes Smuggled Forty-five shipments of Cocaine valued at $4 million each into the U.S. from Mexico. It was 200 kilograms (200 kilos) shipped in coffin sized boxes.
Testimony revealed that it was intended for Distribution in the Memphis Tennessee area. Talk about keeping it in House.
Forty-five shipments of Cocaine at $4 million each is $180 million dollars about one-fifth of a Billion Dollars in Illegal Drugs. But it's only a "Drop In the Bucket" compared to what Fred Smith has smuggled into the U.S. since he first made that deal with the "Boys in Vegas" at Fedex's beginning that Mike Mitchell told of.
He will LIE and say he has NOTHING to hide, but the TRUTH is that's EXACTLY what he does and how he gets away with it. He works a deal with a Drug Cartel to bring their Drugs to his locations in Mexico and he has his people load them into his Fedex Planes. Then he tells his people in Memphis to check "ONLY" this or that shipment for drugs while keeping them "away from His Drug shipments." That way some Illegal Drugs are found that are NOT his. And his go thru EVERY TIME unchecked. Or he just has them flown into another Fedex location that has no inspectors at all. Just like the DEA picture of his Fedex plane flying his "Illegal Drugs" in Boston.
He has perfected his Drug Smuggling Operation using Fedex's planes and facilities just like AFOSI agents said. How many men have Fred Smith had harmed or Killed? The DEA, FBI and others in Federal Law Enforcement agencies know... Ask Them.

U.S. DRUG ENFORCEMENT AGENCY

DEA said this plane was loaded with "illegal Drugs" They stamped the words "Illegal Drugs" on the fuselage.

BOSTON

U.S.A.

U.S. Border

MEXICO

Official D.E.A. Drug Picture of Fedex Planes flying illegal drugs from Mexico to North America. Original picture had arrows pointing from Mexico to Boston.

The original D.E.A. website picture mysteriously disappeared from it's website about the same time that I was almost murdered and left for Dead at my home.

Also mysteriously ...ALL of the medical records of my head wound disappeared from the Christiana Hospital. When I questioned hospital records personnel about how this could happen I was told it was "very unusual." and NOT part of the hospitals policies. They had no idea of what could have happened to my records.

<u>Lesson in History</u>
Something I've learned. ... For many years there were a lot of ships and planes lost in the Bermuda Triangle. Then one man wrote a book about the mysterious vanishings.

But his book had only a "few details." Soon after, many authors began researching the mysteries and history of the Bermuda Triangle and about fifty books were written about the Bermuda Triangle one after another.

Just the "first book" started it. And afterwards a lot more information and facts were revealed.

Fred Smith would rather kill someone than let that happen to him. He doesn't want a lot of writers snooping into his illegal activities and he certainly doesn't want fifty books written about his drug smuggling and whatever other crimes he's involved in or has committed.

I'm sure there are a "few" who knows about it. But they never openly talked about it. They knew better. I didn't.

And I nearly paid the ultimate price for it.

And still might…

Some where out there is more of this story. Somebody knows more about "what air fields" are being or were used. When and how he got his planes across the border (remember this was before 9/11/01) When the borders between Mexico and America were mostly wide open. The names of the pilots he used and the names of the contacts and a whole lot more.

Realize this …

Barry Seal was a major drug smuggler who reportedly smuggled in "billions of Dollars" worth of illegal drugs across the border. Seal didn't have a major company like Fedex to hide his activities.

And where did Seal smuggle them into?….Mena, Arkansas. Just a few miles from where Fred Smith had access to family owned "private air fields and planes."

Both Barry Seal and Fred Smith had cargo planes and access to, and knowledge of private air fields in Arkansas and other places.

Did he know Seal personally? I don't know.

Did Fred Smith and Barry Seal ever do drug business together…I don't know. Yet ! But there are a lot of coincidences. They were in the same state and only miles away. I'm sure they knew of each other. After all, they were "competitors," or were they "partners?"

Barry Seal was murdered by a drug cartel and maybe that's the real reason Fred Smith has so many body guards and keeps them so close?

I was emailing out the DEA picture of his Fedex planes with the illegal drugs in it and had mentioned what others had told me.

Fred didn't want "everybody" knowing that he was smuggling illegal drugs.

Because others with better investigative skills than I have would be digging for more information. After enough stories were written about it, the government would have to come after him.

<u>**And that's why he sent someone to Murder me**</u>

I was just a little guy who had "blown the whistle" on him and his CSS fraud. When he tried to shut me up about his crimes I stood my ground. When he lied and bad mouthed me to discredit me…I took it personal.

When he threatened to put my family out in the streets FOREVER. I'll leave this line blank.

He lives a long ways away. And stays surrounded by body guards because he's a sissy. So he get's to run his lying mouth while hiding under their skirts and behind his corporate lawyers.

It was bad enough that I stopped him and his Fedex company from stealing a billion or more dollars. Then I exposed his Fraud in the newspapers and on 20-20.

When **Pandora's Box** began to open with the DEA picture and a lot of information and talk about him smuggling Illegal Drugs began to spread Fred Smith tried to stop it by taking me out.

I'm not sure if he'll come back or not?

I do feel that by putting this book out I stand a better chance of stopping him than if I don't. And if he is going to send someone back again to kill me either way, at least the TRUTH IS OUT.

The AFOSI taught me that if a crime is going to be stopped …most times it's the media that does it.

It worked for the phony CSS Fraud

It's funny as I look back. All the time I was copying CSS and military documents and secretly taping our conversations, at the time I thought it was me being smart. While they didn't know about the tape recordings, they were making sure I had many copies of Fedex and government contracts, all CSS 1907 tally sheets, plus a lot more documentation and a lot of inside information to take to the newspapers.

I was … only doing what the AFOSI agents wanted and had planned for me to do all along.   They knew the best way to stop Fedex was to go to the media. And since they worked for the government, they were not allowed to.

So they led me to do it for them.

I Hope it Works For Me

The End
The Honest Courier

38062132R00146

Made in the USA
Middletown, DE
12 December 2016